CW01080211

Victorian Disharmonies

Victorian Disharmonies

A Reconsideration of Nineteenth-Century English Fiction

Francesco Marroni

To Prof. Andrew Hiscock,
with my cordial ~~best~~ wishes,

Francesco Marroni

Giulianova, July 10, 2011

The John Cabot University Press, Rome

DELAWARE

Distributed by the University of Delaware Press

Associated University Presses
2010 Eastpark Boulevard
Cranbury, NJ 08512

The paper used in this publication meets the requirements of the American National Standard for Permanence of Paper for Printed Library Materials Z39.48–1984.

Library of Congress Cataloging-in-Publication Data

Marroni, Francesco, 1949-
   [Disarmonie vittoriane. English]
   Victorian disharmonies : a reconsideration of nineteenth-century English fiction / Francesco Marroni.
      p. cm.
   English translation of: Disarmonie vittoriane, with revisions.
   Includes bibliographical references and index.
   ISBN 978-0-87413-090-4 (alk. paper)
1. English fiction—19th century—History and criticism. 2. Social problems in literature. 3. Social conflict in literature. 4. Social change in literature. 5. Order in literature. 6. Literature and society—Great Britain—History—19th century. I. Title.
   PR878.S62M3713 2010
   823'.809355—dc22

                                                2009042752

PRINTED IN THE UNITED STATES OF AMERICA

Contents

Acknowledgments

THIS BOOK APPEARED IN ITALIAN SOME YEARS AGO WITH A SIMILAR title: *Disarmonie vittoriane: Rivisitazioni del canone della narrativa inglese dell'Ottocento* (Rome: Carocci, 2002). Its translation in English has involved a significant, albeit partial revision of my work for at least two reasons. First, while trying to offer a clearer presentation of my ideas, I could not help modifying, sometimes even radically, the linguistic structure of sentences and paragraphs. Second, each chapter has been substantially revised not only in the light of further reflections on the contents and methodology of the original version, but also as a response to useful bibliographical suggestions from, and fruitful discussions with, friends and colleagues.

My first thanks go to Allan C. Christensen for his unfailing support and for his proposal of an English version of my book. Indeed, after reading it in Italian, Allan sent me an e-mail in which he envisaged a larger readership for my interpretation of Victorian fiction as disharmony. He read carefully the drafts of each chapter throughout the translating process, and his keen eye was always extraordinarily helpful in detecting linguistic and semantic "disharmonies"—thanks to his advice the text improved stylistically and gained in *claritas* and economy of expression. I am also boundlessly grateful to Renzo D'Agnillo, old friend and intellectual partner in Victorian discussions and literary walks in Thomas Hardy's footsteps: he was an inspiring reader of my work, while generously helping me in solving many translating dilemmas in the evolution of the English version. I owe a particular debt of gratitude to my dear friend Gloria Lauri-Lucente, who read the typescript at its various stages, always with meticulous perceptiveness and thought-provoking remarks—her detailed and enthusiastic comments have strengthened some theoretical aspects of this book.

My warmest thanks are due also to Massimo Verzella, who, at my implicit pressing request, read the final draft with critical insight

7

and acumen: he was perceptively clever at directing my attention to some minor blemishes that I would otherwise have overlooked. To Raffaella Antinucci I express my gratitude for her very helpful comments on some specific points, and for the gift of a new book devoted to Dickens and London on the very day I concluded my translation, which I tendentiously interpreted as an invitation to continue in my Victorian "progress."

For their precious bibliographical assistance, I wish to thank Mary P. Kane and Eleonora Sasso. Former doctoral students, particularly Silvia Antosa, Valentina Polcini, Saverio Tomaiuolo, and Laura Tommaso, who helped me in various ways: knowingly or not, they provided the unvarying stimulus in workshops and seminars that made this book much the richer.

I also benefited from feedback, advice, and comments of my colleagues of the Center for Victorian and Edwardian Studies (C.U.S.V.E.—G. d'Annunzio University, Pescara, Italy). In particular, affectionate thanks to Emanuela Ettorre, Marilena Saracino, and Enrichetta Soccio, who have always been very supportive and ready to help me in my bibliographical research. But my special thanks are due to Mariaconcetta Costantini, with whom, for over a decade, I have had constant discussion on a variety of Victorian topics during our editorial and departmental meetings and, more frequently, in evening phone calls, when doubts and hesitations besieged my mind.

Finally, as always, love and gratitude to my children, Michela and Jacopo, to whom this book is dedicated.

Victorian Disharmonies

Introduction:
The Victorian Ethos and
the Disharmony of the World

THE VICTORIANS FELT CONTINUALLY BESIEGED BY THE SPECTER OF disharmony and, in response to this dominant fear, transformed their lives into a tireless search for order. From their self-protective perspective, there could be no room for a world that was not built on interpretative codes that united and harmonized all those factors that took on the cast of conflicting forces and transgressive divergences before the accepted norms of behavior. Indeed, nothing was more dangerous for the Victorian mind than the idea of disharmony. The mere recognition of its existence entailed not so much an admission of defeat inflicted by an evil entity, but rather the very negation of the myth of progress and the total disappearance of an axiological viewpoint from which to interpret the signs of a world whose languages and codes were becoming increasingly indecipherable. The struggle against disharmony is therefore the unifying theme of Victorian culture, especially when the various modalities of its artistic productions are considered. Only if order prevailed was it possible to recommend appropriate ethical and behavioral models to the so-called dangerous classes of the nation—a nation profoundly aware of the inevitability of change and the consequent crisis resulting from the continual need for the readjustment and reorientation of the cultural and epistemic basis of society. Hardly a decade of the Victorian age goes by without some fear of an ideological abyss, a sort of moral wasteland in which values become disvalues, and incontestable certainties are unexpectedly transformed into terrible doubts. However smooth, stable, and in place everything appears to be on the surface, underground currents are at work that devour the pillars of Victorian prudence and good sense. The image of a society that was capable of coping with change and could, with every conviction, solemnly

11

advocate itself as the greatest power in the world by bestowing upon Queen Victoria the title of Empress of India (1876) was nothing less than a deliberate response to the call for order. This is how the monarchy reaffirmed its essentially iconic function for a public that felt uneasy with the revolutionary agitations whose palingenetical battle cry was spreading throughout Europe as well as in England. And yet, in my view, it would be rather misleading to limit our focus simply to the contradictions of an era that strove to set itself as an example to the whole world.[1] In fact, unwavering and strong though the British socioeconomic system might seem, it was indisputable that its manufacturing towns were becoming the stage on which the new capitalist class and the industrial proletarians defined their respective roles in terms of a permanent social conflict. In other words, what must be emphasized is the fact that widespread feelings of precariousness and alternating dilemmas affected every sphere of society, causing a sense of fragmentation that only seemed to pave the way for further entropic disintegration, political collapse, and national silence.

In his epigraph to *Howard's End* (1910), E. M. Forster in part embraces the holistic longings of Victorian culture when he writes: "Only connect. . . ."[2] Nine years after the death of Queen Victoria, Forster's novel expresses the same yearning for harmony and reconciliation between opposites, the same affinity between man's different ways of feeling and conceiving his relationship with nature, which Victorian intellectuals had vainly pursued as the only escape from a world condemned to self-destruction. In Thomas Hardy's poem "The Darkling Thrush" (December 31, 1900), the nineteenth century is observed from the perspective of the new century, and portrayed as a corpse over which a desolate spectral grayness looms in a scene of utter ontological nothingness. Such a negative representation seems to suggest that the history of the Victorian age has reached the zero degree of signification, which, from a teleological angle, has led to the triumph of chaos and the disappearance of God.[3] For Hardy, the dysphoric segments of the winter scene and the inability of the poetic voice to interpret the signs of nature reinforce the absence of a dialogic link with the vanishing century as well as an impossibility of achieving a unified vision able to define the destination toward which the humanity of the new century is headed. Far from being out of touch with its time, the line of thought behind Hardy's poem is part of a tradition that, from Carlyle to late Ruskin, presents a haunting and apocalyptic interpretation of the Victorian period.

Carlyle himself, in his monumental work *The French Revolution* (1837), depicts the triumph of anarchy, fully aware that, in more than one point, his own account may be far from any historical truth. With the true spirit of a fire and brimstone preacher, he seeks to give those who govern Britain a lesson in the nightmare of history. In the prophetic tones that pervade every single sentence of his book, the provocative valence of his analyses, and his frequent recourse to biblical quotations to underline his severest warnings, it is impossible not to perceive a completely negative representation of humanity, a humanity more liable to repeat its mistakes than to correct them, and more irrationally inclined toward barbarism than willing to learn from the sad lesson emerging from France. In its messianic dimension, *The French Revolution* affirms the historical necessity of anarchy, while denying it: "For ours is a most fictile world; and man is the most fingent plastic of creatures. A world not fixable; not fathomable!"[4] Carlyle is simply interested in showing that history as narrated by historians is both morally unreliable and void of any didactic purpose, because it is essentially based on lies.[5] For this reason, he proposes a new method characterized by a polemical reinterpretation of the event that has had the most profound influence on the history of Europe:[6]

> Here perhaps is the place to fix, a little more precisely, what these two words, *French Revolution*, shall mean; for, strictly considered, they may have as many meanings as there are speakers of them. All things are in revolution; in change from moment to moment, which becomes sensible from epoch to epoch; in this Time-World of ours there is properly nothing else but revolution and mutation, and nothing else conceivable. . . .
>
> For ourselves, we answer that French Revolution means here the open violent Rebellion, and Victory, of disimprisoned Anarchy against corrupt worn-out Authority. . . . For as hierarchies and Dynasties of all kinds, Theocracies, Aristocracies, Autocracies, Strumpetocracies, have ruled over the world; so it was appointed, in the decrees of Providence, that this same victorious Anarchy, Jacobinism, Sansculottism, French Revolution, Horrors of French Revolution, or what else mortals name it, should have its turn. The destructive wrath of Sansculottism: this is what we speak, having unhappily no voice for singing.[7]

Significantly, Carlyle's rhetoric reads like a linguistic imitation of the anarchy he is describing, and its insistent rhythms effectively convey the dramatic tones of an intensely visionary voice that sees the French Revolution as the great metaphor of history, whose truth can only be grasped once it is freed from its prison of facile interpretative formulas. Thus, the only truth that can be used as a starting point, but that official historiography systematically denies, is the recognition of the French Revolution as a fundamental fracture, and an ultimate historical watershed. Only through the necessity of discontinuity can the forces of Anarchy annul the power of "Authority." In other words, in Carlyle's view, the tensions of anarchy indicate a radical change that is antithetical to the corruption of those in power and the end of all that is necessary for an authentic cultural and moral rebirth. Like a prophet from the Old Testament, Carlyle is convinced that he can distinguish between good and evil, truth and falsity, beauty and ugliness. Driven by his profound palingenetical convictions, he is only able to see visions of disharmony and decadence, and to postpone to an unspecified future time the moment of revelation, in which the spirit will triumph over every form of egoism, especially the rampant, mindless materialism of the present.

Carlyle's essay *Chartism* (1839) can be regarded as a continuation of this dramatic depiction of disorder. His words, which appeal to such objective factors as the discontent of the working classes, immediately recall the main polemical drives of *The French Revolution*. In his questioning of the suffering and revolt of the downtrodden, he presents himself as an authentic interpreter of the times:

> And yet, as we say, it is a question which cannot be left to the Collective Folly of the Nation! In or out of Parliament, darkness, neglect, hallucination must contrive to cease in regard to it; true insight into it must be had. How inexpressibly useful were true insight into it; a genuine understanding by the upper class of society what it is that the under classes intrinsically mean; a clear interpretation of the thought which at heart torments these wild inarticulate souls, struggling there, with *inarticulate uproar,* like *dumb creatures in pain,* unable to speak what is in them! Something they do mean; some true thing withal, in the centre of their confused hearts,—for they are hearts created by Heaven too: to the Heaven it is clear what thing: to us no clear.[8]

The silence of the proletarian masses occupies a world that is very remote from Carlyle's eloquent and prophetic words. But, despite his cultural distance from workers and factories, he proposes himself as the only man prepared to understand the secret text of the historical events that loom on the horizon. From his fiery pulpit he hurls down a series of dire warnings to an audience that, to his agitated mind, seems far too distracted and inattentive and, worse still, insensitive to the perilous clues provided by the historical moment. Following the concept of scriptural interpretation as a decoding of obscure signs—and here the obvious reference is to the Book of Daniel—Carlyle describes the "under classes" as a mass that is incapable of verbally expressing its own suffering. Thus, the antithetical terms *soul* and *roar* find an appropriately unifying element in the adjective *inarticulate.* In Carlyle's emphatic exhortation, the nondisjunction between a positive semantic field (in which *soul* is an index of humanity) and a negative one (characterized by the *roar* of a dangerous beast) is evident in the lexeme *inarticulate,* around which various meanings are made to converge (i.e., a failure to communicate, linguistic incoherence and confusion, and, above all, a lack of connection). The Carlylean stress on the term *dumb* is also significant. Besides its function as an isotopic trait in the first pages of *Chartism,*[9] it serves to associate the silence of the masses with a ferocious and insane destructiveness that, as he explicitly denounces, is on the point of turning into a monstrous creature that is a deathly menace to the social stability of the nation. Nevertheless, for all its savagery and confusion, the industrial proletariat has a heart and soul that must be weighed against its bestial and inhuman aspects. This can only be possible if historical events are deciphered in the light of a truth that may be detected and decoded by those historians who, thanks to their courage and social sensibility, are ready to understand the signs of the times. Carlyle's admonition is very clear: an analysis of the industrial phenomenon must assume as a starting ground not a book of bare statistics or a utilitarian interpretation of industrialization, but "the under classes" and, above all, "the centre of their confused hearts." It is only in this underworld scenery, far removed from historiographic investigation, and apparently of no significance, that an ultimate explanation can be provided.

In short, a harmonious society can be rebuilt, not by the numerous deceitful and futile ministerial reports, but by the power of man's soul: "Tables are like cobwebs . . . beautifully reticulated, orderly to look upon, but which will hold no conclusion. Tables are abstractions, and the object a modest concrete one, so difficult to read the essence of."[10] For Carlyle, the misleading nature of the arguments based on statistics lies in their inability to offer a remedy for the evils at large. Such tables, scientifically compiled as they may be, are as flimsy as cobwebs, since they provide a version of social order that has no relevance with respect to reality. Therefore, he urges a new approach to the problem against the abstract figures of ministerial reports. Paradoxically, however, such an approach involves a return to the past in order to recover the lost harmony that, primarily, implies the recovery of a real aristocracy: "What is an Aristocracy? A corporation of the best, of the bravest."[11] After so many thundering words, what *Chartism* may offer to the reader is a very poor and disappointing reply. His proposal is not a solution to the social unrest and economic fluctuations of the nation. Briefly, his attitude can be compared with the views of the Old Testament prophets who limited their mission to denouncing the evils in the world, while pointing accusing fingers at the corrupt upon whom, sooner or later, divine punishment would eventually be inflicted. Carlyle can only counteract the dominant sense of disorder with a flow of visionary words that become an act of interpretation, an apocalyptic anticipation characterized by the devastating vision of a present destined to be handed over to the forces of chaos.

The Victorian ethos was strongly modified by the profound social and cultural instability deriving from a combination of socioeconomic problems and poor sanitary conditions. Still, the phenomenon that actually rendered the threat of disharmony most tangible was that of the crowd. It was the rise of Chartism that, in the so-called Hungry Forties, brought out into the open and gave national visibility to a working-class movement that, ideologically, posed a real peril for the monarchy.[12] Not only did the Chartist leaders demand political rights for workers, but they also succeeded in "[drawing] together the separate threads of agitation and discontent which already existed."[13] For the Victorians, Chartism meant the march of protesting crowds, which was a totally incomprehensible phenomenon embodying a monstrous violence whose immediate effects meant a fall into savagery. Before the prospect of enormous and anonymous multitudes invading the city streets, the terrified middle classes could only withdraw into the protective space of their own homes to wait for the end of the darkness and the return to the daily routine of business and commerce. The problem is represented not merely by the quantity, but also by the new quality and valence of the message arriving, obliquely, from "this throng of men and women hastening to their labour."[14] While the privileged classes are ready to defend their own territory adopting every sort of weapon, the lower orders long to conquer that opulent space at least with their eyes, so as to construe an alternative urban image, far from their filthy slums and disease-ridden streets. Such a glimpse would pacify their souls and put an end to their precarious and fretful existences spent in the constant search for a job and a home.

If it is true that the crowd embodies the paradigm of violence as its permanent and unique modality of expression (the crowd's image is always equated to violence), it is equally true that its dangers lay in its unpredictability—a crowd does not comply with behavioral norms, rules, or limitations. It represents a form of excess that only leads to a wave of destruction, or, at the very least, the invasion of the territory of bourgeois otherness, and culminates in the chaos of an atemporality that undermines the foundations of the social order. A crowd incites fear precisely because it defies definition. Its sociological coordinates refuse to be interpreted because they do not exist in an identifiable shape, but rather they are the expression of a continual movement that is symptomatic of the new organization of society—an industrial society that would prefer a crowd deprived of its peculiarity, motionless, tamed, and passively obedient to the rhythms and rules of organized labor. A crowd incites fear because it unites and concentrates thousands of individuals and transforms them into a savage and uncontrollable force that has neither a single given behavior nor a dominant voice. A crowd belongs to no one, not even to itself. It cannot be interpreted by any formula; no ritual can dominate it: the crowd is simply the crowd.

The destructive consequences that ensue as a result of the rebellious actions of workers is described with an extraordinary imaginative power by Charlotte Brontë in *Shirley* (1849), which is set in Yorkshire during the Luddite revolts of 1811–12. This novel is one of the first important attempts in fiction to describe the crowd from the point of view of the Victorian bourgeoisie, whose emotional rejection of the phenomenon exposes a lingering inability even to attempt to understand its significance. Of course, there is much more than this in *Shirley*. Thus, the night time raid of the mill is undoubtedly a scene that conveys the extent of the psychological impact caused by the workers' protests. A significant instance of emotional involvement is conveyed by those pages that depict Shirley Keeldar and Caroline Helstone as they are observing from a hilltop the tumultuous crowd in its final assault on Shirley's factory in the valley below:

A crash—smash—shiver—stopped their whispers. A simulta-
neously-hurled volley of stones had saluted the broad front of the mill,
with all its windows; and now every pane of every lattice lay in shat-
tered and pounded fragments. A yell followed this demonstration—
a rioter's yell—a North-of-England—a West-Riding—a West-Riding-
clothing-district-of-Yorkshire rioter's yell. You never heard that sound,
perhaps, reader? So much the better for your ears—perhaps for your
heart; since, if it rends the air in hate to yourself, or to the men or
principles you approve, the interests to which you wish well, Wrath
wakens to the cry of Hate: the lion shakes his mane, and rises to the
howl of the hyena: Caste stands up ireful against Caste; and the indignant, wronged spirit of the Middle Rank bears down in zeal and
scorn on the famished and furious mass of the Operative Class. It is
difficult to be tolerant—difficult to be just—in such moments.

Caroline rose; Shirley put her arm round her: they stood together
as still as the straight stems of two trees. That yell was a long one, and
when it ceased, the night was yet full of the swaying and murmuring
of a crowd.[15]

It may be noted that the phonic convergence of the three lexemes
(cra*sh*—sma*sh*—*sh*iver) breaks up the verbal subject into centrifugal
fragments, a single simultaneous sound whose effect aims at creating a syntactic disorder that is a proleptic configuration of a much
wider social turmoil. Set against the devastating action of the crowd,
any idea of harmony between the classes is smashed into pieces like
the tiny splinters of the factory windows. The struggle witnessed by
the terrified Shirley and Caroline takes on apocalyptic dimensions,
and, as they embrace each other for comfort, their gaze unites, as
if they want to take root in one single perspective capable of assert-
ing their immobility as opposed to the turbulent oscillations of the
masses. Charlotte Brontë's concern here is not with the voice of the
individual worker; nor is it with the dramatization of their misfortunes or, more specifically, their anxiety over being replaced in the
factory by the new machines. Her real concern lies in depicting an
anonymous entity that, on a dark summer night, loses any physiognomic trait of humanity to become the very embodiment of evil. In
Brontë's imagination, the rebellious working-class crowd is compared
to a wild hyena confronting a lion (the legitimate owners of the mill)
in an ultimate struggle between chaos and order, darkness and light.
Through a metaliterary authorial intervention, and in line with the
Victorian novel's conventions, the narrating voice also invites the

reader to acknowledge not so much the "rioters' yell" as the bestiality of the workers' actions and the inhuman and disharmonious effects of the terrible assault scene. By invoking the reader's complicity, the author suggests that the lesson of the Yorkshire Luddite riots is just as relevant for the present day, which is by no means as tranquil as many would like to imagine.

During the stages of the crowd's march on the road and the final assault on the mill, the inhuman yell that arises from the demonstrators, which seems to tear apart the night and last almost for eternity, metaphorically marks a sudden return to barbarity. Accompanying the cry, the enraged workers flow through the streets like a spectral presence, whose thirst for a sort of archaic revenge, in spite of all its acts of vandalism and destruction, will never be quenched. Petrified with fear, motionless and silent as statues, Shirley and Caroline still observe the turbulent scene from a safe distance, though they feel emotionally involved in what is happening under their terrorized gaze. It goes without saying that they function as witnesses exclusively in terms of the private sphere of one's emotions, since their support of the industry's cause stems from their love of two mill owners. As far as the sociopolitical problems of the Luddites are concerned, the two girls instinctively calculate the consequences of the devastation, and, although they are fascinated by the adventurous side of the events, they acknowledge the justice in offering their spiritual encouragement to the cause of the captains of the industry without risking direct contact with the evil embodied in "the mass of cloud, of smoke": "Both the girls felt their faces glow and their pulses throb: both knew they would do no good by rushing down into the mêlée: they desired neither to deal nor to receive blows; but they could not have run away—Caroline no more than Shirley; they could not have fainted; they could not have taken their eyes from the dim, terrible scene—from the mass of cloud, of smoke—the musket-lightning— for the world."[16] Sensitive and palpitating as they may be, by remaining safely protected behind a window, the two girls are performing the function demanded by the sociobehavioral codes of a society that opposed bourgeois rationality to working-class anarchy. Thus, they both are a very explicit embodiment of middle-class expectations regarding the moral confirmation and social legitimacy of matrimony as the culminating point of their individual pursuit of harmony. In their essentially passive state, Shirley and Caroline never place themselves on the same level as the factory workers.[17] Nor do they attempt to understand what exactly lies behind their apparently ferocious and irrational reaction against the introduction of the machines.[18]

The same thematics finds a very different treatment in the fiction of Elizabeth Gaskell, however. While recognizing the potential danger the working classes are capable of representing to the stability of society, Gaskell makes every effort to understand their problems, the values they uphold, the expectations and the structure of feeling that give meaning to their daily lives. That is why she is socially ready to adopt their point of view, leaving aside middle-class prejudices and intolerance. Indeed, only by an imaginatively sympathetic engagement with their world does she feel it possible to give a faithful representation of their hopes and desires. It is into this context of deeply ingrained empathy and fervent religious drives that *Mary Barton* (1848), Gaskell's first novel, should be placed. Undoubtedly, *Mary Barton* is a telling example of the way her approach to the separateness of rich and poor aims to offer an objective and unbiased portrayal of the industrial scene. Although she declared that the protagonist, John Barton, was her hero,[19] the novel can be regarded as an earnest attempt to dramatize the conflict between masters and workers by suggesting the possibility of a social reconciliation in line with the moral teaching derived from her sedulous Gospel reading:

> [John Barton] could not, you cannot, read the lot of those who daily pass you by in the street. How do you know the wild romances of their lives; the trials, the temptations they are even now enduring, resisting, sinking under? You may be elbowed one instant by the girl desperate in her abandonment, laughing in mad merriment with her outward gesture, while her soul is longing for the rest of the dead, and bringing itself to think of the cold-flowing river as the only mercy of God remaining to her here. You may pass the criminal, meditating crimes at which you will tomorrow shudder with horror as you read them. You may push against one, humble and unnoticed, the last upon earth, who in heaven will forever be in the immediate light of God's countenance. Errands of mercy—errands of sin—did you ever think where all the thousands of people you daily meet are bound? Barton's was an errand of mercy; but the thoughts of his heart were touched by sin, by bitter hatred of the happy, whom he, for the time, confounded with the selfish.[20]

The narrator's intervention serves to underline the importance of penetrating the surface of things. Thus, the shapeless mass of people who daily invade the streets of the industrial city is recognized as being made up of individuals whose lives, if given the right attention and consideration, reveal, not the monstrosity of an anonymous crowd, but the sensitivity of real human beings. Gaskell senses the urgency of shaking the privileged classes out of their indifference and forcing them to reassess their superficial judgments of the working classes, and she does this by placing at the center of her story a worker, John Barton, whom she represents dramatically as he is walking the streets at night in search of a chemist to alleviate the suffering of a Methodist friend, lying abandoned in a slum and dying of typhoid fever. But, at the same time, the writer's concern goes beyond Barton himself to concentrate on the diversity and complexity of the individual characters whose destinies can be read as a sort of obscure underground map of hardship, deprivation, and bitterness, all of which make up the indistinct humanity of Manchester.[21]

Paradigmatically, the maze of city streets delineates a topology of mystery. Against the stability of the middle-class house intended as a refuge from outside commercial sordidness, against the warmth and comfort of the domestic hearths around which the members of the masters' families cosily gather, the streets themselves, with their numberless clues of the numberless faces that enact the many stories of the everyday world, disclose an ambiguous, shifting identity. They become the location of a permanent metamorphosis, a space in which the energies of an apparently useless humanity, deprived of any kind of ontological vision, are consumed. Every street in the city, no matter how large or small, underlines this fundamental contrast. Barton's own route takes him from the filthy back streets of the slums to the wide illuminated avenues of the middle-class residential areas where the lavishly decorated shops are the visible signs of exclusion and an ultimate confirmation of the distance between rich and poor. It is precisely the apparently democratic dimension of the street that accounts for its indecipherability: "the lot of those who daily pass you by in the street." The phenomenon of the crowd can be read through these isotopic lines: the impossibility of understanding its language, the unpredictability of its movements in time and space, the obscurity of its ultimate designs. Even if one tries to focus compassionately on a single individual, whether that individual is a ruthless criminal or a young girl disappointed in love, or indeed even the last person upon earth to be blessed with divine light, the mystery lingers on. The street represents the living space of an impossible harmony.

What is more, the labyrinthine streets also contain many potentially interlinking stories, which, far from developing into a clear linear progression, only appear confusing and unreadable, like the chaotically interlacing voices of "wild romances." Significantly enough, in Barton's case, they lead to murder, sin, and self-destruction.

It follows that the democratic space of the street cannot be automatically associated with the positive values of compassion, understanding, and culture. The street often invites crime, and it is also the tragic stage where terrible misdeeds unfold, all of which seem to negate the domestic ideals of the middle classes, who, in the meantime, are engrossed in reading about their own nightmares in the sensation novels of Wilkie Collins, Charles Reade, and Mary E. Braddon. In this sense, it is impossible to imagine a novel like *The Woman in White* (1859–60) without considering the spatial dimension in which the protagonist appears: "There, in the middle of the broad, bright high-road—there, as if it had that moment sprung out of the earth or dropped from the heaven—stood the figure of a solitary Woman, dressed from head to foot in white garments."[22] The street is a place of mystery. Not only that: it is also the melodramatic scene in which the detective pursues the criminal and is more often than not the domain of villains rather than of policemen paid to defend the tranquillity of the privileged classes. The street creates the wild crowd that, by annulling its individual stories, brings about a cultural nullification of the humanity. It may be interesting to recall here what Thomas Hardy noted of the crowds in London in 1879: "As the crowd grows denser it looses its character of an aggregate countless units, and becomes an organic whole, a molluscous black creature having nothing in common with humanity."[23] The reaction of the Victorian intellectuals before the metropolitan masses always seems to be the same. Even in Hardy's case the description of a crowd culminates in a final recognition of its horrible, monstrous presence: "a creature whose voice exudes from its scaly coat, and who has an eye in every pore of its body. The balconies, stands, and railway-bridge are occupied by small detached shapes of the same tissue, but of a gentler motion, as if they were the spawn of the monster in their midst."[24] For Hardy, who, incidentally, had by this time already written *Far from the Madding Crowd* (1874), the London scene is the epitome of disorder, so much so, that in a note dated May 19, 1880, he records his feelings of uneasiness and horror at the idea of living in close proximity to "a monster whose body had four million heads and eight million eyes."[25] In Hardy's vision the masses are associated with a widespread loss of values in Victorian society, which seems more and more entangled in the mad pursuit of purely materialistic objectives. However, what is missing for Hardy, as for other Victorian writers, is a dialectical angle from which the phenomenon can be considered in terms of its historical relevance. What prevails is the tendency to insist on a very reductive mechanical equation: *working classes=nonculture.* Self-righteous people believe that it is precisely this nonculture that leads directly to primitive brutality and an all-pervasive destructive barbarity.[26]

Paradoxically enough, a threatening "organic whole," impervious to any form of teaching, adopts a violent attitude toward those very representatives of culture whom the workers should actually be following. It is no surprise, therefore, if, in *Felix Holt* (1867), George Eliot explores the importance of a cultural awareness in the working classes as the prerequisite for a wise and effectively democratic use of the right to vote. The eponymous hero, who presents himself as a spokesman for the more illuminated workers, bluntly tells the rebels that there is an analogy between poverty and ignorance: "Ignorant power comes in the end to the same thing as wicked power; it makes misery."[27] Power in the hands of the working classes (who are by definition illiterate, rude, and coarse) becomes a destructive power that is diametrically opposed to the cultural heritage of the nation. The very idea that a working-class culture could exist is never even taken into consideration by Victorian novelists, whose imagination invariably works in terms of a genealogy of knowledge that excludes anything that is not directly connected to literary tradition. This ideological conviction leads to a refusal on the part of these writers even to conceive that the proletarian classes could have any association whatsoever with culture. While the cultural forms of the nineteenth century are being transformed by the all-pervasive impact of the industrial revolution, such writers as Eliot keep on interpreting society on the basis of socioeconomic relationships encoded in older forms and conventions, which have now lost their cultural dominance. This is why the only workers who meet with the approval of the governing classes are the fake workers represented by Eliot's hero, Felix Holt, whose defense of the status quo and middle-class morals is a significant example.

Mystery, unpredictability, unreadability: from the point of view of the Victorian intelligentsia, once individuals become a mass, they can only embody a form of moral and cultural disorder whose destructive aims may be imagined, but whose psychological and behavioral coordinates cannot be defined and focused. Since the masses are outside the institutional control and authority, they exemplify the end of the dream for order and, at the same time, the beginning of a new age of barbarism. This is the epistemic basis from which George Gissing takes his cue. Perhaps more than any other Victorian novelist, Gissing senses the implicit danger in these new forms of social organization and concentrates his own artistic effort on the realization of a persuasive social synthesis. Gissing sees the emergence of an organized working class as the first act of an axiological tragedy: the death of that classical culture that, in his view, carried with it a return to the moral virtues and intellectual integrity handed down from ancient Greek and Roman literatures as the supreme forms of human wisdom. John Carey has aptly observed, "Like other intellectuals Gissing deplored the tainting effect of the suburban masses on the landscape as well as on culture."[28] The negative effect of the masses is not limited to the sociological environment, but also extends to the spheres that are more directly dependent on sensitivity and taste. How can a proletarian wonder at the beauty of a landscape, if poverty and hunger prevent him from being able to have an aesthetic appreciation of life? Is it possible to deny the uncontrollable primary needs of the body? When they are hungry, people are only able to think of their own hunger. The danger is that such a condition can only lead to an absence of spirituality whose effects will result in bad taste, ecological insensitivity, savage urbanization, money worship, and a general rejection of authentic cultural values. Gissing is absolutely prepared to subscribe to such an ominous future.

Demos (1886), one of the novels that most evince his awareness of the contradictions of late Victorian society, expresses his absolute terror at the growing importance of the working-class movement. For him, an optimistic approach to the phenomenon can be possible only through a visionary character such as Stella Westlake, who, despite her total lack of knowledge of the working classes, assumes she can interpret their sentiments, in a sort of mythicizing depiction of the proletarian condition: "When she spoke of the toiling multitude, she saw them in a kind of exalted vision; she beheld them glorious in their woe, ennobled by the tyranny under which they groaned. She had seen little if anything of the representative proletarian, and perchance even if she had the momentary impression would have faded in the light of her burning soul."[29] Stella Westlake echoes the socialist views of William Morris, who firmly believed in the basic goodness and honesty of the proletariat. In fact, the woman's ideas are exactly the same as those of her husband, Mr Westlake, "a leader of the socialist movement,"[30] who champions popular utopian values that hark back to a past in which labor had nothing to do with mass production and the ruthless laws of economy and commerce.[31] Nevertheless, it is Gissing's other female character, Adela Waltham, whose words are made to carry greater weight and significance. Having married a laborer who has now become a master, Adela is only too aware of the feelings that rage in the hearts of factory workers and discloses something of her own experiences to her more idealistic friend: "They have not these feelings you attribute to them. Such suffering as you picture them enduring comes only of the poetry-fed soul at issue with fate."[32] Therefore, no possibility of redemption can be envisaged amid the working classes.

In Gissing's view, the gloomy image of "a thronging of released toilers, of young and old, of male and female"[33] is the best literary modality of staging the essential failure of industrialization, which, from a cultural and human perspective, has only led to a society on the verge of anarchy. It is no accident that, in the same year in which *Demos* appeared, he wrote: "I am living at present in Lambeth, doing my best to get at the meaning of that strange world, so remote from our civilisation."[34] In other words, the working-class world is the very antithesis of the harmonious civilized age founded on art and learning with which Gissing, following Arnold's analysis of Victorian culture, would still like to be associated. At the same time, however, he is equally conscious of the fact that the present age, which is insensitive to the world of culture and dominated by a middle-class mentality based on hypocrisy and material wealth, is doomed to disaster. Given this pessimistic representation of contemporary society, it is no wonder that Gissing set his novels in social contexts characterized by social contradictions and political confusion. From an ideological angle, his ideas are far from being unambiguous and coherent. This is why in his narrative works both the ruling bourgeoisie and the proletariat are seen as being equally responsible for producing ugliness and vulgarity everywhere and for destroying the great culture of the past.

If the metropolitan crowds created a "strange world," which eluded control by those in power and operated at a distance from the hierarchically stable space belonging to the dominant classes, then the Victorians could only turn to the past for visions of reassurance and coherence. In many ways, the past provided an ideological basis upon which they could begin to build their dream of order. Looking back to the past seemed the only alternative to the uncertain present, in which the epistemic foundations of society were continually subjected to radical changes, fluctuations, and metamorphoses that rendered the quest for an organizing principle increasingly precarious. Not only was it impossible to envisage a teleological horizon; scientific discoveries also seemed to go against the axiological demands of society.

Significantly, it was the anonymous publication of Robert Chambers's *Vestiges of the Natural History of Creation* in 1844 that would upset the scientific world with its theories of evolution, which, fifteen years before Darwin, suggested a cosmological view that was in evident contrast with the biblical version of the origins of man. Halfway between science and fantasy, *Vestiges* made a deep impact on Victorian public opinion and generated a lively debate around evolutionism that strengthened the moral necessity of confronting a disturbing redefinition of mankind's place in the universe.[35] The Victorians, who were fascinated by this concept of the world that denied the very past that they, in the absence of a stable axiological terrain, were so keen to hold on to, became absorbed by *Vestiges* because they craved to know more about the origins of life: "The book ranged from astronomy and geology to moral philosophy and the prospect of a future life, all drawn together in a gripping cosmological narrative. The early pages described a nebular hypothesis of the universe, showing how stars, and moons had evolved from a gaseous 'fire mist.'"[36] The central part of the book treated the history of the biological and geological development that had led from simple invertebrates to fish, amphibians, reptiles, mammals, and man. Chambers, who believed that the laws of evolution were influenced by a divine will, claims that the crowning moment of evolution was reached by human species, whose conquest of a spiritual dimension together with a rational and intellectual capacity proved that man was moving toward a form of perfection that implied the fulfilment of a dream: "Is our race but the initial of the grand crowning type? Are there to be yet species superior to us in organisation, purer in feeling, more powerful in device and act, and who shall take a rule over us!. . . There may then be occasion for a nobler type of humanity, which shall complete the zoological circle of this planet, and realize some of the dreams of the purest spirits of the present race."[37] Briefly, in a historical context in which the distinction between the scientific and the pseudoscientific appeared difficult to make, a theory emerged, however fictional and imaginary, that denied the historical validity of the biblical account of man's origins. This amounted to an epistemic earthquake. In spite of his prospects for a nobler and purer type of humanity, Chambers's work provoked a series of negative reactions that were in some way a signal of the religious doubts and ontological dilemmas that already existed before the success of his book.[38]

Another feature that increased the feeling of disorientation and discomfort was the link that readers perceived between the phenomenology of the crowds and the emergence of the evolutionary laws, which, as Chambers says in *Vestiges*, has to do with the perception of present-day man as a being dominated by impulsiveness and brutality.[39] The depersonalizing march of the masses, in which the individual is no longer an individual, but a part of an unpredictable and dangerous monstrosity, seemed to confirm the pessimistic interpretation of the future of mankind, whose supremacy over all other species was no longer as clear and definitive as it had been in the past. Nothing new could now be taken for granted. Even when the metropolitan crowds thin out and disperse in different directions, so that the faces become distinguishable in their individual physiognomy, they still recall the expressions of an inferior race rather than one descending from the Old Testament. The negative effects of the factories on men and women, the vulgarity of their behavior, their coarse and disarticulated language, their rags and lack of hygiene only confirm their connection with the beast that no one would want to associate with human beings. To make matters worse, the public imagination now seems to follow a regressive movement in time, since the unstable social fabric of the present moves to the fore dangerous traces of ancient geological eras, obscure and threatening signs from a remote past that take one back to a long night of humanity deprived of God's testimony. The anthilllike cities look out toward an appalling darkness that is simultaneously distant and near.

Thus, seen from a perspective of rationality and order, the anonymous multitude becomes a shapeless entity that appears to have lost every means of discrimination, a category of people whose unruly and wild existences seem exclusively limited to their biological and reproductive functions. In short, the working classes are both a world apart and a mystery. For the bourgeois observer, their faces, their gestures, and their lives are no longer distinguishable or identifiable. Their countenances, their language, their gestures and destinies are all the same. From the 1840s onward, the Victorian imagination sees only an empty, archaic landscape in which bleeding hairy bodies with sunken cheeks and drooping shoulders struggle and fight with one another, prompted by animal instincts and primitive desires. Indeed, this is the scene of the struggle for survival stemming from the idea of an overpopulated territory in which the defense of one life always entails the death of another, who is seen as an antagonist. Consequently, the urban proletariat's completely aggressive view of life terrifies the wealthy classes, whose attitude is imbued with suspicion. They contrast the detrimental negativity of the masses with the positiveness and nobility of the individual, who, as a champion of British civilization, battles against such a process of depersonalizing massification.

If industrialization, with its revolution of the socioeconomic structure, undeniably marked the advent of a hegemonic class together with a new way of conceiving the relationship between the individual and society, it must also be underlined that the depiction of the monstrous physiognomy of the masses embodied a perilous element of discontinuity that, not only highlighted the precarious dimension of social organization, but also revealed how the relationship between present and past was so frail, to the extent of having become practically nonexistent. One may conclude that at the very moment in which they discovered their economic supremacy the Victorians realized that they were alone with their dilemmas, that they lacked stable points of reference and were at the mercy of events they could no longer control. In many ways, society was changing at such a great speed that it was impossible for them to exercise a control on reality. Added to this was the fact that Victorian society was far too conservative to keep up with the changes that were taking place. The more they sensed they were living in a world that lacked a center enlightened by moral authority and historical truth, the more they tried to proclaim their link with a past that, however fragmented and ambivalent, still played a role in their collective imaginary. And against the dark eons discovered by geological science, this stance meant primarily a recovery of the ethical and cultural values from the most authentic of English traditions, that is, the rural tradition of the gentry and ancient nobility.

In sharp contrast to this mobile and variegated background, the unscrupulous materialism of the hegemonic class, and, above all, the continual conflicts between the social classes, is the figure of the gentleman, who, as an ultimate resource to set against the advent of anarchy, is posited as the ideal model of a tradition that embodies values denied by the present world. The gentleman is the representation of an order based not on economic power, but on spiritual strength. He is a figure whose idea of order goes beyond the concept of class and class interest. This is the reason why the gentleman is held up not as an alternative to the anonymity of the masses, but as a moral protagonist who postulates a possible space of cultural mediation. It is not a coincidence that Ruskin, in his strenuous fight against industrial devastation, maintains that the gentleman is a sort of national treasure to defend with tooth and claw, most of all by the working classes, who can learn from him the principles necessary for their moral and cultural growth.[40] All things considered, the gentleman is seen as the only light in a world increasingly torn by apparently irresolvable conflicts, misgivings, and aporias regarding not only the present but also—more extensively—the ultimate sense of life. As Raymond Chapman eloquently puts it:

> The brutality and coarseness which lay beneath eighteenth-century and Regency elegance did not disappear in the age of Victoria. But they were less flaunted, less overtly approved among men who laid claim to breeding, and they gradually diminished in reality. The ideal knight of perfect virtue and gentleness combined with courage had seldom if ever existed outside the imagination. He lived in the pages of Malory and Spenser and he offered an identity for those who were striving toward something better than the morality of the immediate past.[41]

Undoubtedly, the crowd and the gentleman represent the two poles around which much Victorian fiction revolves as it seeks a point of reconciliation between harmony and disharmony, a sort of mediatory terrain between forces gathering around an ideal of chivalry and those that, antithetically, aim to lead to the disintegration and destruction of any axiological perspective. The search for a middle ground implies, from a literary angle, the fabrication of a hero that can be dialogically placed between two apparently irreconcilable worlds. In *Felix Holt*, George Eliot is so convinced by such an endeavor at reaching a mediation that she transforms her protagonist into the real author of the "Address to Working Men" that appeared in January 1868 in *Blackwood's Magazine*.[42]

From this point of view, Anthony Trollope's works are even more interesting. They represent, almost in their entirety, a macrotext that can be read as the most extended and coherent attempt to portray the function of the gentleman in Victorian society while acknowledging, at one and the same time, his conflicts and contradictions. The English gentleman is the true paradigm of Trollope's works. An exemplary embodiment is Plantagenet Palliser, duke of Omnium, the central character of a series of novels who provides an interpretative model for his time.[43] Significantly, with an extremely scrupulous realism, and a technique whereby ideas of conservation and progress are aptly intertwined, Trollope describes through Plantagenet Palliser the condition of the gentleman who, against the gradual loss of the most authentic values of tradition, is presented as a symbol and essence of Englishness:

> Mr. Palliser was one of those politicians in possessing whom England has perhaps more reason to be proud than of any other of her resources, and who, as a body, give to her that exquisite combination of conservatism and progress, which is her present strength and best security for the future. He could afford to learn to be a statesman, and had the industry wanted for such training. He was born in the purple, noble himself, and heir to the highest rank as well as one of the greatest fortunes of the country, already very rich, surrounded by all the temptations of luxury and pleasure; and yet he devoted himself to work with the grinding energy of a young penniless barrister labouring for a penniless wife, and did so without any motive more selfish than that of being counted in the roll of the public servants of England. He was not a brilliant man, and understood well that such was the case. He was now listened to in the House, as the phrase goes; but he was listened to as a laborious man, who was in earnest in what he did, who got up his facts with accuracy, and who, dull though he be, was worthy of confidence. And he was very dull. He rather prided himself on being dull, and on conquering in spite of his dullness. He never allowed himself a joke in his speeches, nor attempted even the smallest flourish of rhetoric. He was very careful in his language, labouring night and day to express himself with accuracy, with no needless repetition of words, perspicuously with regard to the special object he might have in view. He had taught himself to believe that oratory, as oratory, was a sin against that honesty in politics, by which

he strove to guide himself. He desired to use words for the purpose
of teaching things which he knew and which others did not know;
and he desired also to be honoured for his knowledge. But he had no
desire to be honoured for the language in which his knowledge was
conveyed. He was an upright, thin laborious man; who by his parts
alone could have served no political party materially, but whose parts
were sufficient to make his education, integrity and industry useful
in the highest degree. It is the trust which such men inspire which
make them so serviceable; —trust not only in their labour, —for any
man rising from the mass of the people may be equally laborious; not
yet simply in their honesty and patriotism. The confidence is given to
their labour, honesty, and patriotism joined to such a personal stake
in the country as gives them a weight and ballast which no politician
in England can possess without it.[44]

The portrait of Plantagenet Palliser pivots on the concept of work,
regarded as a service rendered to the nation, as a sign of industrious-
ness and struggle. In the form of a recurrent polyptoton, the iteration of the lexemes *labour, labouring,* and *laborious* confers a linguistic
coherence and compactness to the moral definition of the character.
His main qualities derive from the fact that he struggles against the
temptations of laziness and the weakness of fleeting pleasures. Palliser gives a meaning to his own life by investing the social sphere
of his actions with a nobility of soul that corresponds to the nobility
of his social status. In this case, nobility is not only a social category
but also a spiritual one, given that Palliser's sociopsychological behavior—even from a purely theoretical angle—is that of a person
who is seeking to make his way in the world on his own, without any
economic privileges, and driven by the desire to abandon the harsh
path of egoism. Actually, this is not the way things really are or can
be—nor can they be this way—but the rhetorical construction of the
passage is such that the reader is forced to imagine them to be so.
It is significant, for example, that, besides the triple occurrence of
the word *England* (placed at the beginning, just after the first half,
and at the end of the first paragraph of chapter 24 of *Can You Forgive
Her?*), we cannot fail to note how Trollope turns his character into
an element of continuity of past, present, and future ("That exquisite combination of conservatism and progress which is her present
strength and best security for the future") in a moment in which—
the 1860s—the laboring masses were increasingly demanding direct
representation in Parliament.

In Trollope's view, the most evident trait in the figure of the gentleman lies in his capacity to be the exclusive repository of both conservatism and progress; while being a guardian of the best traditions of the past, he is also particularly alert to the signs of change, always paying attention to social intimations from the less privileged classes. Furthermore, one cannot help noticing how Trollope stresses not so much the ethics of work as the triad *integrity-trust-honesty* with the aim of morally confirming Palliser's ability as a politician to represent the interests of the entire nation in every moment of his life, in every gesture that he makes, and in every word that he utters.[45] It must also be added that in his laborious and scrupulous preparation of his parliamentary speeches, Palliser reveals himself as an orator free of empty rhetoric, one who seeks to solve problems by using a realistic language, which appears to be partly an ontological extension of his *dullness*. His sense of commitment, rather than reflecting the brilliant temperament of a born orator, is the opaqueness of a man who aims to conquer the scene through a serious attitude founded on practical solutions to problems: none of Palliser's speeches invokes enticing language that, however gratifying to the ear, has little bearing on reality. It must of course be said that Trollope, with an obvious metaliterary procedure, devotes ample space in his introductory paragraph to the linguistic strategies the politician adopts in his writings: the references to precision and accuracy with which he gives shape to his parliamentary speeches, never uttering a superfluous word, and always avoiding any form of exaggeration in the pursuit of his only objective: the truth. This explains the all-pervading didactic tension that inspires his addresses; his message, devoid of linguistic trappings and useless embellishments, aims to make itself understood by everyone. After all, Palliser's wish to be also remembered for the clarity, honesty, and eloquence of his style can be interpreted as a perfect interface of analogous values that are an intrinsic part of the daily life of the person.

That Trollope attached great importance to his own fictional version of the gentleman becomes evident in his *Autobiography* (1883). After assessing his various productions, and just before compiling a list of his literary works and their respective earnings, a few pages before the conclusion the author recalls: "I think that Plantagenet Palliser, Duke of Omnium, is a perfect gentleman. If he be not, then I am unable to describe a gentleman."[46] Obviously, underlining Trollope's conviction of the moral centrality of his character are not only the recognition of the primacy of the gentleman, but also the need to place his fictional works on the front line of an ideological defense of social harmony. That harmony is structured around the dual virtues of honesty and patriotism that seem to find their most faithful interpreter in Plantagenet Palliser.[47]

Elizabeth Gaskell's attitude toward the gentleman is quite different. According to her analysis of the phenomenon, the relationship between the industrial world and the idea of the gentleman can be founded not so much on the patriotism of the governing classes as on an honest portrayal of the contradictions and contrasts between the past and the present. In line with her enlightened thought, *North and South* (1854–55) presents a problematic version of the figure of the gentleman in John Thornton, a young mill owner who, despite every good intention, and despite his genuine spirit of philanthropy, is forced to succumb to the laws of the market and the fury of the mob. Significantly, after their first encounter, Margaret Hale, the heroine of the novel, outlines to her mother a rather negative description of John Thornton: "About thirty—with a face that is neither exactly plain, nor yet handsome, nothing remarkable—*not quite a gentleman*; but that was hardly to be expected."[48] In Gaskell's narrative decoding of the industrial scenery, it is particularly crucial to emphasize the dominant idea of a gulf between rich and poor that even the most courageous of men will not succeed in bridging. Huge and discouraging though the gulf may be, she makes every effort to stage a fictional dramatization of the physical and moral proximity of the classes. The scene is always the same: the factory, the workers, and the masters. In this connection, John Thornton, who begins his career as an assistant in a drapery, represents a strategic link with the workers for whom he will conduct the "experiments" that, eventually, will lead to his financial ruin. The unfolding of the story reveals that Thornton undergoes no substantial change. But what must be stressed here is that, at the end of his own personal quest for meaning, he is convinced that, to combat class prejudice and intolerance, it is important "[to] bring the individuals of the different classes into actual personal contact. Such intercourse is the very breath of life."[49] Conversely, a more deep-seated and radical transformation takes place in Margaret, who assumes a different and more sympathetic attitude toward the industrialist. Thanks to her new and unbiased awareness of the industrial world, she can appreciate the honest and sincere effort he makes toward encouraging the moral and social growth of his workers. This explains why at the end of the novel, in spite of the failure of his experiments, Thornton emerges as a true gentleman, a figure that, in contrast with Trollope's Plantagenet Palliser, embodies the instability and complexity of the social hierarchy: "His fine figure yet bore above the common height of men; and gave him a *distinguished appearance*, from the ease of motion which arose out of it, and was natural to him; but his face looked older and care-worn; yet a *noble composure* sate upon it, which impressed those who had just been hearing of his changed position, with a sense of inherent dignity and manly strength."[50] In Margaret's eyes, Thornton's financial ruin only confirms his nobility and integrity, in spite of the fact that she had initially refused to attribute to him any sociocultural credibility because of his powerful position as mill owner. Now, however, she seems to detect in his features correctly the signs of past joys—"the old look of intense enjoyment"—[51] almost as if his bankruptcy has magically vanished and the change has only concerned his relationship with Margaret, his workers, and the world in general. Nevertheless, it would be more pertinent to see Thornton as representing something more than a gentleman, and more than a solution against the metropolitan crowds. For Gaskell considers that the category of the gentleman is too inadequate to embody change, and therefore she strives to portray Thornton's transformation more as the effect of a changed visual angle than as a result of the adoption of the mental habit and lifestyle of a gentleman as such.[52] In this sense, it would be more appropriate to identify the real transformation in the novel in Margaret Hale, who, after her decision to save her future husband's factory—which is possible thanks to the unexpected and providential inheritance she receives—fulfills her own ambition of performing an act of altruism.

By placing her female protagonist at the center of the industrial scene, Gaskell delivers a precise ideological message with respect to the relationship between the female universe and society. From her point of view, it is impossible to reduce the role of women to mere dispensers of gentility and domestic love. The experience Margaret acquires through her direct contact with the poorest districts of the town deprives her of those characteristics that, according to the sociobehavioral codes of the time, would have been perceived as being a fundamental element of her natural progression from factory heroine to an angel of the hearth, or, at least, to a woman at the window: an acritical observer of events, a woman typified by social passivity.

On the contrary, after establishing herself in society and dismissing the idea of the seventeenth-century gentleman as the only figure capable of confronting its ills, Margaret manages to make herself heard in her real surroundings and is prepared to envision a future world sustained by those who yearn to work actively for the general good.

Transformed into a monstrous mysterious image, the crowd increasingly becomes a common sight on every city street and, as the process of industrialization intensifies it, produces not only the working-class masses, but also a disquieting throng of prostitutes and burglars, scavengers and beggars, and many other underworld figures who were totally outside the law. As Canetti justly reminds us, "There are no institutions which can be absolutely relied on to prevent the growth of the crowd once and for all."[53] From an ecological perspective, the destructive consequences of the industrial revolution are perhaps even more dramatically evident when one's gaze is turned toward the sky, the ideal space where the voice of man's spiritual yearnings can best be heard. In an imaginary vertical topology, both the inferior level of the pavement and the superior level of the sky have become terribly polluted by the side effects of the new era of industrialization and commercial expansion.

Tellingly, in chapter 7 ("New Scenes and Faces") of *North and South*, the arrival of the Hale family from the south of England is juxtaposed to the vision of the black cloud that, as an initial icon of the industrial landscape, immediately dampens the enthusiasm and curiosity typical of those discovering a new city:

> For several miles before they reached Milton, they saw a deep, lead-coloured cloud hanging over the horizon in the direction in which it lay. It was all the darker from contrast with the pale gray-blue of the wintry sky. . . . Nearer to the town, the air had a faint taste and smell of smoke. . . . Quick they were whirled over long, straight, hopeless streets of regularly-built houses, all small and of brick. Here and there a great oblong many-windowed factory stood up, like a hen among the chickens, puffing out black "unparliamentary" smoke, and sufficiently accounting for the cloud which Margaret had taken to foretell rain.[54]

The crowded streets and the great cloud of smog are the most shocking signs of a present world that has completely forgotten a past that was made up of rural communities and blue skies. The streets and the

cloud convey the negative iconicity of industrialization. Both speak
of a world without light in which, as the protagonist soon realizes,
romance has no space. The cloud that at first seems to be a sign of
change in the weather—a forecast of rain—is really an enormous
mass of smoke that dominates the city like a suffocating vault and
makes the city streets, by-streets and alleys look as hopeless as if they
were the sections of a circle in hell.[55] As with Gaskell, other Victorian
writers cannot help noticing how the sky appears to have become
more and more distant from humanity.[56] Looking up at the sky only
reminds man even more of the disheartening fact that he lives in a
polluted environment that must be intended as the visible representation of a deeper and more unredeemable inner corruption.

"On why is heaven built so far, / Oh why is earth so remote?"[57] asks
Christina Rossetti in 1881. The more the factories and their smok-
ing chimneys impose their antiecological message on the Victorian
landscape, the more the sky seems to distance itself from humanity
and its daily struggles. Darkness prevails over light, utilitarianism
over imagination, and the unnatural over the natural—"It was a town
of red and brick, or of red and brick that would have been red if the
smoke and ashes had allowed it . . . it was a town of unnatural red and
black like the painted face of a savage."[58] With this extraordinarily
powerful image, in *Hard Times* (1854) Dickens transforms the metropolitan environment into a wild physiognomy, thereby conveying to
the Victorian reader his own fear of a return to barbarity, along with
a sense of the unbridgeable distance that separates industrialization
from the best features of English tradition, whose foundations are a
lasting tribute to nature and a staunch defense of its cultural identity.
In short, if it is observed from the new world of the manufacturing
towns, England is no longer perceived as being *England*: the nation
has become an unfamiliar space, an evil entity that denies God and
the harmony of creation and leads people into the depths of hell.
This alien England has lost its ecological mind and, heedlessly, has
abandoned the sky to the spiteful dominion of "interminable ser-
pents of smoke [that] trailed themselves for ever and ever and never
got uncoiled."[59] But probably, in the light of its imaginative tension
and moral symbolism, the most perfect synthesis occurs in the opening page of the third book of *Our Mutual Friend* (1864–65). In one of
the most suggestive openings of Dickens's fiction, the diseases that
pervade the city and the diseases of its inhabitants overlap in an
intense metaphorical dialogism, whose main artistic objective is to

stage a metropolitan scenery characterized by the absolute supremacy of darkness over light:

> It was a foggy day in London, and the fog was heavy and dark.
> Animate London, with smarting eyes and irritated lungs, was blink-
> ing, wheezing, and choking; inanimate London was a sooty spectre,
> divided in purpose between being visible and invisible, and so be-
> ing wholly neither. Gaslights flared in the shops with a haggard and
> unblest air, as knowing themselves to be night-creatures that had no
> business abroad under the sun; while the sun itself when it was for a
> few moments dimly indicated through circling eddies of fog, showed
> as if it had gone out and were collapsing flat and cold. Even in the
> surrounding country it was a foggy day, but there the fog was *grey*,
> whereas in London it was, at about the boundary line, *dark yellow*,
> and a little within it *brown*, and then *browner*, and then *browner*, until
> at the heart of the City—which call Saint Mary Axe—it was *rusty-
> black*. From any point of the high ridge of land northward, it might
> have been discerned that the loftiest buildings made an occasional
> struggle to get their heads above the foggy sea, and especially that
> the great dome of Saint Paul's seemed to die hard; but this was not
> perceivable in the streets at their feet, where the whole metropolis
> was a heap of vapour charged with muffled sound of wheels, and
> enfolding a gigantic catarrh.[60]

The London of Dickens's imagination is not only immersed in a lead-
colored cloud of smog, as is Gaskell's Manchester, but is itself made up
of an enormous agglomeration of vapors that have effectively turned
the city into a living hell, a labyrinthine spectacle of polluting smoke
and poisonous gases, suggesting a great chaos, an apocalyptic vision
very similar to the ominous images that many a time Carlyle describes
in his writings. The evocation of London as "a sooty spectre" makes
the city seem simultaneously the somber background and protagonist of a narrative totally focused on fragmentation and darkness.
Indeed, its buildings and monuments are barely visible, drowned as
they are in a "sea of fog" that can be read as a proleptic allusion to the
filthy waters of the Thames, with its images of death, the indefinable
profile of objects and the mysterious web of individual destinies.

Before Ruskin, and also before the twentieth-century novel, Dickens is able to envisage the death of the sun. And, consequently, the
death of the sky as well: "as if [the sun] had gone out and were col-
lapsing flat and cold." His universe is devoid of an epistemic pivot

upon which reality can take shape; it is a scenery without any points of reference. Everything is evoked in terms of complete negativity. The only vision that can be offered is one of a sheer disharmony that is the natural consequence of a suffocated, ugly spirit that has become nothing but "a gigantic catarrh." The sickness of the body is also a sickness of the soul. The great contaminating cloud is London itself, which, in a single blow, kills the bodies and souls of its inhabitants and transforms them into the fragments of a never-ending night-mare. With his typical sensitivity to color, the writer does not simply describe the cloud of smog, but he also aims at decoding both its psychological traits and its chromatic movements, as if delineating a person's physiognomy starting from the outer margins to the moral nothingness at its center. Thus, in the outskirts of the city the cloud is gray and, shortly afterward, changes to dark yellow and brown. Mov-ing toward the city center the color brown becomes more aggressive and takes on darker and darker tones until it culminates in the rusty black that corresponds to the epicenter of the enormous cloud. One should also not overlook the fact that, from a chromatic angle, the city itself is configured as an apocalyptic scenery, an immense infer-nal machine, a sort of message from the underground that denies any human value and points to the great corruption in the world.

Gerard Manley Hopkins also laments that "the sky is built so far." His journals provide evidence that his eyes were constantly directed toward the sky, wholly involved in an obsessive search for the signs of the divine. And, more precisely, while he is ready to follow and creatively decode the celestial movements, it is in the clouds and in their migrations that the poet seeks to reestablish a sense of beauty. Although Hopkins is greatly aware of an invading pollution, he is still hoping to discover a horizon of total purity, uncontaminated and dialogically prepared to reveal God's presence in the world. Thus, on August 21, 1874, he notes how the smoke exerts its polluting in-fluence well beyond the boundaries of the metropolis: "As we ap-proached Windsor, the London smoke met us rolling up the valley of the Thames."[61] And a month later he writes, "Many coloured smokes in the valley, grey from the Denbigh lime-kiln, yellow and lurid from two kilns perhaps on the shoulders of a hill, blue from a bonfire, and so on."[62] His continual references in his letters to the environmental decay of industrial areas always imply a deprecatory attitude toward the ruling classes: "And our whole civilisation is dirty, yea filthy, and especially in the north; for is it not dirty, yea filthy, to pollute the air as Blackburn and Widnes and St. Helen's are polluted and the water as the Thames and the Clyde and the Irwell are polluted?"[63] This sort of questioning is directly from Hopkins as a *Jesuit poet,* who realizes, to his anguish, the extent to which industrialization has ruined the landscape: the reiteration of the synonyms *dirty, yea filthy* is charged with a moral connotation pointing to a reality that has by now become irremediably compromised: the two adjectives *dirty/filthy* are strategically utilized to reinforce the qualitative and quantitative value of dirt, which, as well as obliterating the natural landscape, seems destined to reduce to zero degree men's capacity to distinguish between good and evil.

Hence Hopkins's quest for an uncontaminated horizon where he can project his remnants of hope. While the poet is studying the sky, the unique focus of his attention are the clouds, the natural clouds whose origin seems to be in the divine breath. As a tireless observer of the metamorphosis of the natural world, he aims at reading the signs of the sky with the same precision as a philologist may read an ancient text. The following are only a few examples of the numerous indications of the profundity of his insights into natural phenomena: "Sunrise at Chagford. There was a remarkable fan of clouds traced in fine horizontals, which afterwards lost their levels, some becoming oblique. . . . Sunset here also. Over the nearest ridge of Dartmoor. Sky orange, trail of Bronze-lit clouds. . . . Grey sky at Hampstead lately. Clouds showing beautiful and rare curves like curds, comparable to barrows, arranged of course in parallels. . . . Mallowy red of sunset and sunrise clouds" (from a note made in 1865).[64] It is only too evident that the young Hopkins is not interested in describing sunrises and sunsets so much as the chromatic and morphological features of a mass of clouds that, in his classifying mind, postulate at once a response and a pursuit of theological derivation. A few years later the poet notes: "July 2. A few showers, fine between. Those fretted mossy clouds have their law more in helices, wave-tongues, than in anything else and it is pretty perceptible. Amber-rose and blue-green on the threads near the sun. . . . Also in the morning pale transparent unpacking white-rose cloud soaked in blue and soon vanishing" (from a note made in 1866).[65] And again: "March 14—Bright morning, pied skies, hail. In the afternoon the wind was from the N., very clod; long bows of soft grey cloud straining the whole heaven but spanning the skyline with a slow entasis which left a strip of cold porcelain blue. . . . March 17—In the morning clouds chalky and milky-coloured, with remarkable oyster-shell moulding" (from a note made in 1871).[66]

It is no exaggeration to talk of a Hopkins nephelometry in such instances: the poet's notebooks contain many pages dedicated to cloud formations, and these descriptions reflect a precise detail of observation that goes well beyond a merely literary description and, at the same time, testify to the scientific dimension of his approach. It is by no means accidental that on the same page the poet often accompanies his verbal descriptions with sketches of clouds as he perceives them, intent as he always is to capture the *inscape* and *instress* of a landscape, the essence and power of objects. This is the alternative vision Hopkins puts forward to the somber and intimidating presence of smog. Against the industrial expansion that only produces ugliness and pollution, he continues to look toward the sky, which he craves to see as being still a euphorically close dimension reflecting God's grandeur.[67]

At the time in which Christina Rossetti was posing her metaphorical question on the remoteness of the sky, John Ruskin was also looking at the sky to ponder on the enormous distance between man and nature. In his view, the general axiological imbalance accounted for a mounting materialism and a parallel loss of spirituality. In his social criticism, he made every effort to understand what had caused so much ruin to the English landscape; precisely because he wanted to believe in "the mutual dependence of all upon all,"[68] his sensibility reacted polemically, and traumatically, before the new industrial economy and its way of organizing work. Therefore, in two lectures delivered in 1884, collected under the title *The Storm Cloud of the Nineteenth Century*,[69] Ruskin presents an apocalyptic picture of the whole century whose visionary language, from a historical perspective, conveys to the reader a terrible intuition of the destruction and self-destruction that marked the early decades of the twentieth century. But apart from the prophetic dimension of the two lectures, what must be underlined is how, in Ruskin's view, the argument is planned more as a moral synthesis of the nineteenth century than as a forewarning of the following decades. In fact, at the beginning of his first lecture Ruskin immediately clarifies his position as great accuser of the present by offering an exalted interpretation of the way the spiritual valence of past centuries was confirmed and reinforced by fine weather:

In those old days, when weather was fine, it was luxuriously fine; when it was bad—it was often abominably bad, but it had its fit of temper and was done with it. . . .

In fine weather the sky was either blue or clear in its light; the clouds, either white or golden, adding to, not abating, the lustre of the sky. . . . The beneficent rain-cloud was indeed often extremely dull and grey for days together, but gracious nevertheless, felt to be doing good, and often to be delightful after drought; capable also of the most exquisite colouring, under certain conditions; and continually traversed in clearing by the rainbow:—and, secondly, the storm-cloud, always majestic, often dazzlingly beautiful, and felt also to be beneficent in its own way, affecting the mass of the air with vital agitation, and purging it from the impurity of all morbific elements.[70]

Behind Ruskin's meteorological description lies a hermeneutical tension aimed at investing with a sacred interpretation the skies of the past, which received a further addition of brightness and beauty from the clouds, as a confirmation of the harmony and solidarity reigning over the natural world. On the level of the human community, this equilibrium and interconnectedness of the elements combined with the belief of living in a well-defined hierarchical society, whose socio-economic organization no one dreamed of questioning. The opposition between past and present has a particular significance within this context. Although the positive adjectives that countermark the axiological horizon of the past (*luxuriously fine*) are contrasted with their antonyms (*abominably bad*), we may say that the conflict portrayed leads to an image of positivity, since it aims at staging the feeling of a divine order. As a result, the very phenomenology of the cloudy tempest is part of an accurate design that tends to exalt God's greatness as the supreme architect of the universe. There was nothing destructive or malicious in the cloud systems of past ages. On the contrary, they exerted their positive effects on nature and mankind, which emerged all the more purified and chromatically beautified. They were the signs of a majestic force that bore witness to the majesty of the creator whose providential will saw in the clouds a source of nourishment for the imagination ("a Divine Power in creation, which had fitted . . . the clouds for human sight and nourishment"). It is most significant that Ruskin uses the lexeme *beneficent*, which, besides implying, by contrast, the negativity of the contemporary climate, also suggests a moral interpretation of the weather.

In the light of the industrial revolution and the manifold problems connected with unbridled urbanization (slum dwelling, lack of hygiene, pollution, ugliness, degrading habits etc.), the weather manifestations are seen as a revelation of something that directly relates to man's destiny. The cloud morphology Ruskin witnesses early in the 1890s speaks of the apocalypse to come. It is no longer simply a case of acknowledging, as in the ministerial reports of the time, the fact that thousands of chimneys in England are spoiling the landscape and emitting so much smoke that it often covers up the sky, for Ruskin, more importantly, detects in the general atmospheric distortion that the factories have produced the first disturbing signs of a new age, an age of darkness that will find its epilogue in the abyss of a great void and the resulting extinction of the human race:

> In healthy weather, the sun is hidden behind a cloud, as it is behind a tree; and, when the cloud is past, it comes out again, as bright as before. But in plague-wind, the sun is choked out of the whole heaven, all day long, by a cloud which may be a thousand miles square and five miles deep.
>
> And yet observe: that thin, scraggy, filthy, mangy, miserable cloud, for all the depth of it, can't turn the sun red, as a good, business-like fog does with a hundred feet or so of itself.[71]

For Ruskin as well "the sky is built so far." Very far indeed. His insistence on the sun's eclipse by a malicious cloud conveys the extent of his obsession and imaginative involvement with ecological issues. While he looks toward the sky in the compulsive search for a harmonious connection between the clouds and the heavens, all that is revealed is the disastrous conflict of spurious elements that no longer relate to one another because they have lost their natural structures. As wide horizons correspond to cramped spaces, goodness gives way to evil, light is obliterated by darkness—the cloud produced by the "poisonous smoke" is envisioned by Ruskin as "a dry veil, which no ray can pierce." Leaving aside his pseudoscientific and pseudotypological definitions of clouds, for Ruskin, the sky no longer exists. All that exists is the representation of a universe that stages only disharmony, disvalues, and fragmentation: "That harmony is now broken, and broken the world round: fragments, indeed, of what existed still exist, and hours of what is past still return; but month by month the darkness gains upon the day, and the ashes of the Antipodes glare through the night."[72] Following Carlyle's social thinking, *The Storm*

Cloud denounces the tight connection between the ruin produced by industrialism and the moral decadence of the Victorian age. As a social thinker who, from a thundering pulpit, had laid great emphasis on the paradigm of mutual dependence, Ruskin can only register that, in the nineteenth-century world, harmony has been broken. Dramatically, Ruskin no longer recognizes around him the signs from which, years previously, he had derived his faith in the possibility of connecting the arts and, indeed, all those activities that represented the triumph of human creativity. He is no longer ready to see the sun in the sky, just as he can no longer see an ordering principle that should determine the right balance of things, human activity at the service of common good, the ethical value of beauty, and, above all, the glorious relationship between man and nature.

There were several intellectuals who rose against the line of thought that stretched from Carlyle to Ruskin. Believing that a new society could be shaped by wisely espousing the new discoveries of science, they directly associated the idea of progress with the progress of England. Briefly, for such thinkers the only possible point of view was one that saw England as the most powerful and forward-looking nation in the world. Nationhood automatically implied patriotism. Consequently, the inhabitants of England were called upon to make their voices heard as English citizens across the face of the earth for the good of the country and the good of all peoples. It is no coincidence that Disraeli, in concluding his speech at the Crystal Palace on June 24, 1872, used a patriotic tone that most emphatically placed England against all the other nations of the Continent: "It is whether you will be content to be a comfortable England, modelled and moulded upon Continental principles and meeting in due course an inevitable fate, or whether you will be a great country,—an Imperial country—a country where your sons, when they rise, rise to paramount positions, and obtain not merely the esteem of their countrymen, but command the respect of the world."[73] Definitely, Ruskin is different from Carlyle.[74] Indeed, if one compares their ideas one will undoubtedly find more points of divergence than points in common. Nevertheless, it is evident that, during the years in which a national image was being forged, their visionary and apocalyptic interpretation of their age generated reactions and protests of writers who, as did Disraeli, believed that England was not only an economic power and "workshop of the world," but also, and above all, a guiding nation whose anti-Jacobin counterattack seemed all the more necessary, primarily because the ideologies influenced by the ideals of the French Revolution had become more and more acclaimed and deep rooted. This explains why Trollope, in defending the national spirit, can depict both Carlyle and Ruskin as the blind detractors of the nineteenth century: "The loudness and extravagance of their lamentations, the wailing and gnashing of teeth which comes from them, over a world which is supposed to have gone altogether shoddy-wards, are so contrary to the convictions of men who cannot but see how comfort has been increased, how health has been improved, and education extended,—that the general effect of their teaching is the opposite of what they have intended."[75] Trollope represents the voice of common sense more than that of the establishment as such. He is an authoritative interpreter of the new national bourgeoisie, quite satisfied with the status quo, and unable or unwilling to look beyond the small sphere of their class egoism and interests. While it is true that, in spite of its contradictions, progress led to improved health, education, and welfare, these were not the parameters upon which the prophets of the nineteenth century had founded their sermons. Their preoccupations regarded the spiritual health of the nation and the fear of a return to barbarity rather than bare statistics that re-garded widespread comfort and increasing exportation. This is pre-cisely the epistemic context to which Matthew Arnold's work *Culture and Anarchy* (1869) belongs. Undeniably, *Culture and Anarchy* marks an important stage in the history of the word *culture*, whose significa-tion is the exact opposite, in Arnold's effort to offer an axiological interpretation of his age, to all that which seems synonymous of bar-barity: "Culture . . . is a study of perfection. It moves by the force, not merely or primarily of the scientific passion for pure knowledge, but also of the moral and social passion for doing good."[76] Arnold's em-phasis is laid on the way the moral dimension of culture is absorbed by society, where, unfortunately, and misleadingly, curiosity is often mistaken for culture (here it must be added that the word *curiosity*, intended in its negative sense, occurs at least a dozen times in the first few pages of the book alone).

Furthermore, when Arnold speaks of perfection he always asso-ciates the term with the adjective *harmonious*, since it is impossible for him to imagine anything, including perfection, to exist beyond a harmonious relationship between the entities of which it is com-posed. What must also be added here is that a lingering element of disharmony in the progress of humanity toward its noblest ethical and cultural achievements is represented by machinery, which, from Arnold's viewpoint, stands for the negation of spiritual liberty and moral vision: "He who works for machinery, he who works for hatred, works only for confusion. Culture looks beyond machinery, culture hates hatred; culture has one great passion, the passion for sweetness and light."[77] In other words, against the social agitations of the present, and also against the temptations of bloody and deathly anarchy and the repulsive forms of a new barbarism, the remedy he suggests points to "the desire for removing human error, clearing human confusion, and diminishing human misery, the noble aspiration to leave the world better and happier than we found it."[78] Ultimately, for Arnold, the real values of life coincide with the values of art, whose ennobling effects, invariably, and cogently, perform a decisive function in the march of civilization as well as in the achievements of man's highest spirituality. Hence, his tendency to stress the morally edifying influence of great works of art and to see the notion of harmony they embody as the only real stronghold against mankind's attempts at destruction and self-destruction.[79] Arnold sees this function, above all, in poetry, which, as he states in *The Study of Poetry*, is the finest hermeneutic tool in its reference to the profoundest level of human sensibility: "More and more mankind will discover that we have to turn to poetry to interpret life for us, to console us, to sustain us. Without poetry, our science will appear incomplete."[80]

In the wake of his theories on the centrality of poetry as a means of interpreting an age, it may be interesting to note that, as a poet, Arnold produced one of the most significant testimonies of the sense of internal discomfort and disorder that plagued Victorian minds in "Dover Beach" (1867). Paradoxically, if we consider his certainties regarding the harmonizing function of literature, the poem conveys to the Victorian reader an image of spiritual disharmony rather than an artistic meaning whose intent is to overcome the poet's contradictions and dilemmas. "Dover Beach" is all the more illuminating in that it was written in the very years in which Arnold was elaborating the thoughts that he would later on express in *Culture and Anarchy*.[81] Divided into four main movements (lines 1–14, 15–20, 21–28 and 29–37), "Dover Beach" dramatizes the contrast between individual aspirations and the cold severity of decades of religious doubts and disheartening aporias. Above all, in the second part, a traumatic clash is staged between the urgent need for definite values and the absolute inability to perceive an axiological horizon from which to reconstruct an order intended as a cultural response to inner chaos. In brief, what is presented is a poet's failure to find answers ready to give an ontological meaning and religious profundity to human life and to banish the nightmare of a world that is becoming increasingly dark and threatening:

21	The Sea of Faith
22	Was once, too, at the full, and round earth's shore
23	Lay like the folds of a bright girdle furl'd.
24	But now I only hear
25	Its melancholy, long, withdrawing roar,
26	Retreating, to the breath
27	Of the night-wind, down the vast edges drear
28	And naked shingles of the world.
29	Ah, love, let us be true
30	To one another! For the world, which seems
31	To lie before us like a land of dreams,
32	So various, so beautiful, so new,
33	Hath really neither joy, nor love, nor light,
34	Nor certitude, nor peace, nor help for pain;
35	And we are here as on a darkling plain
36	Swept with confused alarms of struggle and flight,
37	Where ignorant armies clash by night.[82]

Like many Victorian intellectuals, Arnold contrasts the past and the present to the complete disadvantage of the latter. In his eyes, the present world has increasingly become a sterile wasteland and has distanced itself from those values that he would rather see in operation and euphorically disseminated everywhere. Having lost its guiding and protecting light (23, *bright girdle-furl'd*), man's faith has become a sadly dry voice whose chaotic and fragmentary pursuit is toward nothingness, toward the end of all. The poet projects his melancholic awareness onto the surrounding seascape, creating visions in which any possibility of a positive response to life's various manifestations is utterly denied (33–34, *neither joy, nor love, nor light / Nor certitude, nor peace, nor help*). Not only is there no certainty, but what actually generates an excited reaction (32, *so various, so beautiful, so new*) is nothing more than a pretense, a trick played upon those who still insist on believing in their dreams. Before the collapse of every interpretative framework, love offers the only possible safe haven. Still, in the Arnoldian perspective, love is not given a religious connotation; it simply refers to the private sphere, to the uncommunicative and hidden universe of two individuals who are seen in opposition to a hostile and insensitive world—29–30, *Ah, love, let us be true / To one another!* Apart from the desire for truth—which is presented almost as an ideological refuge against the dominant deceptiveness—in the very moment in which he acknowledges "human misery,"[83] the poet feels forced to reduce his perspective from a cosmic vision to the spiritually contracted choice of two lovers consoling each other. The only reality imaginable seems to be that of a couple before the squalid panorama of a world that, under the glittering veneer of modernity, conceals an old battered, terminally ill body, destined toward a dark barren territory that no divinity can possibly enlighten.[84]

The urge for authenticity and rediscovery does not lead to a renewed faith, albeit precarious and private. The final three lines of "Dover Beach," which begin with a phrase extraordinarily invested with passivity, 35, *And we are here*, dramatize the apocalyptic scene of a cosmos at the mercy of chaotic forces, at the same time that the end of the illusion of progress and history is laid bare. Observed from their private refuge, 21, *The Sea of Faith* appears to the two lovers as 35, *a darkling plain* over which confusion, darkness, barbarity, and the destructive forces of armies' triumph. The end of history is, precisely, this long night in which even the intimate space reserved for love seems completely devoid of significance and carried away into an abysmal space in which all those who still want to believe in salvation are condemned to silence.[85]

History as silence, and history as illusion. The same negative representation of progress can be found in Gaskell's novel *Sylvia's Lovers* (1863), in which the unceasing movement of the sea becomes a metaphor for a time that is unable to break away from its own tautological circularity: "you may hear the waves come lapping up the shelving shore with the same ceaseless, ever recurrent sound as that which Philip listened to in the pauses between life and death. And so it will be until 'there shall be no more sea'. But the memory of man fades away."[86] Philip Hepburn is one of the main characters of the novel, who, after a life of wandering and escaping from his mistakes, feels he has gained salvation when, in disguise, he saves his own daughter from drowning. At this point, only a few feet away from his home, Hepburn abandons himself to death on the beach, in which the rhythmic crashing of the waves seems a deliberate reminder of the vanity of all things. It is significant, therefore, that Gaskell inserts a scriptural quotation—"there shall be no more sea"—which serves to transfer the narrative events to a metahistorical level: "And I saw a new heaven and a new earth: for the first heaven and the first earth were passed away; and there was no more sea" (Revelation, 21:1).

By reminding her readers that the prospect from which Philip Hepburn's tragedy must be viewed extends well beyond historical contingency, Gaskell explicitly suggests that the real protagonist of history is not memory but the human inclination to blindness and oblivion. The transition from one epoch to another is always marked by man's scornful attitude toward older generations, while he is unaware of what is happening just around him. This is a founding paradox of history. In this context, the fourth chapter of *Sylvia's Lovers* contains a Gaskellian digression, which clearly underlines man's blindness before present events:

> In looking back to the last century, it appears curious to see how little our ancestors had the power of putting two things together, and perceiving either the discord or harmony thus produced. Is it because we are farther off from those times, and have, consequently, a greater range of vision? Will our descendants have a wonder about us, such as we have about the inconsistency of our forefathers, or a surprise at our blindness that we do not perceive that holding such and such opinions, our course of action must be so and so, or that the logical consequence of particular opinions must be convictions which at present we hold in abhorrence?[87]

In Gaskell's problematic view, the present evades any sort of analysis. The scientific methodology informing the way Victorian historians and thinkers decode the signs of their times is really only another example of the fictional mechanism with which, culturally, the ruling classes justify the continuation of their power and authority. Gaskell is acutely aware of the geological scale of time and the consequent relativity of every event. Above all, she is convinced that historical interpretations of the present will inevitably be replaced by the interpretations of those who have the advantage of being temporally distant from events. Although she never intended to go against the Victorian grain, it is clear that such an outlook demolishes one of the most fundamental principles on which authoritative figures like Carlyle, Ruskin, and Arnold based their preachings for contemporary society. What Gaskell postulates is a refutation of any form of dogmatic historicism. In fact, it is her view that an unorthodox thought or new ideological pathway, however rejected and slighted by contemporaries ("convictions . . . at present we hold in abhorrence"), could be seen, with the benefit of "a greater range of vision" (i.e., after the elapsing of some decades), under a more positive light, if not as the only way to cope with the problems of society.

In conclusion, we cannot omit to note how her analysis, while affirming the precariousness of the present and the unknowability of the future, regards disharmony as a structural element of change. The dichotomy order/disorder, more than the Arnoldian formula based on the central role afforded to poetry as a means of developing a harmonious society, entails an acceptance of the state of transition and the relativity of all things as the permanent condition of humanity. In this sense, as Gaskell herself writes, the past teaches us that there is no stability for society or the individual alike. And, emblematically, in *Sylvia's Lovers*, such a contradictory character as Philip Hepburn shows the inanity of history in his inability to soothe the pangs of his tormented soul even when, after a deliberate choice of self-effacement, he becomes part of the turbulence of important historical events.

Before Arnold and Gaskell, Tennyson, in one of the most powerful stanzas of *In Memoriam* (1850), imagines a temporality that, by a stratigraphical vision of the earth, conveys a considerable reduction of human aspirations with regard to any practical possibility of man's supremacy over the whole universe:

> There rolls the deep where grew the tree.
> O earth, what changes has thou seen!
> There where the long streets roars, hath been
> The stillness of the central sea.[88]

What is the role of history in comparison with the spatiality and temporality of the cosmos? Tennyson's poetic sensibility perceives the silent depths of the sea where there were once forests, and in the city streets—with their aggressive, swarming crowds—he sees a primordial expanse of water. Such images remind man of the vanity of his struggle for primacy and, at the same time, portray an earth drifting in the galaxy, tossed about by forces and tensions that no scientist will ever be able to investigate.[89] Even far-reaching changes and momentous revolutions are swallowed up into an endless vortex, in the ever-lasting time of a ruthless and inhuman cosmology. Before so much desolation and constant transformation—great or small though it may be—man's only means of defence is his soul that can still feel and suffer. This is the only manner to assert his being in the world. Yet his soul is always on the other side of history. Remorse for guilty acts, terror for a faltering faith, anguish for a serious failing, suffering for a personal tragedy: all such feelings belong to a space that revolutions or social upheavals never reach. And, even when they do, their impact is never decisive. Therefore, while recognizing the geological scale of time, and aware of a society in which individuals are incapable even of raising their eyes to the sky, the soul of man still feels the importance of faith and, in striving for an inner order, it inscribes the silent text of its disharmonies within the vivacious terrain of the Victorian imaginary.

1

A Tale of Two Cities:
Dickens and the Guillotine

CHARLES DICKENS IS NOT THE KIND OF AUTHOR TO WHOM ONE CAN apply a critical attitude that favors simplistic interpretative shortcuts over an attentive analysis of the complex narratological mechanisms that constitute the basis of his literary imagination. This preliminary consideration, to which almost any Dickensian scholar would readily subscribe, admittedly runs the risk of being an authentic truism. Yet, from the angle of critical praxis, much work still needs to be done toward a hermeneutical disambiguation of the writer's fiction. The same holds, above all, for those attempts at radical revision whose methodological means of investigation tend to privilege content (often disguised as pseudostructuralism) at the expense of a critical analysis capable of accounting for the many interconnected levels of literary textualization. Generally speaking, it may be pertinent to point out that only a cogent scrutiny of semiotic dynamic can direct us toward the segnic complexity of which any masterpiece is constructed. Formulas may help us to comprehend the surface of a text, but they cannot explain its essence, originality, or literariness. Therefore, before a reading of *A Tale of Two Cities* (1859) is proposed,[1] it is important to be wary of the risks of facile interpretative generalizations, which, in this case, would mean reducing the novel to a fictional version of the French Revolution, along the lines of Carlyle's *The French Revolution*.[2] Nothing could be further from the truth. *A Tale of Two Cities* is not a novel about the French Revolution, but a novel that adopts that traumatic event as a founding historical framework capable of conveying a vision of the world to be used as a symbolic model for the Victorian age. To put it another way, Dickens assumes the French Revolution as a *pre*-text to provide his readers with a verbal representation of

51

disharmony as an enactment of Evil. What is thematized is a modern and updated revisitation of Evil in which the narrative process is made relevant to the sensibility of those middle-class Victorians who detected in the monstrous metropolitan crowds an analogical connection with the bloodthirsty mob of the French Revolution itself. The novel is, therefore, not the dramatization of the French Revolution. Behind Dickens's literary mind does not lie the awareness of a theoretical Marxist discussion, prepared to find in historical necessity an explanation for the twilight of the aristocracy.

Although Dickens's narrative intentions did not aim at formulating a clear-cut message, George Orwell saw in him a revolutionary thinker manqué. Thus, in a well-known 1939 essay, Orwell makes the following observation regarding the significance of *A Tale of Two Cities*: "He attacks the law, parliamentary government, the education system and so forth, without ever clearly suggesting what he would put in their places."[3] Significantly, Orwell wrote his essay at the end of the 1930 and, from his ideological stance, a narrative text can be regarded as authentic literature only to the extent that it leaves a profound mark on the real world. If one recalls how during the 1930s political commitment and novel writing went arm in arm, it seems only natural that Orwell should accuse Dickens of being incapable of providing a historically adequate analysis of the French Revolution: "From the "revolutionary" point of view the class struggle is the main source of progress, and therefore the nobleman who robs the peasant and goads him to revolt is playing a necessary part, just as much as the Jacobin who guillotines the nobleman. Dickens never writes anywhere a line that can be interpreted as meaning this. Revolution as he sees it is merely a monster that is begotten by tyranny and always ends by devouring its own instruments. . . . The revolutionaries appear to him simply as degraded savages—in fact, as lunatics."[4] In the same years Orwell wrote these words, Lukács also accused Dickens of being trapped by his own Weltanschauung, which, based exclusively on "his petty bourgeois humanism and idealism,"[5] leads him to reduce historical processes to a mere intertwining of private destinies, the so-called privatization of history.[6] In Lukács's view, Dickens does not at all highlight "the connection between the problems of the characters' lives and the events of the French Revolution," which is reduced to "a romantic background."[7] It is unnecessary to emphasize the particular cultural climate in which Lukács wrote his monograph on the historical novel, just as it is unnecessary to denounce the tendentiousness of such an interpretation, or even to hold oneself aloof from a conception of literature as an instrument of historical awareness and democratization of power. Rather, it seems more important to underline that studies of this narrative genre have made substantially little progress after Lukács. To be more exact, what has been missing is an in-depth investigation into the rhetorical-imaginative procedures that control the shaping of history, and that, strategically, define the intricate and multifaceted relationship between history and the individual. We need, in other words, to adopt a methodological approach that is able, without espousing predetermined ideological models, to establish how the text constructs its meaning, and how it arrives at a unified and coherent representation of the world. Only through a linguistic-structural and epistemic-cultural analysis can we confront the very gist of literary complexity.

But to return to the Dickens interpreted by Lukács, certain questions immediately arise. From a linguistic point of view—that is, the level of discourse strategy—, what exactly is meant by the "privatization of history"? And, from a cultural and literary perspective, what are the ideological implications of the concept of a "romantic background"? It stands to reason that, for a correct focus on *A Tale of Two Cities*, we need to go beyond interpretative straitjacket and qualify our critical investigation by keeping in mind the dialogical nature of the narration. At the same time we must emphasize the multilayered tensions of the textual process as a reinvention of dynamic models. On an extrasystemic level, these models have a significant effect on the specific and immanent organization of the novel.[8]

Even Andrew Sanders's anti-Lukácsian defense of the historical validity of *A Tale of Two Cities* ends up by merely opposing one formula against another. He does not attempt to disambiguate the crucial semantic points of the novel, starting precisely from the connection between private lives and public history, to verify how they determine the destinies of the protagonists that culminate in the final scene of the guillotine presented as a sort of Christian altar of salvation. What Sanders writes is very explicit: "History to Dickens is not an escape, or a release, or a relaxation, or even an object of amusement; it is as much of a nightmare as the present can be, even though the present has succeeded in alleviating some of the abuses and prejudices which once made for disorder."[9] *Pace* Lukács, nobody would doubt Dickens's historical awareness. He was imbued with the words of Carlyle's *The French Revolution*. But this does not mean, as David D. Marcus would believe, that in *A Tale of Two Cities* the reader must necessarily find a historical solution as regards the restoration of order: "Like the author of *Sartor Resartus*, Dickens recognised the death of the old order but could not visualise the birth of a new."[10] Obviously this is by no means the function of the novel. The truth is that the literary imagination always and invariably exceeds historical proceedings. Without such an imaginative excess there could never be an embedding of history in the narrative structures of the text which, by convention, must give artistic form to what the historical text can only suggest. This does not entail a denial of history, but rather an awareness of the importance of transcending it. By placing itself above the French Revolution, *A Tale of Two Cities* becomes Dickens's fictional configuration of a possible world and, at the same time, a metaphor for a disharmony that, somehow, continues to speak to its twenty-first-century readers just as it did to its Victorian readers.[11]

A Tale of Two Cities is constructed around two interrelated meaning-generating poles—London and Paris—that are seen as both profoundly diverse and profoundly similar capitals. By playing on such diversity/similarity dialectics, Dickens creates a plot in which the destinies of his protagonists unfold moving between England and France, in line with a narrative development that alternates dynamic and static moments. In this way, the spatial dimension of its metalanguage is marked by a semiotic structuring in which stasis and movement, homologically, refer to the historical dimension (the French Revolution) as well as the private sphere (the individual and metahistorical tensions of the protagonists as they strive to fulfill their personal desires). In his unraveling of the narrative threads in which public life, affects private life and vice versa, Dickens evokes neither the great figures nor the real-life protagonists of the French Revolution. In contrast with Carlyle's vision,[12] which nevertheless inspired *A Tale of Two Cities*, Dickens's strategy is to give priority to actions occurring on an antiheroic and everyday level, artistically involved as he is in decoding the signs and sociocultural languages of historical marginality. As a result, the actual contexts of the revolution are shown solely from an angle functional to the events narrated in the novel, without providing even a glimpse of the wider and epistemically more relevant context of the historical protagonists. This does not mean that the novel's pluridiscursivity and plurivocality are in any way limited. On the contrary, its broad context and double spatial polarization allow them to function fully within a fervidly visual sensibility aiming at the staging of a scene in which the good and evil sentiments of humanity meet and clash.

From the perspective of Dickens's literary imagination, *A Tale of Two Cities* presents two narrative levels that correspond to the *historical text* (the French Revolution of whose places, names and events the reader has at least a general knowledge) and the *fictional text* (the unraveling and interlacing of the lives of the characters who belong to different worlds and are the bearers of tensions, desires, and alternatively converging and conflicting voices). On every level of the semantic-structural organization of the novel, these two texts are intensely interrelated to create a dialogism that bestows the whole process of signification with a compactness and coherence that makes *A Tale of Two Cities* such a great work. What also cannot be denied is that, as far as the plot is concerned, historical facts are seen as a useful terrain in which to implant the evil that is potentially concealed in every individual. This negative link between the historical dimension and the private sphere charts a fundamental axis that becomes the testing ground to verify the extent to which each character is capable of opposing resistance to the temptations of destruction and wickedness. Robert Alter justly observes that "the treatment of history in *A Tale of Two Cities* does possess a certain imaginative authority because it generally concentrates on history as the medium of implementation of evil."[13] There is no doubt that evil is presented as a proairetic area of nondisjunction between the individual and the masses, between subjective sensitivity and the bloodthirsty crowds of the revolution. If the individual can always be undeniably carried away by the crowd, then, it is easy to conclude that even the mildest person can be swallowed up by the delirious masses and, solely for the pleasure of participating in the collective orgy, be transformed into the most ferocious and gory of all those in revolt.

It is precisely the incipit of *A Tale of Two Cities*, with its emphasis on the contrasting forces that govern the age (the year is precisely 1775), its peculiarly apocalyptic cadence of Carlylean derivation, and, above all, its rapid sequence of contradictions, that defines the patterning of nondisjunctive elements and places in close syntactic and isocolic contiguity completely antithetical moral values:

> It was the best of times, it was the worst of times, it was the age of wisdom, it was the age of foolishness, it was the epoch of belief, it was

the epoch of incredulity, it was the season of Light, it was the season of Darkness, it was the spring of hope, it was the winter of despair, we had everything before us, we had nothing before us, we were all going direct to Heaven, we were all going direct the other way—in short, the period was so far like the present period, that some of its noisiest authorities insisted on its being received, for good or for evil, in the superlative degree of comparison only.[14]

The paratactic organization of the opening sentences conveys a moral dimension that, deliberately abstracted from its sociohistorical coordinates, invests every word with a prophetic tension and immediately recalls the figural intensity pertaining to Bible preaching. The insistent iteration of the segment *it was* underlines the idea of distance striving toward proximity (*the period was so far like the present period*), given that the present and the past are assimilated in the same rhetorical vigor culminating in the evocation of heaven and its contrary. It is interesting to note that Dickens, clearly with the intention of attenuating this linguistically aggressive tone, omits the lexeme *Hell* in preference of a periphrasis. Nevertheless, as a result of the specific morphological-syntactical parallelism (*we were all going direct to heaven / we were all going direct the other way*), the solution in no way weakens the force of the impact; it connotes the scene rather as a blind race toward the "season of darkness" evoked earlier. The verbal configuration tempts one to conclude that the copresence of conflicting images itself recalls a specific verse from Ecclesiastes (1:17) in which the Preacher speaks of wisdom and folly: "And I gave my heart to know wisdom, and to know madness and folly: I perceived that this also is vexation of spirit." *Wisdom* and *folly* are the words that immediately represent the antithetic polarities between which humankind wavers in its race toward the two alternatives of the Christian faith: heaven and hell. Consequently, the long enumeration of antitheses must be read as a preparation, on the one hand, for the general framework in which the lesson of the Christian acceptance of events will be inscribed in the conclusion of the novel. On the other hand, there is no doubt that the light/darkness dichotomy upon which *A Tale of Two Cities*, symbolically, textualizes its meaning also marks the extreme case of words disguising reality. But, as the narrator knows very well, real life almost always moves within intermediate territories, in which the hyperbolical distortions of rhetorical writing have no function.

It cannot go unnoticed, moreover, that the underlying apocalyptic vision points to a representational extremity of human life, a critical threshold beyond which is situated that terra incognita already evoked in the novel's initial words. Precisely because of the paradoxicality of the vision, everything and nothing, fullness and blankness, become mutually exclusive. It is in this context, characterized by verbal excess and dichotomic exaggerations, that the rapid sequence of antitheses paves the way not to a gratifying clarity, but to an enormous interpretative confusion. What emerges is a sort of blackout that is primarily the effect of a deadlock in which the authorial voice seems to be trapped at the end of his analysis: the oppositions simply lead to the representation of a circularity in which the only conclusions drawn encourage the belief that past and present are very similar. Yet the same argument also implies an incitement to deny the value of history both as an experience and as a lesson for humankind.[15] In effect, such an impasse seems to belong exclusively to the "noisiest authorities," who, with their "superlative degree of comparison," are presented to the reader as the only ones that subscribe to the dualistic language of the novel's opening. Wisdom and folly, light and darkness, heaven and hell, everything and nothing, are the antonymous pairings of a more general disharmony of the world, which is also the disharmony of the ruling class, whose blindness makes them unable to read the signs of the times. Certainly, it is a blindness belonging to the rulers of that time (the historical context indicates precisely the year 1775) as well as the hegemonic class of the present (1859—the year of publication of *A Tale of Two Cities*—has been defined as "a turning-point" in the history of English culture).[16]

The story of the "two cities" is a narration focused on a similarity and a difference. Paris and London unfold their destinies along routes whose origins lie in their respective mighty hearts; routes that from the metropolitan center project out toward an external space; routes that often cross over to delineate the trajectories of new encounters and new human mappings. Thus, the mail coaches of *A Tale of Two Cities* travel between the two capitals carrying the protagonists with their sometimes fictitious and sometimes true stories. However, the historical and cultural dialogue that is established between the two capitals makes no progression and leads to *nothing* rather than *everything* since humanity is incapable of progressing, captured as it is in the net of its eternal passions: not the progressive linearity that leads to happiness, not the propulsive movement of a story that fulfills the utopia of a common welfare, but a circular process that, continually returning to its beginning, frustrates the human ambitions, caught between illusions and contradictions, of a radiant future. As the following words from Ecclesiastes warn: "There is nothing new under the sun" (1:9). To put it briefly, the antitheses of the opening sequence give a linguistic form to the confusion in the world and, as a result of their parallel oppositions, are also isotopically linked to the two cities of the novel, which, in many ways, thematize the impossibility of a truth *within* the web of history as well as the prevalence of noise (that is, of violence and barbarity) over the desire for communication and comprehension among men.

The first narrative sequence proper in which the Dover mail advances toward Dover on a cold November night is permeated by this resistance to communication: "There was a steaming mist in all the hollows, and it had roamed in its forlornness up the hill like an evil spirit, seeking rest and finding none."[17] The nighttime scene is rife with a negativity in which the image of an evil spirit gives an ethical-axiological continuity to the "darkness" of the opening sequence, which is, proleptically, imposed as the dominant valence of the narration. The following words, too, which no longer concern the inhospitable and threatening environment, but the human element, further corroborate the dysphoric dimension of the scene: "The Dover mail was in its usual genial position that the guard suspected the passengers, the passengers suspected one another and the guard, they all suspected everybody else, and the coachman was sure of nothing but the horses."[18] As far as the morphosyntactical texture is concerned, suspicion gives rise to a sort of chain reaction that culminates, after the triple occurrence of the lexeme *suspected*, in a dysphoric *nothing*. What is introduced is not a microcosm of collaboration, of light and harmony, but a space dominated by an internal and external darkness of which the passengers' mutual mistrust becomes the clearest symbolical evidence. This dehumanizing loneliness of the individual is paradoxically opposed to the "human" dimension of the horses, which, from the standpoint of the coachman, are the only beings to be trusted, ready to perform their tasks without protesting against the cold and the wet and immune to the profound diffidence that permeates all those in the mail coach. The aim of Dickens's narrative modality in the first part of *A Tale of Two Cities* is not so much to thematize the loneliness of a group of travelers who are strangers to one another and have no desire whatsoever to make one another's acquaintance, as to introduce mystery intended as the fundamental paradigm of human behavior. The narrator presents the actions of the characters, reveals their aspirations and feelings, penetrates into their thoughts, but ultimately there always remains a margin of obscurity, an unfathomable territory: it is the space of *nothingness*. And it is precisely this impenetrable inner marginality that, resisting even the boldest imagination, stimulates and inspires the narrative voice to wonder over the destiny of men, as at the beginning of chapter 3 ("The Night Shadows"), while the mail coach advances toward Dover:

> A wonderful fact to reflect upon, that every human creature is constituted to be that profound *secret* and mystery to every other. A solemn consideration, when I enter a great city by night, that every one of those darkly clustered houses encloses its own *secret*; that every room in every one of them encloses its own *secret*; that every beating heart in the hundreds of thousands of breasts there, is, in some of its imaginings, a *secret* to the heart nearest it! Something of the awfulness, even of Death itself, is referable to this. No more can I turn the leaves of this dear book that I loved, and vainly hope in time to read it all. No more can I look into the depths of this unfathomable water, wherein, as momentary lights glanced into it, I have had glimpses of buried treasure and other things submerged. It was appointed that the book should shut with a spring, for ever and for ever, when I had read but a page. It was appointed that the water should be locked in an eternal frost, when the light was playing on its surface, and I stood in ignorance on the shore. My friend is dead, my neighbour is dead, my love, the darling of my soul, is dead; it is the inexorable consolidation and perpetuation of the *secret* that was always in that individuality, and which I shall carry in mine to my life's end. In any of the burial-places of this city through which I pass, is there a sleeper more inscrutable than its busy inhabitants are, in their innermost personality, to me, or than I am to them?[19]

As the journey toward Dover continues in the darkness and fog, each of the travelers is no less unintelligible than the night landscape. To render the idea of hermetically closed individualities even more explicit, the narrator foregrounds all his own astonishment regarding the humanity that he sees as the mystery of all mysteries. Almost as if intending to decelerate the progress of the mail coach, the story hesitates to present bare facts and creates strategies of postponement, moments of irresolution. This takes us to a further narratological consideration. Before passing on to the main narrative events, Dickens, more than anything, intends to prepare, for the benefit of his readers, the hermeneutic tools with which they can focus more clearly on the ties between individual destinies and the French Revolution. He thereby dispels any doubts about providing any idea of history that is not one of an enormous disharmony.

Nothing could be more tragically impenetrable than a great city asleep at nighttime, a cluster of houses and a series of confined rooms huddled together in the dark. This Chinese box–like topology of the metropolis designates the thresholds that the writer's piercing eye must cross before confronting the individual, whose heart, that final and impassable threshold, is the location of a mystery par excellence. Nothing can penetrate its mysteries. Not even the liveliest and boldest imagination can lay bare its innermost thoughts. This opaque territory of every human being, ontologically, defines itself as a covert space that resists any interpretation and concedes nothing to either the narrator's or the historian's readings. The isotopy of secrecy constitutes one of the semantic axes upon which the story is constructed: the five repetitions of the lexeme *secret* in the preceding quotation may already be seen as a hermeneutic warning for those who, erroneously, expect the French Revolution to be interpreted by a narrator who embraces the idea of history: "profound secret and mystery to every other . . . its own secret . . . its own secret . . . a secret to the heart nearest to it." Secrecy is not a question of distance or proximity and has nothing to do with the social strategies of honest dissimulation or skillful deception. It is not the cold conscious choice to raise a defense barrier in order to protect one's vital space from the aggressiveness of others. It is nothing connected with the sociohistorical dimension.

In Dickens's conception of individuality, secrecy is an ontological condition that expresses in the most quintessential way the separateness of every being from the anonymous and nonanonymous mass that makes up the rest of humanity. From this angle, as is explicitly stated by way of conclusion ("the secret that was always in that individuality"), secrecy and individuality amount to the same thing. And yet, what the narrator detects in the inaccessibility of the human soul is by no means a positive self-definition and self-expression on the part of the individual being. On the contrary, he perceives it as a space that rejects life in its innumerable daily manifestations. Paradoxically, the innermost and secretive chamber of our soul ends up, by invariably eluding an exchange with external life and experience, as a part of us that is exposed to the dominion of Death. This latter, through the trope of personification, establishes an intratextual dialogue with the Darkness of the intense ouverture of *A Tale of Two Cities* to define an ontological framework that focuses on the continuity between life and death. To put it briefly, life is the word that is uttered (i.e., the inner life that reveals itself), while death is the word that is concealed (i.e., the buried inner life, hidden from others). It follows that the secret (the secret that resists the devastations of time) is the bond that every human being has with death, precisely for the reason that every individual carries to the grave the things never revealed to anyone, either because the individual did not want to reveal them or because he could not. In this sense of absolute closure, the secrecy of human beings, in Dickens's cemeterial responsiveness, is no different from the mystery that every grave retains forever. The final question leaves no room for doubt: "In any of the burial-places of this city through which I pass, is there a sleeper more inscrutable than its busy inhabitants are, in their innermost personality, to me, or than I am to them?"

Nevertheless, the narrator seeks to establish a dialogic relationship with the city. Like Wordsworth is in "Composed upon Westminster Bridge," he is especially fascinated by the evocation of its "mighty heart." Besides the unfathomable heart, the unfathomable stories connecting individual life to the metropolitan universe work hauntingly on Dickens's imagination, stimulating him to set up an analogy between the city and its inhabitants. The mystery involves the opposition between being and appearing that, in a really extraordinary way, belongs both to the cityscape and to the individuals living within it. An inside and an outside, a visible and an invisible reality: these dichotomies actively nourish a more general disharmony. The façades of the houses reveal very little of what is inside just as the faces encountered in the streets reveal nothing of the identities of their owners. There are no physiognomic rules that account for the many cartographies of what is axiomatically invisible. Thus, if the inside of a book is open for a few moments, it is only to show that its purpose is to be closed: "It was appointed that the book should shut with a spring, for ever and for ever, when I had read but a page." Dickens, of course, is not lamenting the total illegibility of the world. He is simply affirming that the hermeneutic level of our reading will never be able to fathom its profundity and the entirety of its mystery, but will be forced to stop at the ultimate threshold, at a point very close to the revelation of the truth which, in any case, remains out of reach.

The whole of the first part of *A Tale of Two Cities* (which corresponds to the first section, significantly titled "Recalled to Life") is structured around the paradigm of the inscrutability of individual human behavior and, homologically, the inscrutability of collective destinies. Consequently, to return to the scene of the journey and the three characters in the mail coach, what clearly emerges is the total isolation of each passenger, to which corresponds, not only a total lack of solidarity and communication, but also an anguishing sense of vulnerability and precariousness: "So with the three passengers shut up in the narrow compass of one lumbering old mail coach; they were mysteries to one another, as complete as if each had been in his own coach and six, or his own coach and sixty, with the breadth of a county between him and the next."[20] This is the psychological-behavioral framework in which the writer inscribes his narration inspired by the French Revolution: not a grand historical canvas adopted as a founding ground upon which to stage fictional events, directly involving important or tiny figures of history, but the interstitial image of a silent mail coach, a scene in movement that refuses to be focalized. Indeed, it is not the narrator's intention to depict the scene, but rather he wishes to actualize an effect of visual and phonic fading out. Admittedly, darkness, vapor, and fog are agents of a dissolving that also *dissolves* the imposing outlines of the two cities, while showing the careful toiling of a mail coach, which, being neither in Paris nor in London, seems to be wandering lost in a maze, breathless and terrorized, in search of a solitary ghostly figure from history. Nevertheless, the mail coach does not lose its traces in the night fog: the heavy numbness of the travelers is interrupted by a messenger on horseback with an urgent letter for Mr. Jarvis Lorry, of Tellson's Bank in London. Before he sets off again, the man on horseback is entrusted with a message to take to London "RECALLED TO LIFE."[21] The banker's three words are given orally, but Dickens reports them as if they were the headlines of the front page of a daily newspaper. This sensational episode, however cryptically encoded, triggers off a mixture of curiosity and suspicion in the other passengers, a suspicion that is further heightened by the fact that Mr. Lorry is a banker whose pragmatic thoughts have notoriously little to do with supernatural phenomena. The curiosity of the passengers is the psychological factor that, according to literary conventions, motivates the curiosity of the reader, who suddenly realizes that there is no imaginative discontinuity between the spectralization of the night landscape and the specter reunited to his body with which during the journey Mr. Lorry engages in silent conversation.[22]

A recurrent metaphor in *A Tale of Two Cities* is that of resurrection, which, in Dickens's narrative discourse, establishes an ontological and moral dialogue of proximity with the change of heart. In both cases, what takes place is a transformation that, as indicated in the syntagm "recalled to life," is decidedly invested with Christian overtones. Within the complex network of parallelisms and contrasts that distinguish the plots and subplots of the novel, it is the story of Dr. Alexandre Manette—the "resurrected" man—that is placed at the center of the French Revolution. His personal plight takes the form of an explicit exposure of the decadence of the French aristocracy that makes him a victim of the abuses and injustices at the origin of the people's insurgence. At the center and at the margins of the revolution: Dr. Manette does not share the same world of the revolutionaries because he belongs to a different class and culture. Thus, he does not represent anarchy and barbarity, but the positive values of human understanding and cultural sensitivity; he does not preach democracy but believes in the power of the conscience to react against injustice. Yet some questions may legitimately be asked at this point. For example, why exactly has Dr. Manette been imprisoned in the Bastille for eighteen years? What precise crime has earned him such a hard sentence? When we consider that the mail-coach journey toward the "resurrected" man occurs in November 1775, the events leading up to his imprisonment obviously date back to 1757. This is the year in which a young doctor, who is witness to the harrowing scene of the death of a young girl abused by two brothers of the Parisian high aristocracy, decides to report the fact by writing a private letter to the minister with the intention of demanding justice. This courageous act, however, only produces the immediate effect of another injustice. In his prison memoirs, Dr. Manette recalls the epilogue of the episode featuring the family of the marquis St. Evrémonde as its ruthless protagonists: "The Marquis took from his pocket the letter I had written, showed it me, burnt it in the light of a lantern that was held, and extinguished the ashes with his foot. Not a word was spoken. I was brought here, I was brought to my living grave"[23]: buried alive in the Bastille, the tomb of the living. The founding idea is that of a man buried alive, swallowed up into the bowels of the earth, and

completely concealed as a result of attempting to challenge the laws
of the powerful by denouncing their misdeeds.

This being the previous story, the recovery of Dr. Manette's lost
identity, his metamorphosis from a ghost of the past to a man of the
present, can only be brought about by disinterment, an activity that
entails principally a recovery of the memory: it is important to dig
deep down if the body is to be recovered from the psychological ruins
of trauma, and if the soul is to be saved from the trauma itself and the
individual restored to the ontological continuity of its own personality. This is no easy task, however, because what has to be investigated,
confronted, and decoded is the mystery of Dr. Manette with the secret of his past and long deathly silence. Significantly, while the mail
coach proceeds toward Dover where Mr. Lorry is to encounter Lucie,
the daughter of the "resurrected" doctor, not only is there a parallelism between the dark journey and the darkness in which the victim of aristocratic cruelty has lived for eighteen years, but images of
disinterment haunt the banker himself and lead to melancholic and
apocalyptic visions: "After such imaginary discourse, the passenger
in his fancy would dig, and dig, dig—now, with a spade, now with a
great key, now with his hands—to dig this wretched creature out. Got
out at last, with earth hanging about his face and hair, he would suddenly fall away to dust. The passenger would then start to himself, and
lower the window, to get the reality of mist and rain on his cheek."[24]
In his practical interpretation of the world, Mr. Lorry is incapable of
imagining the metaphorical implications of disinterment. What his
imagination projects is actually a macabre vision of the living dead.
The fact that he is obsessed by the idea of digging is evident when,
in the dining room of the Royal George Hotel in Dover, prior to his
encounter with Lucie Manette, he abandons himself to a reverie that
culminates in the image of an excavation: "As the day declined into
the afternoon, and the air, which had been at intervals clear enough
to allow the French coast to be seen, became again charged with mist
and vapour, Mr. Lorry's thoughts seemed to cloud too. When it was
dark, and he sat before the coffee-room fire, awaiting his dinner as
he had awaited his breakfast, his mind was busily digging, digging,
digging, in the live coals."[25] "Digging, digging, digging": digging in
the search for a lost image, digging to recover the dreams of his childhood, and digging to find a light in the darkness. If the obsessive
imaginings of the banker are anything to go by, man's main activity
seems to be one of continual excavation, or, rather, restoring things

to life in the sense of redesigning the map of the past so that memory prevails over oblivion: the oblivion of events, the oblivion of ideas, and the oblivion of human beings. Forgotten by everyone, buried in a dungeon in the Bastille, Dr. Manette is found and restored to life. In Mr. Lorry's statement it seems that everything can be summed up in the words he utters to the messenger: "This is a secret service altogether. My credentials, entries, and memoranda are all comprehended in one line, Recalled to Life, which may mean anything."[26] Once they find themselves in the presence of the prisoner, Mr. Lorry and Lucie Manette realize that the "resurrected" man is merely a body without a soul. The person discovered may have the same body as Dr. Manette, but his weary soul lies elsewhere. For his resurrection to be complete, all the broken ties between his past and present need to be reestablished. Once the body is restored to life, the soul has to be dragged out of the darkness. And this is a much more difficult and delicate process.

Who is the Dr. Manette of 1775 if not a man whose memory is like an empty room in which words and gestures are meaningless? For his daughter and the banker his face appears a blank that has nothing to communicate: "No human intelligence could have read the mysteries of his mind, in the scared blank of his face. . . . They tried speaking to him; but he was so confused, and so very slow to answer, that they took fright at his bewilderment. . . . He had a wild, lost manner of occasionally clasping his head in his hands, that had not been seen of him before; yet, he had some pleasure in the mere sound of his daughter's voice, and invariably turned to it when she spoke."[27] It is a confused, bewildered man without historical-social coordinates who has been exhumed, and who tries to protect himself from external sounds, a man who feels crushed by the heavy weight of the world as it unfolds before him. Indeed, the experience of being disinterred and freed from imprisonment seems no less traumatic than the extreme experience of death. His new birth implies an abandonment of the *other*—that is, of the lonely man in the Bastille, the man who for eighteen years spent entire days at his shoemaker's bench. The abandonment, finally, is that of the prisoner who no longer knows Dr. Alexandre Manette but answers to a new and absurd identity: a number and a place: "One Hundred and Five, North Tower."[28]

The encounter with his daughter, Lucie, and Mr. Lorry does not produce the miracle of a sudden harmonious reuniting of body and soul: for just as there are two cities in the story, there are also two souls in the doctor-shoemaker. To the eyes of his saviors, Dr. Manette seems to be a man from the underground who rejects the real world with the same force with which he rejects the light that blinds his eyes. He resists the notion of having to appear in the world. Alexandre Manette is precisely the ghost that his daughter was afraid of meeting: an infinitely lonely being who, like a robot, fills his time by performing the same recurring gestures of a shoemaker working to complete, in his repetition compulsion, the killing of his real identity. The shoemaker, in other words, works like a madman to deface the last real remnants of a young doctor who, many years previously, had had the courage to denounce the injustices inflicted on the French people:

> The faintness of the *voice* was pitiable and dreadful. It was not the faintness of physical weakness, though confinement and hard fare no doubt had their part in it. Its deplorable peculiarity was, that it was the faintness of solitude and disuse. It was like the *last feeble echo* of a sound made long and long ago. So entirely had it lost the life and *resonance of the human voice*, that it affected the senses like a once beautiful color faded away into a poor weak stain. So sunken and suppressed it was, that *it was like a voice underground.* So expressive it was, of a hopeless and lost creature, that a famished traveller, wearied out by lonely wandering in a wilderness, would have remembered home and friends in such a tone before lying down to die.[29]

The insistence on Manette's voice indicates the measure of his silence. After such a lengthy imprisonment, he is no longer capable of communicating with and relating to the outside world, which, for him, is a wasteland, a desert that produces in him only a lingering death wish—it is not society but the underground world that is Manette's natural element. His voice, which he has not been able to use for eighteen years, and which he has forgotten how to use, is the obvious sign of his social death. It is not only the indicator of the silence of his body, but also the silence of his soul, a place of forgetfulness that triumphs over memory. While the other characters underline the miracle of his resurrection, the prisoner only longs for the silence of death, which, from a psychobiographical angle, means the total physical and spiritual annihilation of Dr. Manette. His endless, painful inner journey in the search for the signs of his past has been a fruitless one and can therefore lead only to death. Bewildered and confused before Lucie, he can only ask whether she is his jailer's daughter. Following one of the recurrent *topoi* of Victorian fiction,[30] the father's recognition of his daughter occurs only when he focuses on her golden hair. Their embrace is an affective response to an aesthetic-physiognomic impact:

> Her golden hair, which she wore in long curls, had been hurriedly pushed aside, and fell down over her neck. Advancing his hand by little and little, he took it up and looked at it. In the midst of the action he went astray, and, with another deep sigh, fell to work at his shoemaking.
>
> But not for long. Releasing his arm, she laid her hand upon his shoulder. After looking doubtfully at it, two or three times, as if to be sure that it was really there, he laid down his work, put his hand to his neck, and took off a blackened string with a scrap of folded rag attached to it. He opened this, carefully, on his knee, and it contained a very little quantity of hair: not more than one or two long golden hairs, which he had, in some old day, wound off upon his finger.
>
> He took her hair into his hand again, and looked closely at it. "It is the same. How can it be! When was it! How was it!"[31]

This scene is important because the golden light of Lucie's hair initiates the defeat of the darkness that still persists in the man's heart. Typical of Dickens's melodramatic strategies, the recognition does not happen once and for all as a climactic moment in the bond between father and daughter. On the contrary, it is never taken for granted, for there always remains a temptation in the "resurrected" man to return to the underground, and to be only a number, living in the constant obsession of his activity as a shoemaker and therefore ignoring change. Self-protective and unconscious as this attitude may be, it unquestionably entails ignoring those people who have made him revisit his past and relive the scenes of an inexpressible pain that have led to his separation from his family and his physical and moral "burial" in a tower in the Bastille.

Paradoxically, all of his past suffering seems summarized in the scrap of rag in which he has kept "one or two long golden hairs"— they have been, and remain, the extremely fragile link between the man and his past, an intimate, delicate, and precious link that somehow sets off an imperceptible, yet authentic internal movement toward the unknown girl. Thus, Dr. Manette can only wonder what mysterious event has made the lock of hair he has kept in the folded rag so similar to the girl's hair. If his sensations are real, then the whole world surrounding him is a pretense, a fiction that he cannot and must not trust. If, instead, it is not a fictional scene, then he does not exist and is merely a ghost living the strange experience of being among the living. This, in short, is the reaction that lies behind his confused state. As soon as Dr. Manette has regained his freedom, what the change has involved for him is the discovery of a life suspended between darkness and light, the very state of nondisjunction to which the incipit of the novel refers. For many years after being taken back to England, Dr. Manette continues to be persecuted by his past: the mental imprisonment persists even when everything should help him to feel free. Indeed, during his identity crisis, in the middle of the night, he walks back and forth in his room and, in the search for salvation, takes up his shoemaker's tools and works with the same absorbed concentration as prisoner "One Hundred and Five, North Tower." Thus, "a low hammering sound in his bed-room"[32] is a warning to his daughter of the reemergence of his hell, the reaffirmation of the dysphoric polarity, the surrender to an immense pain that no filial affection can apparently wipe out. For his integration into the community to be complete, he has to cross over other thresholds. These other experiences are connected with an acceptance of the French Revolution and its "hard, hard history,"[33] and his definite spatial displacement to London, where, in the end, he finds domestic bliss in a quiet house in Soho, together with his daughter, Lucie (conveniently married and mother to a child called Lucie) which, topologically, configures a moral reply to the antiworld of death, violence, and savagery represented by the Bastille.[34]

The title of the second book of *A Tale of Two Cities* is "The Golden Thread." It is an explicit reference to Lucie Manette's blond hair, whose symbolization, set in the melodramatic climax of her encounter with her father, represents the euphoric polarity of the diegesis. The chromatic quality of Lucie's hair constitutes both a mnemic-fabulistic sign as well as a unifying element that, in its peculiarly gendered encoding, emerges as the only morally gratifying thread within the complex web of lives and events. It is the golden thread that leads to the final domestic scene in which the virtuous characters, while cosily sitting in front of the fireside, enjoy a sort of psychological compensation by telling stories of a revolution that is also a story of two cities. The golden thread also intermingles the lives of three men who have three distinct functions in Lucie Manette's life: Dr. Alexandre Manette (her father, who embodies a deep-set anguish deriving from his memory of the injustice he suffered), Charles Darnay (her husband—i.e., Charles Evrémonde—who thematizes the nightmare of history), and, finally, Sydney Carton (the devoted worshipper and the sinner who fulfils his desire for redemption in the form of a real moral resurrection).[35] This triadic actorial structure includes, on the one hand, the similarity relationship between Charles Darnay and Sydney Carton, who, in the numerological organization of *A Tale of Two Cities*, actualizes the idea of coupling, or, rather, the number 2 that is expressly cited in the title. On the other hand, besides Lucie's "golden thread," the three characters are linked by the theme of death since, in many ways, Manette, Darnay, and Carton more than once imagine dialogue with their own respective dying selves.

Like Dr. Manette, Charles Darnay undergoes the trauma of an act of injustice when, in 1780 he is tried by an English court for high treason against the monarchy and is only saved by the entrance of his double, Sydney Carton, who dismantles the whole accusation against him by showing the ease with which a person's identity may be mistaken. The facts contested refer to his crossing of the chan- nel on board a packet ship five years previously while traveling to- ward London in the company of Lucie Manette, her father, and Mr. Lorry. Apart from the double identity of the accused (Charles Dar- nay, the English gentleman, is in contrast with Charles Evrémonde, the French émigré), what must be immediately noted is the extraor- dinary way in which the destinies of Dr. Manette—the doctor buried alive in the Bastille by the marquis St. Evrémonde—and Charles Darnay, or Evrémonde, saved from hanging by the vital testimony of his resemblance to Carton, are interlinked. Immediately after his acquittal, Darnay meets Carton. Eloquently, they engage in the fol- lowing exchange, which, from a narrative point of view, may be seen as an indirect prolepsis:

"Do you feel, yet, that you belong to this terrestrial scheme again, Mr. Darnay?"

"I am frightfully confused regarding time and place; but I am so far mended as to feel that."

"It must be an immense satisfaction!"

He said it bitterly, and filled up his glass again: which was a large one.

"As to me, the greatest desire I have, is to forget that I belong to it. It has no good in it for me—except wine like this—nor I for it. So we

are not much alike in that particular. Indeed, I begin to think we are
not much alike in any particular, you and I."

Confused by the emotion of the day, and feeling his being there
with this Double of coarse deportment, to be like a dream, Charles
Darnay was at a loss how to answer; finally, answered not at all.[36]

Carton's question is by no means out of place. His gesture saves the
accused man from a death that was already prepared to comply with
its destructive mission. Now, with his return to the world of the living, Darnay still feels in a quandary. He experiences a liminality that
is all the more ontologically powerful in that he is forced to conceal
his true identity from everyone. It is no accident that he, fully aware
of being a *liminal persona*, has confessed earlier to Carton: "I hardly
seem yet . . . to belong to this world."[37] With respect to the paradigm
of belongingness, Carton too cannot see the reasons why he should
belong to "earthly schemes." He feels like a tragic outsider, a man
destined to an existential marginality that no heroic gesture will ever
redeem: "I care for no man on earth and no man on earth cares
for me."[38] The fact that he is an alcoholic further underlines his desire to be elsewhere and to assume as his own personal strategy the
ideology of nonbelongingness, since the society in which he lives
offers no moral reasons for living, apart from his devotion to Lucie.
Despite his *contemptus mundi*, it is Lucie who is the only credible and
appeasing response to his thirst for affection; she embodies all that
he craves but knows he can never possess. As he confronts the image
of the perfect gentleman in Darnay—"a young man of about five and
twenty, well-grown and well-looking, with a sunburnt cheek and dark
eye. His condition was that of a young gentleman"—,[39] Carton cannot help noticing that, apart from their physical resemblance, their
lives and destinies are divided by an unbridgeable distance, which
denotes a cluster of inner values in Darnay that he cannot recognize
in himself.

For his part, Charles Darnay detects a further element of ontological confusion in his double ("frightfully *confused* regarding time and
place. . . . *Confused* by the emotion of the day") that brings home to
him the sense of an entirely problematic relationship with the world
that is almost always invested with a dreamlike and painful marginality. As can be easily seen, despite the major differences in their
respective characterizations, the three men who are linked by Lucie
Manette's golden thread share an existential destiny that is strongly

marked by the mystery of life. In fact, their lives are directly inscribed in Dickens's discourse around the impenetrability and indecipherability of the soul, and his definition of secrecy as something that is totally excluded from life and, consequently, open only to death. Thus, it is significant that Carton—the only one of the three who is not forced to face death while in a prison or a courtroom—defines his role in terms of mortality, or, to put it more plainly, in terms of death. He confesses to Lucie his most complete and sincere devotion to her, without forgetting to declare: "I am like one who died young. All my life might have been."[40] When Carton discloses his love for the girl, every word he utters really seems to belong to a man who is not only without a future but already dead. He is metamorphosed by his own words into a mere ghost, who, while postulating the essential secretiveness of his individual identity, has finally decided to lay bare his most intimate aspirations and deep-rooted desires: "'If it had been possible, Miss Manette, that you could have returned the love of the man you see before you—self-flung away, wasted, drunken, poor creature of misuse as you know him to be—he would have been conscious this day and hour, in spite of his happiness, that he would bring you to misery, bring you to sorrow and repentance, blight you, disgrace you, pull you down with him. I know very well that you can have no tenderness for me; I ask for none; I am even thankful that it cannot be."[41] The self-destructive and self-denigrating tension of Carton's words is an index of the urgency of a religious sentiment that is linked with his ultimate choice to sacrifice his own life in order to save Darnay's and, above all, to save a family that, from his point of view, has as its moral pivot the woman with whom he is hopelessly in love. As he continues to open his heart to Lucie, Carton lays bare the peculiar nature of his aspiration, which goes beyond historical processes and individual destinies. What he desires is an actual resurrection:

> "If you will hear me through a very little more, all you can ever do for me is done. I wish you to know that you have been *the last dream of my soul*. In my degradation I have not been so degraded but that the sight of you with your father, and of this home made such a home by you, has stirred old shadows that I thought had *died* out of me. Since I knew you, I have been troubled by a remorse that I thought would never reproach me again, and have heard whispers from old voices impelling me upward, that I thought were silent for ever. I have had

unformed ideas of striving afresh, beginning anew, shaking off sloth and sensuality, and fighting out the abandoned fight. *A dream, all a dream, that ends in nothing,* and leaves the sleeper where he lay down, but I wish you to know that you inspired it."[42]

In Dickens's novels, memory often plays a decisive role in determining the transformations of the soul, which, by altering the ontological status of the individual's inner universe, postulate a significant turning point in men's destinies. In this sense, Carton's meeting with Lucie sparks off a series of recollections—the return to life of lost "old shadows"—whose images reveal values that he had believed cancelled forever by his cynical, skeptical, and destructive attitude. From his defeatist silence, new, reassuring voices move forward to enlighten his path toward the possibility of redemption. Nothing can undo the negative vector of his life, but there is still the possibility of a battle that implicitly involves a desire to combat evil and to defend goodness. The personality that moves into sight in his confession is no longer a negative "I" doomed to sink into nothingness. On the contrary, it is an "I" that projects itself out toward humanity at large, which, thanks to the golden thread that Lucie offers him ("I wish you to know that," Carton repeats twice), now appears to him in all its dimension of positive solidarity. Yet, in spite of his goodwill, even his desire to struggle and assert goodness becomes a form of failure: for the only thing Carton has left in his life is his encounter with Lucie, to whom he entrusts "the last dream of [his] soul."

In his moral intransitivity, in his ontological short-circuiting, Carton "abandons" life without making the ultimate choice of death. At this point in the novel, he is a dangling man, lost in his liminality, in the expectancy of an event that will somehow offer him a final possibility to abandon the limbo territory he occupies and affirm his desire for goodness. The extreme cynicism that assails him as he takes his leave of the girl reconfirms his ontological wavering between the desire for change and the practical impossibility of being different: "An hour or two hence, and the low companions and low habits that I scorn but yield to, will render me less worth such tears as those, than any wretch who creeps along the streets."[43] The street, which is topologically antithetic to the microcosm of domestic space, is negatively connoted and countermarked as a space of perdition, while the eddying crowd seems to engulf Carton and deliver him once more to the forces of evil.

But this is not to be the case. Lucie Manette marries Charles Darnay while in France the risk that the discontent of the people will escalate into revolution becomes increasingly evident. In the third book ("The Track of a Storm"), which is set in 1789, the revolutionary storm involves Charles Darnay, who, after being identified and recognized as the marquis St. Evrémonde, is accused of the crime of emigration and transferred to the Parisian prison of La Force. After his eventual acquittal, he finds himself implicated in the responsibilities of the French aristocracy when the discovery is made that his wife's name is Lucie Manette, and that she is the daughter of Dr. Alexandre Manette. It is at this point that the doctor's manuscript, which contains a precise and detailed account of the cruelty of the Evrémonde family, is read out in court. What is the document discovered among the ruins of the fortress if not a new "disinterment" of Dr. Manette's heart-rending past? It is also, ironically, a resurrected text that is to be decisive in convincing the court to apply the death sentence to the person the doctor has always known only as Charles Darnay.[44] Thus, his memories from the past resurface to pin down the aristocracy to its responsibilities as it reveals, in the convoluted network of relationships between private and public, a textualization whose truth is grafted onto the historical necessity of the revolution, for, indeed, who would question the cruelty of the aristocracy? If it is true that "[Darnay] had voluntarily relinquished a title that was distasteful to him, and a station that was distasteful to him,"[45] is it fair to make him the only one to pay the price for the sins that his noble family have committed not only in the past decades but also in the past centuries? From the moment in which Darnay-Evrémonde's life is projected on the ideological horizon of the revolution, the aristocrat is no longer seen as an individual but as an enemy of the people—his antiaristocratic gesture and his words, honest and heartfelt though they may be, are unable to blot out his historical iconicity stained with crimes, injustice, and violence. His noble title automatically inscribes him in a sign system for which his head is worth just as much as the king's, both of them belonging, as it were, to the same symbolic category. And this semioticization of Darnay-Evrémonde is amply confirmed by the reading of the numerous pages of Dr. Manette's manuscript: "A terrible sound arose when the reading of this document was done. A sound of craving and eagerness that had nothing articulate in it but blood. The narrative called up the most revengeful passions of the time, and there was not a head in the nation but must have dropped before it."[46] The document recalls the scene of its composition, evoking the image of an intellectual who, in his extreme despair, like a survivor from a shipwreck on a desert island, entrusts his very last message in a bottle thrown out into the limitless expanse of water. However, Manette's is no ordinary narrative; it is not the simple request for help or the letter of someone condemned to death. It is a text that is marked by its own historical valence, since it speaks of the injustice in the world, particularly the injustice that reigns in France. Besides, the idea gained from Manette's papers is also that of writing as a means of rediscovering the gift of words, no matter if it is only a written word. If absolute segregation for Manette means the anguishing silence of the world, his choice to write opens up the possibility of an encounter with the Other—through his writing, he can imagine a silent interlocutor, an absent addressee who makes his loneliness less psychically shattering. Considering that a word is always marked by an explicit or implicit dialogical vector, language invariably contains the desire to connect with other people's words, which is an index of civility and culture. After the document has been read, however, the reply is only a "terrible cry" that is a denial of language and the most evident indicator of a bloodthirsty barbarism. Darnay-Evrémonde's condemnation to the guillotine becomes the great occasion for Carton to move into view and free himself from his moral sloth. As his double, Carton takes the condemned man's place before the guillotine and faces death.

In so doing, he becomes an agent against devastation, in defense of those domestic values symbolized by Darnay and Lucie Manette's family—in defense, that is, of the middle class serenity of which the little world of Soho, protectively distant from the ferocious revolution, seems to be the authentic epitome. The closure of *A Tale of Two Cities* therefore foregrounds Dickens's alternative to the insulting mob and bloody scaffolds of the French Revolution:

> "I see Barsad, and Cly, Defarge, The Vengeance, the Juryman, the Judge, long ranks of the new oppressors who have risen on the destruction of the old, perishing by this retributive instrument, before it shall cease out of its present use. I see a beautiful city and a brilliant people rising from this abyss, and, in their struggles to be truly free, in their triumphs and defeats, through long years to come, I see the evil of this time and of the previous time of which this is the natural birth, gradually making expiation for itself and wearing out.

"I see the lives for which I lay down my life, peaceful, useful, prosperous and happy, in that England which I shall see no more. I see Her with a child upon her bosom, who bears my name. I see her father, aged and bent, but otherwise restored, and faithful to all men in his healing office, and at peace. I see the good old man, so long their friend, in ten years' time enriching them with all he has, and passing tranquilly to his reward.

"I see that I hold a sanctuary in their hearts, and in the hearts of their descendants, generations hence. I see her, an old woman, weeping for me on the anniversary of this day. I see her and her husband, their course done, lying side by side in their last earthly bed, and I know that each was not more honoured and held sacred in the other's soul, than I was in the souls of both.

"I see that child who lay upon her bosom and who bore my name, a man winning his way up in that path of life which once was mine. I see him winning it so well, that my name is made illustrious there by the light of his. I see the blots I threw upon it, faded away. I see him, fore-most of just judges and honoured men, bringing a boy of my name, with a forehead that I know and golden hair, to this place— then fair to look upon, with not a trace of this day's disfigurement— and I hear him tell the child my story, with a tender and a faltering voice.

"It is a far, far better thing that I do, than I have ever done; it is a far, far better rest that I go to than I have ever known."[47]

After his dramatic portrayal of "the disjointed time"[48] of a world gone astray, after his narration focused on the triumph of chaos over the individual's desire for ordering principle, and, again, after the annihilation of every palingenetic prospect through the effects of a revolution that, disastrously, has transformed civilization into a wasteland, the narrator stages the end of the night. Sydney Carton's words before the guillotine may be seen as the representation of a euphoric connection of past, present, and future: the visionary drive of a man sacrificing his own life to save another's allows for a possible future unity and order, and it simultaneously gratifies the reader's expectancy of an ending. It suggests a better world to come for everyone and, above all, the victory of justice over tyranny, discrimination, and violence. In Carton's verbal configuration, the guillotine is soteriologically transformed from a symbol of barbarism into a symbol of his own redemption as well as that of humanity in general. The victim is no longer Darnay-Evrémonde's double who chooses to die on the scaffold to save, for the second time, a man of whose life he knows barely anything. In the end, he becomes the figural representation of an *imitatio Christi* who resolves the initial antithesis between Darkness and Light to the advantage of the latter. He also anticipates, and partly inaugurates, the era in which "a beautiful city and a brilliant people" will reemerge from the abyss of despair and sin. In brief, describing his resurrection Carton also describes the resurrection of the world.[49]

Hence, it is no accident that as the condemned man, hand in hand with a young seamstress, is about to offer his head to the "ministers of Sainte Guillotine,"[50] he recites the words of Christ from the gospel (John 2: 25–26): "I am the Resurrection and the Life, saith the Lord: he that believeth in me, though he were dead, yet shall he live: and whosoever liveth and believeth in me shall never die."[51] *He shall never die*: the final image of a heroic figure who, after his radical internal metamorphosis, shows his readiness to succumb to the guillotine as a symbolic reiteration of Christ's sacrifice is in perfect accordance with the semantic universe that unifies and characterizes Dickens's macrotext. But there is even more than this. If it is undeniable that, diegetically, it is Alexandre Manette who is "recalled to life" in the first book, retrospectively, after reading the ending, it is easy to see that the man who has really been "resurrected" is the one who can now rise as a symbolization of the palingenesis of society. That man is Sydney Carton. From his ontological marginality as double, from the ancillary position of one, physiognomically, and psychologically, depending on another's identity (Carton is Darnay's double and not the opposite), he moves to the center of the stage. In this way, he becomes the protagonist of a text in which his resurrection is narrated *in the* progeny of Darnay-Evrémonde, whom he has saved from the guillotine (and who thus becomes another "resurrected" man). The protagonists "recalled to life" are precisely the three men who, through the magical influence of Lucie's golden thread, find a way to establish for themselves a place beyond death, and thereby to defeat death. But it is equally true that only Carton can declare that "he shall never die" it is light of this biblical phrase (the defeat of death and the eternity of life) that we are invited to read Dickens's message in defense of a continuity that only belongs to the private sphere of genealogies, against history as inane circularity, and as incapacity to provide an alternative to the great anarchy of the French Revolution. Carton will not die in eternity both because he thematizes the Gospel of John by making the guillotine his cross, and because in his mental picture he imagines a boy who has been named after him—Lucie Manette and Darnay-Evrémonde's son—becoming a wise judge and administrator of the law. What he has been unable to do, because of his excessive devotion to debauchery and laziness in pursuing a career as a lawyer, his hyperbolic and elated imagination projects into a radiant future in which his dreams will come true.

The theatrical epilogue of Carton's story is a perfect thematization of the Dickensian idea of the mystery governing the behavior of all men and that—as was seen in the opening words of chapter 3—defines an impenetrable space withdrawn from social life and from humanity itself. However, in the scene of the guillotine the mystery is disclosed, for how can the permanence of the mysteriousness of Carton's tragic fate be read, if not as a testimony of the divine origin of man? From this point of view, Carton appears to embody "the mystery of a Person,"[52] as proposed by Carlyle: mystery as an ontological attribute that characterizes the individual in terms of a final positive assessment of his personality.[53] The text of Carton's vision establishes an immediate dialogical connection with Dr. Manette's document, given that both of them are produced in the same condition of liminality and are presented as acts of testimony whose content intervenes further to interlace—in a significant genealogical continuity—Lucie's "golden thread" with the lives of the three men who have performed, even though with different roles, a common function toward the construction of a bourgeois order.

With respect to the linguistic structuring of the ending, it must be observed that Carton's words recall not so much the rhetorical style of the biblical prophets as John Bunyan's *The Pilgrim's Progress* (1678). Just as the visionary passages of *The Pilgrim's Progress* are rendered through the anaphoric iteration of the phrase *I saw*,[54] the same happens on the level of the morphosyntactic organization of the flow of Carton's discourse. His visionary observations move, with an insistent verbal representation, from the scenes of the revolution of the present to the overjoyed image of a future characterized by the private happiness of the individual. Furthermore, as *A Tale of Two Cities* is centered on the contrast between two cities, Bunyan's text also dramatizes the antithetical images of the "City of Destruction" and the "Celestial City," which indicate the protagonist's journey from sin to salvation according to a moral itinerary that, at several points, corresponds to Carton's. The vision of the "beautiful city" reveals Carton's apocalyptic desire to enter the New Jerusalem rather than a euphoric and historically credible metropolitan scene projected into the future. Even in this respect, Dickens's hero follows the same itinerary as Christian in *The Pilgrim's Progress.* Nevertheless, unlike that of Bunyan's character, Carton's journey toward the scaffold becomes a sort of Way of the Cross during which the inhuman cries and derision of the crowd do not affect his serenity or that of the young seamstress who shares his destiny—"She kisses his lips; he kisses hers; they solemnly bless each other."[55] In short, Sydney Carton becomes the central focus of the scene on the scaffold not so much because he dies, not because his head is cut off by a blade, but because he manages to transform his sacrifice into a spectacle, an impressive event that is not to be easily forgotten. It is only in this way that he can give a meaning to his life and resurrection before the executioner and the guillotine, whose lugubrious presence somehow allows the narrativization of his sacrifice for the benefit of the "spectators" of the times to come. "The tale of two cities," from this point of view, becomes the story of Sydney Carton, which, with the repetitions of its nominations ("a child upon her bosom who bears my name . . . a boy of my name") and narrations, in its passing from one generation to another, champions the primacy of the domestic values of the new English middle-class mentality.

From Dickens's historical perspective, the French Revolution is finally subsumed into the image of the guillotine, which, through Sydney Carton's beheading, postulates the eradication of any private sphere from its "language" based on institutionalized violence. At the same time, thanks to the blade that establishes and legitimizes the idea of Christlike sacrifice, Carton becomes a new prophet who can speak of the alternative world. Now, from his ideologically oriented pulpit, he can envisage a future society in which all conflicts are resolved and the sacred serenity of domestic life becomes the triumphant representation of harmony. Before the epilogue, the revolutionary events spark off a series of metaphors insistently referring to a great and uncontrollable whirlpool that annihilates everything and consigns everything to chance. The text hereby configures history as the circular movement of a vortex whose relentless, centrifugal action negates and extinguishes every individual desire and every private drive toward self-realization. In a way, it is the crowd that, despite its anonymity, plays a dominant and unifying role on the historical stage.

Needless to say, behind the portrayal of a bloodthirsty, ferocious, hungry mob lies a petty bourgeois attitude that equates the crowd with anarchy, violence, and brutishness—and this is an ideologeme that we find at the inception of Dickens's textualization.[56] On the one hand, there is the domestic sphere of Lucie Manette and the three men tied to her by the "golden thread" of virtue and piety; on the other, the indistinct mass of those who, while giving visibility to history, correspond to forces that lead directly to savagery and bestiality, to the negation of every human sentiment; those who have "a tigerish smear about the mouth" and who, at every possibility, are only too ready to spell out the word *blood*, their most urgent longing: "one tall joker so besmirched . . . scrawled upon a wall with his fingers dipped in muddy wine-lees—BLOOD."[57] By making the lexeme *blood* function as the hypogram of the revolution, Dickens conveys a very precise message to his reader, who cannot fail to infer the connection made between the desire for blood and ignorance, which, in their perverse and inextricable web, are presented as the premonitory signs of popular revolt. The fact that the narrator imagines all the negativity looming on the horizon of the poor Parisian suburb of Saint Antoine as an evil cloud must not be underestimated:[58]

> And now that the cloud settled on Saint Antoine, which a momentary gleam had driven from his sacred countenance, the darkness of it was heavy—cold, dirt, sickness, ignorance, and want, were the lords in waiting on the saintly presence—nobles of great power all of them; but, most especially the last. Samples of a people that had undergone a terrible grinding and regrinding in the mill, and certainly not in the fabulous mill which ground old people young, shivered at every corner, passed in and out at every doorway, looked from every window, fluttered in every vestige of a garment that the wind shook. The mill which had worked them down, was the mill that grinds young people old; the children had ancient faces and grave voices; and upon them, and upon the grown faces, and ploughed into every furrow of age and coming up afresh, was the sign, Hunger.[59]

It is the cloud on Saint Antoine that emblematizes the ills of a people who, at the end of their tether, are prepared to burst and inundate the nation with their threatening floods of blood, ignorance, and violence. What must be noted here is that the Parisian lumpenproletariat seem to entrust their destiny to history, because history means change. And, in their case, every sort of change is better that the present predicament. In other words, they nourish their expectation with the belief that the unfolding events of history will bear those signs implying their liberation from the "nobles of great power." But, on the contrary, the image of the mill, ironically, epitomizs the idea of a circularity that, rendered also in the morphosyntactic structuring of the discourse (especially in the polyptoton *grinding, regrinding, ground, grinds*), accelerates the progressive destruction of the humble while preparing the way for death. The mill is the iconic staging of Hunger—"the sign, Hunger"—that stands out as the dominant figure in the scene. It is no coincidence that Blood, Ignorance, Hunger are the personifications of a morality tale centered entirely around the tragic events of the French Revolution. It is no ordinary hunger that is personified, but the hunger that has been besieging the agonized Parisian suburb for so long—the hunger of those waiting to rebel. The profound sense of their revolt resides in the narrator's lexical choices, which not only qualify hunger in detail by presenting its various consequences, but also partly justify its lethal conclusion:

> It was prevalent everywhere. *Hunger* was pushed out of the tall houses, in the wretched clothing that hung upon poles and lines; *Hunger* was patched into them with straw and rag and wood and paper; *Hunger* was repeated in every fragment of the small modicum of firewood that the man sawed off; *Hunger* stared down from the smokeless chimneys, and started up from the filthy street that had no offal, among its refuse, of anything to eat. *Hunger* was the inscription on the baker's shelves, written in every small loaf of his scanty stock of bad bread; at the sausage-shop, in every dead-dog preparation that was offered for sale. *Hunger* rattled its dry bones among the roasting chestnuts in the turned cylinder; *Hunger* was shred into atomics in every farthing porringer of husky chips of potato, fried with some reluctant drops of oil.
>
> Its abiding place was in all things fitted to it. A narrow winding street, full of offence and stench, with other narrow winding streets diverging, all peopled by rags and nightcaps, and all smelling of rags and nightcaps, and all visible things with a brooding look upon them that looked ill. In the hunted air of the people there was yet some wild-beast thought of the possibility of turning at bay.[60]

However obsessively reiterated and obviously apparent, the moral qualification of hunger is presented as an emblem of a fact that no governor can see. What the word *hunger*, which is repeated seven times, shows is a sort of huge inscription that runs throughout the entire nation. The anaphoric construction of the phrases indicates the narrator's intention to dramatize a play called *Hunger* through a series of rapid scenes that reveal not only the extent of its omnipresence but also the way Hunger is the real name of "a spectre [who] is haunting Europe."[61] Dickens seems to be telling his reader that hunger no longer belongs to the starving individual who says "I am hungry," but rather has become a tautological totality that, self-referentially, declares, "Hunger is hungry." This is the paradox that the writer's narrative tension thematizes precisely to make us understand how, by eliminating the subjective voice, the following phase is inevitably one in which the beast will gain the upper hand over man.

In his textualization of Hunger as a necessary historical event, together with his search for a verbal order intended as an alternative to revolutionary disorder, the writer insists on the notion of circularity.[62] In doing so, the trope of repetition (see, for example, the parallel syntagms *A narrow winding street* and *other narrow winding streets*) becomes linguistically representational of the idea of revolution as a great and senseless vortex of history—a maelstrom marked by a totalizing disharmony. It is no accident that after defining the initial agitations of the revolution, "a great storm in France, with a dreadful sea rising,"[63] the narrator insists on the water metaphor to describe the agitations of the inhabitants of Saint Antoine, led by Ernest Defarge and his wife (and here it is important to remember that the revolutionary couple keep Dr. Manette under their care immediately after his release from the nearby Bastille), like a centripetal vortex that drags everything into its frantic circular movement: "As a whirlpool of boiling waters has a centre point, so, all this raging circled round Defarge's wine-shop, and every human drop in the caldron had a tendency to be sucked toward the vortex."[64] The attack on the fortress of the Bastille becomes an uncontrollable tide, a human mass that, having given their lives to hunger, now have nothing to lose and rage with "the furious sounding of a living sea,"[65] against the symbol of the ancien régime until, after four hours, a white flag signals that the siege is over and that the Bastille is in the hands of the rebels, who do not waste a second to inundate it with their bestial presence: "so tremendous was the noise of the living ocean, in its irruption into the fortress, and its inundation of the courts and passages and staircases."[66] The swirling images predominate over all the others and, in their insistent repetition, thematize the great disharmony that from the suburban quarter heads toward the center of Paris like a dark and uncontrollable flood:

> The sea of black and threatening waters, and of destructive up-heaving of wave against wave, whose depths were yet unfathomed and whose forces were yet unknown. The remorseless sea of turbu-lently swaying shapes, voices of vengeance, and faces hardened in the furnaces of suffering until the touch of pity could make no mark on them.
>
> But, in the ocean of faces where every fierce and furious expres-sion was in vivid life, there were two groups of faces—each seven in number—so fixedly contrasting with the rest, that never did sea roll which bore more memorable wrecks with it. Seven faces of prisoners, suddenly released by the storm that had burst their tomb, were car-ried high overhead: all scared, all lost, all wondering and amazed, as if the Last Day were come, and those who rejoiced around them were lost spirits.[67]

This human sea conveys the scene belonging to the Last Judgment in which tombs are opened and bodies reunited with their souls. Dick-ens sets up an imaginative series of associations between the rebellion of the people and the apocalypse, both of which will end only with the conclusion of the narration. Revolution is no longer revolution: it has metamorphosed into chaos. Before the reader there is a stage on which the personifications of Chaos, Blood, Hunger, and Ignorance play their respective roles, while waiting for the arrival of the prima donna, "The Vengeance." On this occasion, chaos, the sea, and the crowd are one and the same force, which, "black and threatening . . . destructive . . . yet unfathomed . . . yet unknown . . . remorseless," com-pletes its performance thanks to the semantic contribution of Venge-ance, which is the nickname of one of the "heroines" of the people's revolution: "The Vengeance, uttering terrific shrieks, and flinging her arms about her head like all the forty furies at once, was tearing from house to house, rousing the women."[68] Once again the mass of women, guided by The Vengeance, flow through the streets like a whirling, orgiastic flood that no barrier can hold back: "With these cries, numbers of the women, lashed in blind frenzy, whirled about, striking and tearing at their own friend until they dropped into a passionate swoon, and were only saved by the men belonging to them from being trampled under foot."[69] It is almost as if the evil cloud of Saint Antoine itself has generated the sea—a monster born with the purpose of spreading contagious wickedness throughout the world. It is as if the struggling elements have made a temporary truce in order to destroy every form of humanity in man and, regressively, consign its existence to a ruthless primal bestiality: "In such risings of fire and risings of sea—the firm earth shaken by the rushes of an angry ocean which had now no ebb, but was always on the flow, higher and higher, to the terror and wonder of the beholders on the shore—three years of tempest were consumed. Three more birthdays of little Lucie had been woven by the golden thread into the peaceful tissue of the life of her home."[70] In his insightful and far-reaching study of crowd behavior, Canetti acutely observes: "The word 'ocean' is the final expression of the solemn dignity of the sea. The ocean is universal, it reaches everywhere, it touches all lands: the ancients believed that the earth itself swam on it. If it were possible, once and for always, to fill the ocean, the crowd would have no image of its own satiability."[71] The revolution continues like a mad whirlwind, attracting everything to it, annihilating everything, and turning everything into a great force that devours men, whether they belong to the enemy or wear the Jacobin cockades: the image of an ocean that has no ebb reveals the extent to which the world has come to be under the sway of disharmony. It is a disharmony whose effects, as have been seen, also involve Lucie Manette's golden thread. Safe in her domesticity without shadows, Lucie measures time by the birthdays of her daughter, who, in line with a circularity pertaining to every level of textual organization, is also called Lucie. But the juxtaposition of the two contrasting scenes (*three years of tempest* vs. *Three more birthdays*) proleptically assumes that the other city will also be dragged by the great wave of the revolution into the square in which the guillotine has been erected: "One year and three months. During all that time Lucie was never sure, from hour to hour, but that the Guillotine would strike off her husband's head next day."[72] Nevertheless, Lucie's husband is spared the bloody blade of the guillotine since fate has bestowed on him a double that, in a certain sense, is the gift of a second life. Sydney Carton is converted to play the role of someone who must be removed and eliminated for the good of humanity. Such a coincidence—that is, the emergence of the *other*[73]—is rightfully associated with the mysterious dimension that Dickens believes he can see within every individual soul, for not everything can be rationally explained simply because light is never only light, and darkness never only darkness. Opacity prevails over *claritas*: there is no bedrock on which to build a stable interpretation. There are areas that cannot be ultimately defined. It is precisely within these areas of nondisjunction that the narrator constructs his stories about the French Revolution.

Although the ocean overwhelms the whole of the French aristocracy, it is not able to overwhelm the man who, by renouncing his own name, has manifested a social consciousness that overcomes the narrow limits of the cruel and inhuman nobility. Darnay-Evrémonde's head is spared neither because he has had a moral conversion, nor because the revolution has ceased to perform its devastating activity. The truth is that the private sphere of Soho is saved thanks to an act of shrewdness that finds its fundamental support not in the concealment of a nobleman's identity, but in a physiognomical coincidence, or, to be more precise, the fortunate encounter with a double who seeks to convert himself by becoming a Christian martyr. It is undeniable that the "resurrected" man Darnay-Evrémonde, together with Lucie Manette, also espouses the values of bourgeois orthodoxy, which, with every means, seeks a comforting response to its hidden terrors in the tranquil limited spatiality of domestic life.[74] In Dickens's imagination, the natural consequence of this reassuring separateness entails a recognition of the supreme importance of heart and home over genealogical privileges and the economic interests of an increasingly selfish and corrupt world. Consequently, while individuals may find existence in part redeemed in the domestic sphere, there is no possibility for redemption in the regions in which history operates and unfolds its plots.

2

Wilkie Collins, Death, and the Labyrinth of the Letter

WHEN ABOUT TO PUBLISH HIS SERIALIZATION OF THE DEAD SECRET[1] in *Household Words* in January 1857, Wilkie Collins's major concern was to convince critics and readers alike of his independence from Dickens, whose popularity was at its height. Collins wanted to secure his own literary identity and market, particularly since, in his earlier works, he had given the impression that he was Dickens's imitator and continuator, if not his actual epigone. How could a writer who had already revealed remarkable inventiveness with such novels as *Basil* (1852) *Hide and Seek* (1854) and a collection of short stories, *After Dark* (1856), distance himself from the awkward Dickensian shadow? Although he could recognize no particular qualities by which to define himself aesthetically, he was aware of the fact that he had to adopt an approach that could not be instantly traced to Dickensian themes and techniques, and that would mark the definite end of his period of literary apprenticeship. Thus, without renouncing certain strategic-fictional methods that already anticipated the textualization of such important novels as *The Woman in White* (1860) and *The Moonstone* (1868), Collins attempted to achieve in *The Dead Secret* what he himself defined as "the poetry of everyday truth."[2] To be underlined is not so much that *The Dead Secret* reveals an evident search for certain thematic paths corresponding to his own innovative views, nor that it represents a transitional stage toward the writer's mature period in the 1860s, but rather that it makes some significant metaliterary observations regarding the novel form and its transformations.

However, another point must be made clear. While it is not irrelevant to speak of truth in the case of the sensation novel, it is important to add that this particular kind of truth has no philosophical implications. More precisely, what is meant by truth is a point in which every mystery is explained and any order, momentarily disrupted, is restored. Truth is deeply ingrained in mystery, and this truth is the other side of the mystery to be reached and disclosed after a long trial. In a way, truth may also be regarded as a hidden document that will eventually clear up a crime, a mischief, and whatever has been covered by secrecy and silence. Therefore, it would be rash to see truth in Collins as operational in everyday life, as something that, at least in his purely theoretical intention, would seem to anticipate the "hard truths" that lie behind the lives of the humble people described by George Eliot in chapter 27 of *Adam Bede* (1858).[3] For him, the phrase "everyday truth" does not have the social and axiological connotation that it does for Eliot. On the contrary, it refers to those acts of *transgression* that are concealed behind the thousand various gestures of everyday life. Briefly,—and this is a feature Collins shares with all the other writers of sensation fiction[4]—what stimulates his imagination are certain events that appear to others as normal and conventional, but that are really terrible and indecipherable, and all the more so for the very fact that they take place between the four walls of domestic life, and far away from the grand scenes of the Gothic tradition. By treating such events, these "domestic stories" shed a light, in a way that differs from Eliot, on the dark forces of the human soul and question its most basic certainties. These "silent" events undermine the foundations of the reassuring image that Victorian society projected of itself.[5]

In the case of *The Dead Secret*, Collins adopts a strategy of essentialization of the secret by means of a letter that is the repository of a hermeneutic power that the characters both tend toward and distance themselves from. Everything is functional to this writing of the truth, while the other expedients that usually characterize sensation fiction remain dormant, or, at the very least, more or less unconscious, behind the scenes of the novel. This is what distinguishes *The Dead Secret* from Collins's other works. His deliberate renunciation of most of the stylistic elements of the genre entails an entrusting of his plotting of the domestic drama to the disruptive forces of a text (the letter) inscribed within another text (the novel). As a result, the narrative development hinges on the writing of the letter, which, considering the peculiarity of its contents, becomes an unavoidable structural principle whose wide-ranging impact affects the destinies of the main characters.[6]

The Dead Secret is a novel about a letter: a single letter that, being both a confession and a testamentary act, tells more about the power of words than about the characters themselves. Its message is a vector whose meaningful excess (i.e., semantic surplus) evades the control of the very people who have signed it. *The Dead Secret* is the story of this overdetermined letter, which, unlike the many letters scattered in various Victorian narratives, acts as a pivot to the actions and thoughts of the characters. More importantly than the actual secret it contains, its words give form to the destinies of the characters as well as the novel itself, which, precisely, unfolds along a span of time extending from the moment of the production of the epistolary writing to the moment of its discovery. Thus, besides imposing its own language of a truth that postulates a return to order and daily life, the letter impresses its ethical-behavioral intentions onto a metaliterary code that, as shall be seen, controls the beginning and end of the novel and actualizes a marginalization of the main characters with respect to the primacy given to the rhetoric of the narrative language.

"Can she have told him?"[7] The words Mrs. Treverton's faithful maid, Sarah Leeson, repeats to herself immediately introduce the theme of secrecy. As she wonders in anguish whether her mistress has ever summoned the courage to speak to her husband, Captain Treverton, Sarah Leeson not only verbally constructs the key point of *The Dead Secret* but at the same time exhibits her emotional involvement in the revelation. It is no accident that a few pages later the maid asks her mistress the same question she has asked herself: "Have you told my master?"[8] The disinterment of the secret is rendered all the more urgent by the fact that Mrs. Treverton is on her deathbed: a situation of ontological liminality that calls for a liberating act that will allow the woman to die at peace with herself. If Mrs. Treverton is the repository of a secret which is shared by Sarah Leeson, the behavior of the latter remains a mystery. Her unrelenting questionings and fearful trembling, her palpitating way of acting on the stage of secrecy, go well beyond the submissive role belonging to a maid. Briefly, what is evident is that at Porthgenna Tower, a large country mansion on the west coast of Cornwall, a course of action is being charted in which a mistress and maid are to be interpreters of a fiction of transgression on equal terms, both of them attempting to restore order to a disconnected reality. Because of her impending death, Mrs. Treverton feels she can no longer hide from her husband the fact that their only daughter, Rosamond, was not born of their marriage, but is the daughter of Sarah and a miner who tragically died before he could marry the maid.

This is precisely "the poetry of every-day truth" that Collins intends to explore. From a literary angle, Collins's aim is to show how a sensational event drawn from the new social reality may become an imaginative text whose inspirational fountainhead is truthfulness ("every-day truth"). In fact, the semantic core of *The Dead Secret* contains the story of a child effectively stolen from a maid in order to gratify the paternal desires of a husband. In polemical contrast to Victorian socioeconomic and religious norms that conceptualized the family as an institutional pivot as well as a guarantee of stability, the novel is structured around a paradigm of inheritance and origin that destabilizes the family. But what can an origin be without the implication of an end? Death interrogates the conscience of the dying person, when he/she must make a final decision without delay: how to make an exit from the worldly scene, and how to conclude the pattern of his/her life, and to what extent to unburden his/her soul from guilt, sins, and secrets. In Mrs. Treverton's case, after an existence built on lies, an ultimate single act of truth seems to provide her with a way to confront death. This ultimate choice means that she also has to relive the beginning. Because she lacks the necessary courage to reveal her deceit directly to her husband, Rosamond's story and her obscure origins are set down in writing:

> The writing case, with a sheet of note-paper on it, was placed upon Mrs. Treverton's knees; the pen was dipped into the ink, and given to her; she paused, closed her eyes for a minute, and sighed heavily; then began to write, saying to her waiting-maid, as the pen touched the paper: "Look."
>
> Sarah peered anxiously over her shoulder, and saw the pen slowly and feebly form these three words: —*To my husband.*
>
> "O, no! no! For God's sake don't write it!' she cried, catching at her mistress's hand—but suddenly letting it go again the moment Mrs. Treverton looked at her.
>
> The pen went on; and more slowly, more feebly, formed words enough to fill a line—then stopped. The letters of the last syllable were all blotted together.
>
> "Don't" reiterated Sarah, dropping at her knees at the bed-side. "Don't write to him if you can't tell it to him. Let me go on bearing

what I have borne so long already. Let the Secret die with you and die with me, and be never known in this world—never, never, never!"

"The Secret must be told," answered Mrs. Treverton. "My husband ought to know it, and must know it. I tried to tell him, and my courage failed me. I cannot trust you to tell him, after I am gone. It must be written. Take you the pen; my sight is failing, my touch is dull. Take the pen, and write what I tell you."[9]

This is the crucial scene of *The Dead Letter*. Although the two women maintain their relationship of complete complicity, the real mother and the fictional mother now respond in different ways on the basis of the life/death opposition. On the one end, Sarah Leeson, who belongs to the side of life, has no desire to carry on her shoulders alone a burden that, until that moment she has shared with her mistress; the idea terrifies her and she attempts by every possible means to exclude herself from the paralyzing scene of the epistolary writing. On the other hand, the woman who is on the threshold of death— "the beckoning hand of Death was signing to her from the Gates of the Grave"[10]—wants to relieve her guilty conscience by entrusting her double, the woman who has played her role as mistress during the childbearing time, with a message that signifies the exposure of an act of transgression. The maid's extreme anxiety culminates in an impulsive gesture of protest in which she tries to stop her mistress's hand, a reaction that can be explained by the fact that Sarah does not want to see reactualized, even though only in epistolary writing, her condition as a fallen woman. Such a reactualization would put at the fore her divided self and this is why she immediately begins to suffer moral qualms and to evince psychobehavioral disturbance.

But even on the point of death, the roles of maid and mistress must be respected: even while dying, Mrs. Treverton asserts her authority as director of the final scene. If Sarah Leeson wants the secret to die with both of them ("Don't write to him"), Mrs. Treverton replies with an opposite determination ("It must be written")—that finally results in her decision to write a letter to her husband. The moment of writing leads, significantly, to another act of complicity. Feeling her energy to be temporarily reviving, Mrs. Treverton begins to write the letter, which will later, however, be completed by the maid, who complies with her mistress's wishes only after the latter threatens that in case of disobedience her ghost will return from beyond the grave to punish the maid: "Write, or I shall not rest in my grave. *Write, or as true as there is a Heaven above us, I will come to you from the other world!"*[11]

Resorting to her former experience as theater actress, Mrs. Treverton organizes the sequence of her death in a series of dramatic procedures culminating in the writing of the letter, which becomes the structural center around which the whole narrative development revolves and depends. To be underlined here is the obsessive attention with which the maid observes the pen, the object of a silent battle and vehicle of a decisive gesture that entails the end of a lie. It may also be noticed that the word *pen* is repeated no fewer than eleven times and always with a particular emphasis, almost as if the pen rather than the actual letter were materializing the secret.

The insistent reference to the writing materials, in the confrontation between the mistress and the maid, highlights Sarah Leeson's passivity, for in spite of her moment of rebellion, she agrees in the end to write and so to play the role of accomplice even in the last act of Mrs. Treverton's life. In this case, it is the mistress herself who puts the pen between her fingers ("Closing her fingers mechanically on the pen that was thrust between them."[12] The climax is reached when, in a further submission to the urgency, Sarah Leeson is forced not only to write the text of the letter but also to countersign it as an accomplice:

> Her eyes recovered their steady look of intelligence; and, when she again addressed her maid, reiterating the word "Write," she was able to enforce the direction by beginning immediately to dictate in quiet, deliberate, determined tones. Sarah's tears fell fast . . . but she wrote submissively, in wavering lines, until she had nearly filled the two first sides of the note-paper. Then Mrs. Treverton paused, looked the writing over, and, taking the pen, signed her name at the end of it. . . .
>
> "Sign!" she cried, beating her hand feebly on the bed-clothes. "Sign Sarah Leeson, witness. No! —write Accomplice. Take your share of it; I won't have it shifted on me. Sign, I insist on it! Sign as I tell you."
>
> Sarah obeyed; and Mrs. Treverton taking the paper from her, pointed to it solemnly, with a return of the stage gesture which had escaped her a little while back.[13]

The reader knows nothing about the text of the letter, apart from the opening phrase (*—To my husband*), which thereby gives a hint of the nature of its contents. In providing this hint, Collins consciously distances himself from the narrative conventions of the genre, which always leave the mystery to be solved at the end. But in accord with the conventions, the narrator's emphasis is on *how* the letter comes to be written and not on its contents. Significantly, the initial pages of the first chapter focus on the dramatization of an act of writing that, by becoming the main event, is also depicted as a watershed between a *before* and an *after*, from which there is no turning back. Once the letter addressed to the man who has been the victim of the deceit has been composed, the manner in which the letter was written rather than its contents will give shape to subsequent events. The context prevails over the text, the scenic modality over the practical encoding. As a result, it is the clash between Sarah and Mrs. Treverton regarding the epistolary writing that determines a disorder that is resolved into order only when it is actually read by the destined recipient. To put it another way, the fact that Mrs. Treverton is at peace with herself after she completes her confession does not imply any restoration of order; on the contrary, the event is only the beginning of new deceits and secrets that will continue to conceal the dead secret, the secret par excellence.

The nature of the bond between the mistress and the maid is, in reality, much more complex than the opening scene of the novel allows the reader to perceive. Normality and order are paradigms that do not belong to Mrs. Treverton's life. Having arrived from the "obscure stage of a country theatre,"[14] she continues to act a part in an unconscious desire to hold on to her theatrical personality even after becoming mistress of Porthgenna Tower. She also forces her maid to "act out" a script that entails an exchange of roles, epitomizing thereby a symbolic upheaval of social harmony. In the diegetic framework of an explicit dramatization of the contrast between "the strong nature of the mistress and the weak nature of the maid,"[15] the plot links them both on a fictional and on a real level that acquires an existential valence. Sarah agrees to recite the role of her mistress and undergo a sort of physical and psychical dispossession of her own body whereby she forgets she is a servant. Thus, once she is forced to resume the behavioral codes of a subordinate, she cannot help feeling a profound and radical identity crisis. Becoming a divided self, she has to cope with the guilt feelings deriving from a traumatic fracture: she has rejected her maternal role by renouncing her daughter and her association with the innocent happiness of childhood. The script has imposed on her the part of a childless servant, while nature persists in claiming her rights to a very different role in life. The claims of nature and maternity are, in this context, both on the side of psychic order and behavioral continuity.

The episode in which she is forced to countersign a letter whose text she has played no part in producing places Sarah in a position of extreme involvement in her mistress's existence. In this inextricable interlinking of destinies, the maid's identity is no longer clearly defined and seems rather to be blurred into a different personality, which she is unable to recognize or control. After the letter-writing scene and the subsequent swearing on the Bible, and, above all, after the death of her mistress, a disintegrating, confusing, and inescapable vortex possesses her. She is no longer the Sarah Leeson of the script imposed by Mrs. Treverton, but neither is she any longer the Sarah Leeson *before* Porthgenna Tower: "Lost in the labyrinth of her own thoughts,"[16] "She lost herself in a maze of useless conjecture"[17] From an ontological angle, the woman loses herself in a mental maze whose chambers can be compared topologically to the Gothic and labyrinthine structure of the north wing of the house,[18] which becomes a point of convergence of her thoughts and obsessions, and, almost in imitation of her mistress, of her desire for death as well.[19]

"Swear that you will not destroy this paper, after I am dead."[20] In conformity with her self-dramatization and her desire to control events even after her death, Mrs. Treverton forces the maid to take an oath that she will not destroy the letter, which, however, is not to be seen outside the walls of Porthgenna Tower. Her death prevents the actualization of the third and most fundamental stage of the oath: that of immediately consigning her written confession to Mr. Treverton. Partly because she wants to withdraw from her mistress's orders and partly because she does not wish to see Mr. Treverton suffer, Sarah refuses to hand him the letter, justifying herself by the fact that her mistress did not have time to make her take an oath on this specific point. It goes without saying that Sarah Leeson poses the moral problem of interpreting the thoughts of the deceased woman—an honest interpretation of her last wishes would mean consigning the letter, but since she does not swear to this, the maid ends up by choosing a solution that, without violating her duties, allows her to avoid afflicting pain on the recipient of the message. Sarah decides to hide the letter in an abandoned wing of the mansion, the "Myrtle Room." She performs this act of testamentary occultation after adding a further message to her mistress's text in which, with puritanical zeal, she explains the reasons that force her to make her choice: "Whether for good or for evil, the fatal Secret was hidden now—the act was done. There was something calming in the first consciousness of that one fact. She could think more composedly, after that, of herself, and of the uncertain future that lay before her."[21] Thus, the epistolary text whose exclusive function is that of revealing the truth is deprived of its dramatic strength, in the sense that any practical performance of the confession is barred: the secret continues to be buried and relegated to a space that annuls the transgressive valence of its significance and effectively delays the moment of its reemergence. But what is the woman's response before the prospect of an "uncertain future"? Incapable of reacting positively, she has only one way out: to escape. Sarah Leeson escapes from Mrs. Treverton and from the scene of her deathbed. In particular, she is continually haunted by the image of her dead mistress in her role of unflinching persecutor post mortem—in brief, she flees from her mistress's ghost. Her desire to escape from Captain Treverton, and, indirectly, from Rosamond herself, is no less impelling. Not having had the courage to consign the letter, she now does not even have the courage to go through daily life any longer because, in one way or another, it would entail continually having to "recite" her fictional role as a maid faithful to the memory of Mrs. Treverton. Sarah escapes also, and above all, from the letter and from the room in which it is hidden. The confessional text, buried in the most inaccessible part of the house, doomed to dust and silence, stands out in her restless mind like a temptation that she may give in to at any moment. The woman runs away from the Myrtle Room, which, in spite of its promising name—the myrtle is a symbol of Venus and therefore of love—appears to her as the very epitome of the sin it contains. Ultimately, she escapes from Porthgenna Tower, which represents everything belonging to this mysterious world: the people and the sense of deceit, the letter and the protagonists involved in the confession, the phantoms and the echoes of the great theatrical mechanism conceived by Mrs. Treverton.

Sarah Leeson is a character who bases her life on a paradigm of uncertainty and ambiguity. She is very similar to Elizabeth Gaskell's "grey woman,"[22] whose face bears the signs of premature old age along with a physiognomic map revealing the blurred gaps of her psychic landscape. Hence, her experience of the dilemma concerning *how* to escape before actually succeeding in her plan of flight: What kind of traces should she leave behind? Should she just simply escape, or offer some sort of explanation to the captain, who, as the innocent victim of an intrigue, would never understand the motives for such a hasty disappearance? Significantly, and in perfect coherence with her dilemmatic personality, the maid decides to leave a message, another confession, which, from one point of view, should demonstrate that any action she has taken has been in good faith: "As rapidly as her pen could form the letters, she wrote a few lines addressed to Captain Treverton, in which she confessed to having kept a secret from his knowledge which had been left in her charge to divulge; adding, that she honestly believed no harm could come to him, or to any one in whom he was interested, by her failing to perform the duty entrusted to her; and ending by asking his pardon for leaving the house secretly, and by begging, as a last favour, that no search might ever be made for her."[23] This is yet another letter around the secret. Urged by a more or less unconscious desire to stimulate Mr. Treverton's curiosity and, at the same time, frustrate it, the woman declares the duty she has been entrusted with as well as her desire not to honor it. Therefore, the secret remains a *dead secret*, which thickens the mystery around her unannounced departure, itself a mirror and consequence of the hidden letter in the Myrtle Room. However, her escape from her responsibilities and from Porthgenna Tower does not liberate her from those ghostly events. Now, the dead woman to whom she had lent her body and soul is *inside* her. Her mistress is a negative presence, a spiteful, tormenting specter that will never allow her a moment of peace and tranquillity. In many ways, Sarah Leeson's letter is a recognition of her inability to free herself from the burden of the past.

"When you go to Porthgenna, *keep out of the Myrtle Room*."[24] These words, which Sarah Leeson (alias Mrs. Jazeph) whispers to Rosamond in the middle of the night, summarize her reaction when, after an extraordinary series of circumstances, she encounters her natural daughter no less than fifteen years after the death of Mrs. Treverton. In fact, the second part of *The Dead Secret* begins after many years have elapsed and culminates in the encounter between the former maid and her daughter. Three crucial events take place during the time lag and, from a merely structural perspective, may be epitomized as follows:

a) *Event*: Rosamond secretly marries Leonard Frankland, who has become blind as a result of eye strain from "watchmaking occupations"[25] for too long in his boyhood. *Place*: Long Beckley, "a large agricultural village in the midland counties of England."[26] *Character*: Dr. Chennery, vicar of the parish and "historical memory" of the Treverton family.

b) *Event*: Immediately after his wife's death, Captain Treverton sells Porthgenna Tower to Leonard Frankland's father, who is a prosperous trader seeking to acquire an aristocratic status. *Place*: an unidentified village near Long Beckley, the captain and daughter's new residence. *Character*: Andrew Treverton, the captain's misanthropic brother, who, having insulted Mrs. Treverton, is no longer on good terms with the family.

c) *Event*: A few months after the marriage, while on their way to Porthgenna, Rosamond and Leonard are forced to stop because Rosamond falls ill and gives birth prematurely to a boy child. *Place*: West Winston, a small village in Somerset. *Character*: Mrs. Jazeph is hired as a nurse by the young couple, who are blocked in West Winston.

By coincidence, Sarah Leeson is informed of the young couple's intention to settle down in Porthgenna. Terrified by the idea that Rosamond may find out the truth, and incapable of reacting, the woman enters a phase of abnormal behavior. At one level, Sarah is always servile, silent, and docile in her manner, but, at another level, her comportment is obscurely mysterious. What emerges is a woman with a "strangely scared expression in her eyes,"[27] consumed by a psychic instability verging on madness. In a night time world of gothic tensions, while all the others are asleep, the woman walks about like a ghost whose agitations have vaster social implications.[28] Her restlessness suggests something terrible that seems to derive directly from Mrs. Treverton. In a dimension of fiction and death, a destructive pact unites the two women.

The strange behavior of the nurse leads Leonard Frankland to make a drastic decision. Mrs. Jazeph (Sarah Leeson) is dismissed, and, once more, her choice is to escape. But, thanks to the help of Dr. Chennery, Rosamond manages to find out from her misanthropic uncle's maid the exact whereabouts of "the Myrtle Room" and, finally, arrive at the revelation of the secret. Apart from the complicated series of events that lead to the discovery of the truth, it is important to point out here that Sarah is presented as a woman on the run until the moment of her death. She confesses to her uncle, Joseph Bauschmann, whom she visits in Truro in the search for help: "As every one sees me! All people's eyes seem to look through me; all people's words seem to threaten me."[29] In her obsessive neurosis, the looks and words of others have an extraordinarily petrifying effect on her. Lost in a maze of sensations and contradictory thoughts, she can only indicate her existence by incessantly moving about with the monomaniacal idea of keeping the secret a *dead secret*. She thus first tries to prevent anyone who may have that intention from entering the room that holds the secret, then tries to remove the letter from its hiding place.

What is revealed in the epilogue is quite obvious. Sarah Leeson's mental prison is the result of a hypersemanticization of the message,[30] all the more so when we realize that the "disinterment" of the letter produces less distress than expected. Not only is there less distress, but thanks to the unearthing of the truth, and therefore the recognition of her role as mother, Sarah is removed from the scheme of destiny organized by Mrs. Treverton and restored to her real identity. She is, therefore, no longer a character who has to recite a script in which the *dead secret* has a central role, but a mother who, by rediscovering her daughter, finally finds her moral if not psychic salvation:

> "Look!," she said. "There she is as she always comes to me, at the close of the day,—with the coarse, black dress on, that my guilty hands made for her,—with the smile that there was on her face when she asked me if she looked like a servant. Mistress! Mistress! Oh, rest at last! The Secret is ours no longer! Rest at last! My child is my own again! Rest, at last; and come between us no more!"
>
> She ceased, panting for breath; and laid her hot, throbbing cheek against the cheek of her daughter. *"Call me 'Mother' again!" she whispered. "Say it aloud; and send her away from me for ever!"*
>
> Rosamond mastered the terror that shook her in every limb, and pronounced the word.[31]

Another page containing a deathbed scene: to be underlined here is not the gothic trope of the haunting ghost, but the continuation of the complicit relationship between maid and mistress. It is not a coincidence that their pact is definitively, and automatically, broken when Sarah Leeson's natural role by right is recognized. As the scene renders very clearly, a direct correspondence can be perceived between the presence of Mrs. Traverton's ghost and the acknowledgment of

Sarah's identity as mother. It is only once Rosamond pronounces the word *mother* without any hesitation that Mrs. Treverton's shadow abandons the dying woman, whose painful self still lives in a land of psychic disorder and social confusion. On the one hand, the extent of Sarah's textual introjection is so great that the moment in which she expresses her wish to be liberated from it, she cannot help going back in her memory to the strategies of deceit and disguise: the very beginning of a totalizing disharmony. On the other hand, it is undeniable that the exchange of roles is at the origin not so much of the loss of her maternal rights as of the psychic split that marks the inception of her social and ontological death. The beginning (Mrs. Treverton's death) and the end (Sarah Leeson's death) are linked in a circular pattern played by the pair mistress/maid, whose diegetic functionality encloses the fictional text. It is clear that beyond the boundary of this deep-structured circularity there is no longer space for mystery and its representations.

In other words, the rediscovery of the letter breaks a seemingly everlasting and indissoluble bond between the two women. Sarah's recovery of her own identity overlaps with the regained mental sanity of a woman who, in the end, is able to give expression to the love for her daughter. It is superfluous to add that the moment in which Sarah regains happiness—". . . How happy we shall be together now!"[32]— coincides with the moment of her death. This is the epilogue that literary convention reserves for the fallen woman as the final seal of an irreversible liberation from evil. Furthermore, the fact that the story of the dead secret develops over a period of time that witnesses, in diegetic and temporal extremes (incipit/explicit), the disappearance of the two protagonists is also significant. Placed at the beginning and at the end of the diegetic design, the destructive and self-destructive event of the two women allows for the reading of the fictional text (the story they fabricated) as a location of death. In this connection, their respective deaths should be read as the sign of an ultimate negativity that, by opposing pretense against the reality of *real* life, models a world in which no horizon of truth is visible.

"I prophesy that we shall see ghosts, and find treasures, and hear mysterious noises—and, oh heavens! What clouds of dust we shall have to go through."[33] With these words Rosamond expresses her desire to go beyond fiction and to hypostatize a realistic reading of the world. The dust she refers to, after her ironic references to gothic tropes, has nothing to do with the underground labyrinths in which the most terrible misdeeds have been performed, but is rather the index of an immobility she rationally intends to fight against. For Rosamond, dust is simply dust in the sense that it can evoke only its everyday materiality. It is a metonymic dust whose thick layers on furniture and everywhere will be only a fastidious minor obstacle from the moment she enters the north wing of the mansion whose architectural vitality and dignity she wants to restore.[34]

If the female pair Mrs. Treverton/Sarah represents a polarity of fictional theatricality, Rosamond, on the opposite extreme, may be seen to stand for a vision of realism that, above all, entails accepting responsibility without following the gender conformity connected with femininity.[35] This is clearly evident in her decision to marry Leonard, in spite of his blindness,[36] which leads to her assuming a social role reserved for male competence, precisely because of her husband's disability. Whatever her education in terms of moderation and verbal self-limitation, whatever her natural sensitivity and reserve, Rosamond is always unambiguous and rational, always prepared to make decisions and take the lead in any situation. In no way inclined toward vagueness of language, she always speaks directly, almost cruelly in her speech's realistic tension. Thus, in her first encounter with Sarah Leeson in the role of nurse (a coincidence that is functional to the textualization of the contrast between mother and daughter), Rosamond's reaction is spontaneous and immediate:

> "Gracious goodness! *Who are you?*" exclaimed Rosamond. "A woman or a ghost?"
> Mrs. Jazeph's veil was up at last. . . .
> "*Who are you?*" repeated Rosamond. "And what in the world do you stand there for—between us and the sunlight?"
> Mrs. Jazeph neither answered nor raised her eyes. She only moved back timidly *to the farthest corner of the window.*[37]

Rosamond's surprised reaction, and, most of all, her double question to the recently appointed nurse bring to light her perspective of the world. Her emphatic repetition of the interrogative *who are you?* underlines her immediate sense of Sarah-Mrs. Jazeph's incongruous presence in the home of a young couple who are doing their best to care for a child born prematurely. Not only does Rosamond lean on the side of realism, but her words also indicate her perception of the negativity of Sarah, who, as already noted, herself a figure of death and mortality, raises a barrier against life "between us and the sunlight." Briefly, the relationship between the natural mother and her daughter, even though socially "illegitimate," is characterized as an opposition between Sarah's enigmatic silence and Rosamond's authentic words. Paradigmatically, binary oppositions between darkness/light and life/death emerge that, on careful consideration, can be seen to encompass two completely different ways of relating to the world. Sarah's physical and psychological contraction corresponds to the vitalistic expansion of her daughter, who, thanks to her decision to embark on a detective investigation, is destined to occupy the moral center of the story. To put it more explicitly, this attitude means her reappropriation of Porthgenna Tower together with the expulsion of its ghosts and secret letters, which have transformed it into an intricate web of dysphoric and destructive psychobehavioral tensions.

If we continue to analyze the mother/daughter dichotomy, we cannot help noting that for Sarah movement implies the search for a dark corner seen as a place to conceal and bury the secret that besieges and torments her mind. Liminality is the peculiar trait of her existential condition, and, interestingly, her favourite moment is nighttime because it conceals her from other people's eyes: "she was hidden by the curtain. . . . Her shadow stole darkly over the bright picture which the doctor had been admiring. . . . Although her face was necessarily in shadow in the position which she had chosen, the doctor saw a change pass over it when Mrs. Frankland spoke."[38] In addition, her natural color is a gray tending toward black, her favorite posture is that of someone crouching in a hiding place— even though she is not pursued by anybody she permanently feels like a trapped animal.[39] Nevertheless, Rosamond does not allow herself to be overcome by terror at the decidedly extravagant behavior of the nurse. But, in line with her prevalently practical behavioral code, she makes Mrs. Jazeph/Sarah Leeson the object of her own personal analysis:

> "What an odd woman she is!" whispered Rosamond.
> "Odd, indeed," returned Mr. Orridge, "and desperately broken in health, though she may not confess to it. However, she is wonderfully neat-handed and careful, and there can be no harm in trying her for one night—that is to say, unless you feel any objection."

"On the contrary," said Rosamond, "she rather interests me. There is something in her face and manner—I can't say what—that makes me feel curious to know more of her. I must get her to talk, and try if I can't bring out all her peculiarities."[40]

Behind Rosamond's words lies something more than mere curiosity. From the viewpoint of social and institutional roles, she is about to initiate detection work that does not really pertain to the female sphere. It follows that Rosamond will study the clues she receives after a series of coincidences to such an extent that she will manage to discover the truth about her own self. As a result, a spirit of investigation prevails in the young woman culminating in the crucial moment of recognition brought about by the reading of "the fatal letter,"[41] which, for Rosamond, signifies, on a social level, her fall from aristocracy to the less prestigious role of servant.

For to be the illegitimate daughter of a tin miner and a maid means being excluded from the world toward which she feels more especially attracted. And yet—and herein lies the powerfully transgressive impact of *The Dead Secret*—the loss of her status does not entail the loss of Leonard's love, or the loss of Porthgenna. Collins's powerful polemic against the Victorian mind-set lies precisely in the recognition of ties and rights that go beyond the social ladder and even a person's economic condition. Against every form of melodrama, the rhetorical expedient with which Rosamond conveys the dilemmas and uncertainties of her new condition to her husband is all the more significant. Again, her words are very explicit in their hypothetical morphosyntactical construction; they never betray her own idea of moral integrity and behavioral coherence: "Suppose I had been a servant—the servant who had helped to nurse you in your illness, the servant who led you about in your blindness more carefully than anyone else—would you have thought much, then, of the difference between us? Would you—."[42] Leonard shows no hesitation at all. By accepting Rosamond in her new guise as "love-child,"[43] from the angle of the Victorian ethos, he confirms a moral and cultural primacy that no longer belongs to a pyramidal vision of society in which the fixity of class and social identities is postulated. What is suggested is a world in which it will no longer be necessary for a woman to hide her maternity, even when it concerns a union not consecrated by matrimony: "Don't let us refer again to the past: I know all I ought to know, all I wish to know of it. We will talk of the future, mother, and of happier times to come."[44] Once again it is Rosamond who enucleates, against the passivity of her mother, a positivity that implies, in the first place, the certainty that the future will not and must not belong to secrets like that of the letter hidden in the Myrtle Room. The emerging axiological conception appears all the more explosive if one thinks that, as a result of a series of family events, Rosamond will not even lose the considerable inheritance received after selling Porthgenna Tower to Leonard's father, thanks to the decision of the misanthropic Andrew Treverton to renounce a property that belongs, by natural right, to his "niece" Rosamond.

The final pages of *The Dead Secret* postulate a new interpretation of the nature of social bonds and a new axiology that contrast with the traditional ways of understanding the values on which the British nation is founded. In this unorthodox portrayal of society, the nobility of the soul is considered to be more important than nobility inherited by right. In many ways, nobility is equated to truth and honesty. In her revolutionary praxis, as well as at the various behavioral levels (private and public), Rosamond is coherently following a line of stark realism, against fictional manipulation and duplicity. The crowning moment of her courageous tracking down of the hidden text (i.e., the truth of her origin) is represented by her decision not to destroy the letter but to read it word for word to her husband. If for Sarah it is true that the discovery of the confessional document ends her tormented wanderings and releases her mind from the ghost of Mrs. Treverton, it is nonetheless also true that the hypersemanticization of the letter ends precisely at the moment in which the accurate account of the facts surfaces. With the solution to the mystery and the restoration of the social order—a social order in which it is at last possible to live without secrets and ghosts—Rosamond and Leonard are able to set their relationship with the world on more certain and lasting values than those of social status and wealth. In the explicit, as a sort of moral seal, Leonard expresses in no half-terms the lesson that he has learned from his wife: "The highest honours . . . are those which no accident can take away—the honours that are conferred by LOVE and TRUTH."[45] Love and truth are projected into the idyllic territory of a new world. This idealized world, at the very moment it is hypostatized, transforms into an antiworld everything that the couple have left behind them: all the pretense and intrigues, the letter and its contaminating ghosts, the secret rooms and their paralyzing narrative disseminations, all the disvalues and disaffections, the darkness of the soul and the scenes of death.

"More women write novels now than men. What is to prevent me from trying? The first great requisite, I suppose, is to have an idea of a story; and that I have got."[46] To regard Rosamond's words simply as a concise metanarrative digression would be a drastic simplification of *The Dead Secret*. It may therefore be pertinent to ask why Collins drags in the question of women and the novelistic genre. From a diegetic point of view, Rosamond's words must be read in the context of her newborn awareness of change that, primarily, seems to imply a feminization of society. In this connection, she feels the urgency of mediating between the fiction of the past and the realism of the future in order to establish the social and ontological continuity of her genealogically complicated personal story. She adopts this mediating process as a strategy to convey to her husband the unpleasant truth of her fall to the rank of servant, without thereby limiting or spoiling her identity. Her self-defense also involves the urgent need to write the final chapter of her mother's sad plight in line with the narrative principle of a pacifying explicit: "How would you end it, love?"[47] Leonard only answers her question after the whole letter has been read. At this point, the epistolary text becomes a psychoanalytical tool that offers the interpretative key of the story his wife has just narrated. Rosamond's fiction thus coincides with and is naturally grafted onto the fiction exposed by the letter—her real origin emerges in the form of a writing that is also a form of unmasking. The novel that she would have wanted to write has, in reality, already been written in the letter—"The letter will explain"[48]—which, until the very last moment, dictates its laws made up of past events that no narrator's hand can correct.

But there is a final point to be highlighted. The device of telling her mother's story—which is also the story of her own life—by using the fictional strategies of her own time has a very interesting epistemic significance. In her self-representation as a potential novelist, Rosamond chooses to adopt a literary code so as to make her story more captivating for her husband; transgression, genealogical disorientation, and mental disorder seem to be under control when they fit in a conventional literary framework. By assuming the peculiar position of a narrator, she is able to say what, until that moment, may have seemed unimaginable if pronounced simply, and exclusively, by the daughter of Sarah Leeson. Once the right sentiments have been stimulated, and once their dilemmas have been dramatized with skillful narrative techniques, she can demand of her husband the understanding and the answer that would otherwise have been denied her. Even in this choice, Rosamond embodies a female typology that Collins presents to the reader as an antithetic model to the literary conventions of the time.

3

Cousin Phillis:
Illness as Language

Illness always entails a metamorphosis that, in a way, fore-grounds more than a mere bodily transformation. If it is true that sickness projects the body beyond the limits of normality, it is equally true that this new territory can be defined as a space where the sufferer's voice has lost both its authority and its identity. Following Kafka, we could say that every pathology is a *Verwandlung*, a sort of combination of physical change, psychic instability, and social marginalization. Thus, when a patient begins to realize the full meaning of his new state, he cannot help becoming an observer of the signs emerging from his sick body, which seems progressively transformed into an object of medical investigation, and this reifying process is the first step toward the discovery of our precarious balance between being and nonbeing. Clearly, the patient's interpretative capacity is directly dependent on the extent to which his diagnosis is the result of a real detachment from the materiality of his body. Paradoxically, while he is trying to restore the lost equilibrium between mind and body, he needs a distancing from his physicality in order to obtain a clearer focus on its bodily language.

In other words, illness highlights the antithesis of body and soul, one of the polarities on which identities are built: body and soul, visibility and invisibility, materiality and immateriality, fact and fiction, life and death. Visibility refers always to the body, which testifies to its being *there*, an emblem of passivity and docility to analysis and to all those therapeutic procedures involved in malady—a sufferer is regarded as a person who is no longer the agent of his own actions, and, by the same token, his sick body is inevitably and clinically forced to inaction. In contrast, invisibility pertains to the sick person's mind, whose main activity is a silent and painful self-investigation and, eventually, a self-interpretation. So, beneath the surface of bodily inaction it is possible to detect the intricacies of many psychic itineraries to be understood as a natural response to the sufferer's fears of physical destruction and loss of ontological integrity. In the throes of an analytic activity aimed at the recreation of that body/soul unity that the new pathological state is jeopardizing, a patient's mind performs a double conflicting function. This function depends, at once, on the body (acted upon and passive) and on the soul (acting and active). Malady means separation and centrifugal movement, whereas our fight against malady manifests our longing for a permanent psychic center.

With respect to the nature of change, we may easily conclude that a pathological sign often reveals itself in a sudden and unexpected way. The more sudden the change is, the more tragic is the impact of illness on our daily life. The very beginning of *Die Verwandlung* offers a convincing example of this kind of response: "Als Gregor Samsa eines Morgens aus unruhigen Träumen erwachte . . ." ("As Gregor Samsa awoke one morning from uneasy dreams ...").[1] One morning the Kafkaesque hero wakes and discovers that he has been transformed into a disgusting insect. Now his radically metamorphosed body is no longer his own but the tablet on which the text of his own death is being written. Such a discovery is traumatic. His mind must immediately cope with a bodily transformation as well as with the personal abnormality that malady implies and publicly exhibits.

A man or a woman who loses his/her physical unity makes of his/her body the immediate object of meditation and scrutiny. The sufferer's mind is immediately called upon to understand and interpret that body in order to restore a coherent meaning to his life—to understand the ailing body means to repossess it. And, needless to say, this is not an easy task to perform. From another perspective, we might say that the body is the surface on which, as a rule, what is made visible and readable is always hidden from the eyes of others. Consequently, when a pathological condition posits its semiotic norms, the body becomes the place where the mental landscape can be detected and possibly understood in its manifold aspects. Its language cannot be made of words precisely because the sufferer has no words to describe his condition but those of his malady; the inner self finds at last in the symptoms evinced by the bodily frame a significant way of communicating with the external world. Still, being doomed to inaction, this person cannot freely express his feelings through his real voice; other people will vicariously interpret and verbally convey his wishes and ideas, which, considering the deep-rooted cultural and behavioral prejudices of the others, will be deprived of any positive communicative value. As a consequence, the patient's social personality will only reveal that the fundamental bridge between his self and the others has wholly collapsed. Essentially, being forbidden to declare in simple and clear-cut words what the majority refuses to know—that is, malady as a condition of potential insanity, malady as a language poised between being and nonbeing—the sick voice is pushed into the narrow paths of a silence wherein no redeeming parable is made audible to the world without. Yet, strange though this may sound, to a sick person the words describing his/her malady are more important than the malady itself: Words of hope, words of despair. Words of gratifying positivity, words of annihilation.

To what extent does a patient's world depend on the other's language? And to what extent do we feel that our own "normalcy" is undermined by the sick person's abnormality? Why do we often assume that malady means more than we can infer by adopting a pathologist's angle? Briefly, I believe that, since malady epitomizes and foregrounds the ontological insecurity that we daily experience, our prevailing reaction is to negate the sick person's verbal narrations.

This is all the more true for the Victorian mentality, whose sexual mainstay is represented by the conviction that transgression is a pathological state, which becomes much more dangerous and destructive when a female subject is involved in events that do not respect social codes. If there is no room for the sick person's voice, what is immediately at his/her disposal is the body. As a forced choice, the body language communicates with its signs/symptoms, which, in the most extreme and paradoxical example, can involve a radical physical transformation, the metamorphosis into another entity and, possibly, the metamorphosis into a huge and repellent insect. This is a case in which malady can be understood as a most complete flight from one's body—a flight into a total annihilation of one's personality. The Kafkaesque *Verwandlung* is, from a literary angle, a great metaphor for diversity, whose unrealistic exaggeration, immediately conveyed by the very first sentence, does not diminish the extraordinary impact of the story on the reader's sensibility.

However, the kind of transformation that more frequently takes place in Victorian narratives concerns not a total metamorphosis but, more traumatically, a physical distress whose consequences are mental confusion and ontological darkness. It is a psychophysical condition that, from a medical perspective, can be labeled as depression and neurasthenia. The scenery of this sort of personal drama is often the domestic sphere, where the minutest movement produced by the body/mind duality seems further intensified by the suffocating and limited room in which Victorian heroines are confined. The embodiment of their yearnings and emotions cannot go beyond this controlled space simply because any form of externalization is seen as a form of weakness. What is clear about the Victorian heroine is this: the redefinition of her own body's boundaries always involves a redefinition of her mind's social and psychological territories. In line with this pathological externalization of inner monstrosities, Kafka's Gregor Samsa is simply a hyperbolic version of the necessary physical metamorphosis that mental malady always produces and foregrounds.

As far as social change and malady are concerned, we can say that one of the most illuminating Victorian narratives is *Cousin Phillis* (1863–64), which can be read as Elizabeth Gaskell's attempt to give a most complete representation of the way change produces a destructive effect on those who still rely on old values and old modes of life. But, more than a story centered on the new reality of locomotives and factories, *Cousin Phillis* can be read as the silent drama of a heroine whose body and soul are tempted and eventually half-destroyed by the enticing language of a complex and barely decipherable changing world.

First of all, the story of Phillis Holman is also the *story* of the way her malady is narrated. Significantly, the narrator of *Cousin Phillis* is her cousin, Paul Manning, whose interpretative power is strongly conditioned by his direct involvement in Phillis's illness, not to say by his deep attraction to her beauty and his possible love for her. In this regard, it is important to note that the first time Paul arrives at Hope Farm to pay a respectful visit to his distant relations he immediately meets a universe that is as far from the external world as one can imagine. So, when he goes back to the railway office in Eltham, where he serves as an apprentice under the young railway engineer Edward Holdsworth, he can easily draw the conclusion that Hope Farm is a place of purity and innocence. Being an independent minister and a farmer, the Reverend Holman founds his moral authority and teaching on the Bible and on the natural cycle of the seasons, even though he is only too ready to accept those technical improvements and scientific discoveries that are an exalting expression of the age of progress. But, despite the open-mindedness of the pater familias, we can easily see that Hope Farm appears more like an Edenic garden than a farmstead whose daily routine is made of hard work and scanty meals.[2]

The first image of Phillis epitomizes the very idea of stability combined with beauty and innocence. In his hyperbolic and luminous representation of his new-found cousin, the narrator delineates a portrait that is in perfect contrast to Phillis's unstable and physically weak bodily frame at the end of the story:

> I see her now—cousin Phillis. The westering sun shone full upon her, and made a slanting stream of light into the room within. She was dressed in dark blue cotton of some kind; up to her throat, down to her wrists, with a little frill of the same wherever it touched her white skin. And such a white skin as it was! I have never seen the like. She had light hair, nearer yellow than any other colour. She looked me steadily in the face, with large, quiet eyes, wondering, but untroubled by the sight of a stranger. I thought it odd that so old, so full-grown as she was, she should wear a pinafore over her gown.[3]

In focusing on Phillis's positive response (she was "untroubled by the sight of a stranger"), the narrating voice is indirectly anticipating the "troubles" caused by this openness, which is more the result of innocence than of a deep-rooted interest in what really happens in the external world. The anticipation of trouble is further intensified in the final remark concerning the "pinafore": Paul cannot help noticing a discrepancy between her mature and full-grown body and the way she is dressed. Clearly, behind this visual contradiction lies an invisible and partly unconscious clash between what she longs to be and what her overprotective parents are educating her to be. Apparent here is Phillis's association with physical well-being and *integritas*, without any inklings and symptoms of that ailing body from which she will eventually try to escape.

"I see her now—cousin Phillis."[4] The narrating voice is giving full play to a memory that seems to connect the first meeting with his cousin to a mythical time, in which everything was part of a stable and satisfying landscape. Thus, if Hope Farm means timelessness and health, it also means the unstable dimension of that kind of perfection. Of course, this small and innocent world cannot last forever, simply because the same rule that applies to every human being applies even to the Holman family—everyone has inevitably to cope with change and mutability. But it is barely necessary to stress that the Reverend Holman is fully conscious that society is rapidly changing even though he cannot understand that transformation will enter his own family circle before long. From a psychological and ontological angle, his blindness is still more evident: he is unable to see Phillis's physical maturity and so the absurdity of her infantile dress. What is more, he seems in many respects a biblical figure, whose idea of order and harmony is based on a patriarchal view of his role: his words are imbued with truth and wisdom, his gestures are always solemnly precise, his orders iterate a daily ritual that ignores temporality intended as change and evolution. At suppertime, his personality assumes its most evidently patriarchal function:

> We were called back into the house-place to have supper. A door opening into the kitchen was opened; and all stood up in both rooms, while the minister, tall, large, one hand resting on the spread table, the other lifted up, said. . . . "Whether we eat or drink, or whatsoever we do, let us do all to the glory of God."
>
> The supper was an immense meat-pie. We of the house-place were helped first; then the minister hit the handle of his buck-horn carving-knife on the table once, and said, —
>
> "Now or never," which meant, did any one of us want any more; and when we had all declined, either by silence or by words, he knocked twice with his knife on the table, and Betty came in through the open door, and carried off the great dish to the kitchen, where an old man and a young one, and a help-girl were awaiting their meal.[5]

The vulnerability of such an idyllic and highly ritualized rural setting pertains to its innermost core. Strong and stable though Hope Farm may appear, its social structure is fragile and weak. Paul Manning cannot help feeling that the passing of time as experienced in the Holman family is totally different from the temporal flux he experiences at work. Significantly, it is the Bible associated with Phillis's father that offers him a mode of interpretation when he first meets Phillis and her mother: "I felt as if I were somebody in the Old Testament. . . . Was I like Abraham's servant, when Rebekah gave him to drink at the well? I thought Isaac had not gone the pleasantest way to work in winning him a wife."[6] Obviously, in tracing a biblical parallelism, the narrator wants to convey more his sense of remoteness and primal innocence than his role as "Abraham's servant," which he seems to reject simply because Rebekah was actually Isaac's cousin.[7] At the same time, what Paul is saying is that the most striking features of Hope Farm are its tranquillity made up of a meaningful silence and the perfect harmony of the surrounding landscape.

Illness plays an important role in *Cousin Phillis,* but in its initial manifestation it has nothing to do with Hope Farm. Entering from the external world, change and malady are the factors that will plant the seed of destructiveness in the Holman family. The Reverend Holman's words candidly express the simplicity and openness of his family with respect to the arrival of the railway line to Heathbridge: "now that railroads are coming so near us, it behoves us to know something about them."[8] Here the focus falls on Holdsworth, who, in his emphatic way, the narrator describes as a perfect man: "He's a regular first-rate fellow. He can do anything."[9] Holdsworth is the hero who has conquered Paul's imagination and whose enterprises are at the center of Paul's narratives to the people of Hope Farm: "The minister used to listen to my accounts of Mr. Holdsworth's many accomplishments and various adventures in travel with the truest interest, and most kindly good faith."[10] From a linguistic point of view, Holdsworth and Phillis are rhetorically united in the memory of Paul, who, in his fictionalizing narration, applies the same hyperbolic code of excess to both his cousin and his friend. Thus, before he appears in the flesh at Hope Farm, the young engineer's life is narrated and interpreted by Paul, who does his best to make his ideal portrait as credible as possible.

In terms of Holdsworth's acceptance within the domestic order of Hope Farm, one cannot help noticing the crucial event of his illness. Partly putting into question his role as hero of the new technological adventure, the illness seems at once to humanize him and to make him a privileged recipient of the Holmans' sympathy and solidarity— "he was very ill for many weeks, almost many months."[11] But the point I wish to stress is not the Holman family's response but the matter of bodily *integritas.* From the perspective of subjective pathology, Holdsworth introduces into the rural idyll of Hope Farm the signs of bodily disorder together with, to use a Hardyan definition, "the modern vice of unrest":[12] "The morrow was blue and sunny, and beautiful; the very perfection of an early summer's day. *Mr. Holdsworth was all impatience* to be off into the country; morning had brought back his freshness and strength, and consequent *eagerness to be doing.* I was afraid we were going to my cousin's farm rather too early, before they would expect us; but what could I do with such *a restless vehement man as Holdsworth* was that morning?"[13] Holdsworth's approach to reality is conducive to instability and mobility. Yet, observed from the perspective of the peaceful harmony of Hope Farm, he is not a dangerous invader but simply a man recovering from a malady. After the critical experience of his illness, it is only too natural for the Holman family to be openly unprejudiced toward him. This attitude, at the very beginning of Holdsworth's stay, atones for his superficiality and easy going manners, which seem to be more the feedback of his recovery than a superficial streak in his temperament. His way of speaking is, to be sure, quite opposite to the severe and formal language that dominates the personal interrelationships of Hope Farm, where every sentence reverberates with a biblical resonance.

Essentially, the young engineer introduces into the stable world an element of linguistic doubt and indeterminacy that forces Phillis to assume a silent attitude before a male cultural predominance: "This was a style of half-joking talk that Phillis was not accustomed to. She looked for a moment as if she would have liked to defend herself from the playful charge of distrust made against her, but *she ended by not saying a word.*"[14] Silence is the only way she can cope with Holdsworth's linguistic playfulness—this is the response of a girl who is wholly unable to understand and interpret the guest's gestures and words, which she can only accept as a form of vitality and exoticism. Holdsworth opens up before her eyes a social scene that is much larger and richer than the farm where she has been living. But, in so doing, he does not explain to her that the society he is from is also marked by cultural ambivalence and psychological complexity. Indeed, his personality seems to be shaped by two conflicting sides: the playful side, mainly characterized by the fascinating description of his travels through Italy and Europe at large, and the earnest side pertaining to his professional ambition and desire for self-fulfillment.

By the Reverend Holman's standards, Holdsworth's linguistic attitude is not spotless, in the sense that he seems too mundane and affected. But Holman is unable to connect his "suspicion that [Holdsworth's] careless words were not always those of soberness and truth"[15] with Phillis's falling in love with him. The self-enclosed community of Hope Farm takes for granted that Phillis needs no other love but her parents'; they do not have any suspicion that behind the pinafore she wears lies a sexuality that is beginning to claim its own behavioral and affective territory. Confronted with Phillis's exigency of self-expression, her parents can only find a misleading answer— they keep on imagining that she is still the innocent creature they have been treasuring in their hearts over the years, while deliberately ignoring the fact that her psychological and physical maturity is pushing her imagination beyond the narrow boundaries of domesticity. With respect to the young woman's silent dissatisfaction, Thomas Recchio has astutely noted that "her life at Hope Farm, wonderful as it may seem, is for her nothing in comparison to the fullness of knowledge and experience she can imagine."[16] Phillis's "unspoken dissatisfaction" involves a text of secrecy that no one is able to interpret correctly. This loneliness can be regarded as the seed of a personal drama that, through the torments of psychological and ontological fragmentation, will find its culminating moment in her "brain fever"[17] as a consequence of Holdsworth's sudden departure for Canada.

"Phillis! did we not make you happy here? Have we not loved you enough?"[18] What this brief quotation shows is not only the Reverend Holman's blindness as pater familias but also a censorious attitude that makes Phillis feel guilty of having betrayed her parents' expectations. The patriarchal voice puts the stress on the fact that secrecy is not proper behavior for a girl—secrecy corresponds to an indirect sin that cannot be atoned for in a world made of verbal honesty, in a world where "[Phillis] had such a complete reverence for her parents that she listened to them both as if they had been St Peter and St Paul."[19] On the contrary, Holdsworth adopts a linguistic code strongly based on allusion and indirection, not only when he is dealing jokingly with Phillis, but also when more serious topics are involved. His answer to Paul's question concerning his attachment to Phillis is a perfect indicator of his linguistic opacity: "Love her! Yes, that I do. Who could help it, seeing her as I have done? Her character as unusual and rare as her beauty. God bless her!"[20] At the same time his answer makes Phillis a heroine of a fable more than the real protagonist of a true love story—"She lives in such seclusion, almost like a sleeping beauty"[21]—giving a fuller expression to his view of Hope Farm and its people as a sort of flight from his demanding professional world. Ultimately, his words manifest his conviction that the farm is characterized by a timelessness that means repetition and immobility. This is the kind of context that the engineer could accept only during his convalescent days, but now, with his body's *restitutio at integrum* he cannot imagine a world that is not that of continual change and new professional experience.

Thus, when Holdsworth makes the sudden decision to leave for Canada, he consciously exhibits uncertainty and ambiguity about his future because he does not want to disappoint his friend. Although he is fully aware that Heathbridge and Hope Farm already belong to his past, he hints at a possible return, shedding a false and distorting light on his real plans and motivations: "I will go to-night. Activity and readiness go a long way in our profession. Remember that, my boy! I hope I shall come back, but if I don't, be sure and recollect all the words of wisdom that have fallen from my lips. Now where's my portmanteau?"[22] Once Holdsworth has completely recovered, he suddenly disappears from Phillis's daily routine without a leave taking. What the yearning girl immediately realizes is that she can rely only on an interrupted love discourse, on a love message that is not a real pledge, on words that do not correspond to reality.

Finally, the only thing that he leaves Phillis is the impossibility of explicitly expressing her love for him. She finds herself on a dark path leading to silence and passivity, which also means the painful recognition of her failure to understand and to give a final shape to the fragments of her experience:

> I purposely looked away from Phillis, as I thus abruptly told my news.
> "To Canada!" said the minister.
> "Gone away!" said his wife.
> But no word from Phillis.
> "Yes!" I said. "He found a letter at Hornby when we got home the other night—when we got home from here. . . . He bade me thank you most gratefully for all your kindnesses; he was very sorry not to come here once again."
> Phillis got up and left the room with noiseless steps.[23]

The girl can be singled out here as the weak link in the family chain that guarantees the axiological continuity of Hope Farm. Phillis's silence signals the beginning of a personal drama in a communal context in which harmony and order are so much taken for granted, so much part of the daily routine, that it is impossible for her parents to interpret her "noiseless steps" and her decision to disappear as an intimation of her ontological crisis. Whereas her parents' words express their innocent astonishment at the breaking of the news, Phillis evinces a response that means not only that words fail her, but more exactly that she has already entered a life-threatening stage: the pathologization of her disillusionment is stronger than her will to believe in Holdsworth's return to her. Confronted with his unexpected departure, ending a love discourse that has not culminated in an explicit and gratifying pledge, the heroine sees her future life as a blank wall. The event marks the end of her girlhood and her inability to enter a new and more complicated phase of her life. From a somatizing perspective, she intuits her destiny as a fall into an ontological chasm in which her individual subjectivity will experience a harmful and devastating ordeal.

Brought up in the conviction of a perfect correspondence between word and meaning, she has discovered, thanks to Holdsworth's linguistic skills, that a speech can have more than one meaning. What is more, just after hearing Paul's news about his friend, she discovers how Holdsworth's ability with languages can be easily transformed into linguistic betrayal. What are all his words worth if he has abandoned her without a sign of love, without a message of hope? What meaning can be attributed to their long hours spent together, passionately reading Italian passages from Dante's *Inferno* if the words that united her longing life to his were so poor and weak? Apparently, she cannot cope with a world that has suddenly become complex and unreadable. While it is true that words fail her, it is equally true that her body becomes the tablet on which she is given the possibility to inscribe her anguish. When some time after Paul's news she leaves her room for supper, she already exhibits signs of a physical metamorphosis:

> The supper was ready; it was always on the table as soon as the clock on the stairs struck eight, and down came Phillis—*her face white and set, her dry eyes* looking defiance to me, for I am afraid I hurt her maidenly pride by my glance of sympathetic interest as she entered the room. *Never a word did she say—never a question did she ask about the absent friend*, yet *she forced herself to talk.*
>
> And so it was all the next day. She was *pale* as she could be, like one who has received some shock; but she would not let me talk to her, and *she tried hard to behave as usual.*[24]

What is perhaps less immediately obvious here is the narrator's attempt to offer an interpretation of what is visible (the paleness of her face, etc.) and what is invisible (*she forced herself to talk*; *she tried hard to behave as usual*)—a significant transformation in Phillis's behavior that his sympathetic attitude has enabled him to perceive. On the face of it, nothing has changed: supper is served at eight o'clock sharp as ever, the Reverend Holman continues to combine farming and preaching, the people of Hope Farm invariably follow the same work schedule from daybreak to sunset. Upon closer inspection, however, we realize that all has changed: the silence that invades the house has nothing of the "tranquil monotony"[25] that communicated to Paul the sense and value of eternity[26] during his first stay at the farm. It is a silence that can be defined now only in the context of an impending tragedy whose final scene has still to be acted.

When Paul meets Phillis and her parents again on Christmas Day, he cannot fail to read on her body the "story" she is not able to narrate: "I only saw her paleness after we had returned to the farm, and she had subsided into silence and quiet. Her grey eyes looked hollow and sad; her complexion was of a dead white."[27] Her physical decline evinces more and more the signs of her psychic shrinking, which entails also a flight from the daily world into a territory of loneliness, pain, and unanswered cries: "While my head was down I heard a noise which made me pause and listen—a sob, an unmistakable, irresistible sob. I started up." Confronted with this explicit expression of pain, Paul is ready to offer his sympathy, but "she held her hand out of my grasp, for fear of detaining her."[28]

What must also be pointed out about the narrator's interpretative role, however, is his inability to understand the full extent of Phillis's psychic condition, characterized by a most complete passivity. The idea that a sympathetic and helping family circle can offer a good shelter from any form of personal shock seems to inform his skin-deep response to the heroine's growing physical distress and decay: "I stood still and wondered. What could have come to Phillis? The most perfect harmony prevailed in the family, and Phillis especially, good and gentle as she was, was so beloved that if they had found out that her finger ached, it would have cast a shadow over their hearts. Had I done anything to vex her?"[29] What is startling is that the same blindness that hampers the sympathetic action of Phillis's parents is evident in Paul, whose questions will lead him to offer her solace made of deceptive and mystifying words: "He had never spoken much about you before, but the sudden going away unlocked his heart, and he told me how he loved you, and how he hoped on his return that you might be his wife."[30] As a result of this revelation, which is more the offspring of Paul's helpful desire than a realistic representation of Holdsworth's leave taking, Phillis reaches "an almost heavenly happiness."[31]

Words can kill; words can save. Words can convey comfort and happiness; words can convey despair and sorrow. The narrator seems to take up Holdsworth's role on a stage in which linguistic skills play a much more important function than sheer facts.[32] There is, however, a substantial difference: now language is used not to conquer her heart, but to cure her body, whose decline is all the more shocking to Paul as he feels he is responsible for what has proved Holdsworth's intrusion in the world of Hope Farm.

Secrecy and silence are the props upon which Phillis constructs her unsteady and fictional edifice devoted to Holdsworth as a lover who will return from Canada and make her a happy wife. But her construction soon crumbles when Paul receives a letter from his friend announcing his marriage with a French Canadian woman—"Paul, I think we need never speak about this again, only remember you are not to be sorry."[33] After reading the letter, the first words that Phillis speaks to her saddened cousin is not to abandon their line of secrecy and silence:[34] she seems to be convinced that by not speaking of her inner drama she can mitigate her suffering. Again, words are the true protagonists of our destinies. And, in Phillis's case, written words rather than spoken become the key to reading reality; ostensibly they seem to overreach the real in a way that intensifies her pathological response to a strong emotion.

The final stage of Phillis's calvary is marked by Paul's sense of guilt, which becomes more and more intense as he discovers the way in which her body tries to express the words of pain that her voice is forbidden to pronounce: "once my eyes fell upon her hands, concealed under the table, and I could see the passionate, convulsive manner in which she laced and interlaced her fingers perpetually, wringing them together from time to time, wringing till the compressed flesh became perfectly white. What could I do? I talked with her, as I saw she wished; her grey eyes had dark circles round them and a strange kind of dark light in them; her cheeks were flushed, but her lips were white and wan. I wondered that others did not read these signs as clearly as I did."[35] "What could I do?" Behind the narrator's question lies the important recognition that he is the only one who can properly read Phillis's language, whose signs are not words but symptoms opening up a frightening territory dominated by silent sorrow and self-destruction. Equally important is the fact that his attention is totally focused on a single part of her body—to be more precise, on her hands—scrutinizing it almost with a medical attention in order to find a "therapeutical" answer to the question that everyone sympathetically posits to himself when confronted with a sufferer: "What could I do?" As will be easily recognized, he is unable to decode the external signs of her body in all their pathological implications—Phillis's concealed inner torments and the progressive instability of her identity give rise to a movement of self-marginalization that is further enhanced by a secrecy that is the most direct effect of a repressive society.

Not surprisingly, a more traumatic result of a cultural mentality that represses female sexuality is a sense of guilt that will be clearly expressed in the culminating moment of the heroine's crisis: "I am so sick with shame!"[36] Precisely because the girl has at last had the courage to reveal the origin of her physical and psychic distress, she can now also lay bare that sexuality whose importance her parents have failed to understand: "'I loved him, father!' she said at length, raising her eyes to the minister's face."[37] This is more than a simple declaration of her affective and sexual needs. Behind this simple expression—"I loved him, father!"—we cannot help perceiving the index of a revolt against patriarchy and Victorian gender ideology. Yet Phillis's rebellious words are unexpected and can be accounted for only when her extremely high degree of mental confusion is taken into consideration. Therefore, more than an act of conscious rebellion, her words are the instinctive manifestation of an exasperated mind on the verge of a mental and physical breakdown—which actually happens immediately after her verbal outburst:

> Probably the father and daughter were never so far apart in their lives, so unsympathetic. Yet some new terror came over her, and it was to him she turned for help. A shadow came over her face, and she tottered toward her father; falling down, her arms across his knees, and moaning out,—
> "Father, my head! my head!" and then slipped through his quick-enfolding arms, and lay on the ground at his feet.

> I shall never forget his sudden look of agony while I live; never! We raised her up; her colour had strangely darkened; she was insensible.[38]

This climactic scene marks the beginning of what we can define as Phillis's voyage in the dark. From now onward it will be her diseased body that speaks for the girl, whose "new terror" emerges from her inability to disentangle her life from a confusing past and from a meaningless future. At the same time the gulf between father and daughter can also be regarded as a consequence of her linguistic determination to affirm the rights of her freedom as a woman. Indeed, her self-representation goes against the family grain and postulates a personality beyond the sacred boundaries of strict paternal control. But, despite the courageous affirmation of her love and disillusionment, the crucial words are those referring to her father as the only saving figure on whom she can rely. Interestingly enough, the climax of *Cousin Phillis* defines an image of patriarchal authority that is rather contradictory. While the negativity of the role of Phillis's father in terms of her psychological and social growth is dramatized, he is eventually reinstated as a pivot of family life.

At this point secrecy no longer makes sense in Phillis's inner landscape: she has declared her feelings, thereby triggering her aching transition from girlhood to womanhood and, spatially, from the self-enclosed and simple universe of Hope Farm to the complexities and intricacies of the wide world. Although Paul is the only one who has shared her secret, it is also true that, once he has lost in Phillis's eyes that psychological authority bestowed on him by complicity, he cannot help but limit his role henceforth to that of a passive chronicler of the sad story of a heroine abandoned by her lover. Significantly, the stages of the girl's disease, the beginning of "a sleep which was the crisis, and from which she wakened up with a new faint life,"[39] are not part of his narratorial experience. He is not admitted into the sick room, where only her parents nurse the sufferer.[40] We are given to understand that Phillis's body, whose brain fever functions as a language to express the full extent of her mental turmoil, will resist any form of closure but that of the disease itself. No happy ending will gratify the reader, but only Phillis's vague idea that "we will go back to the peace of old days. I know we shall; I can, and I will."[41] Her journey is defined by these final words, which indicate that illness and physical distress will have negative effects on her mind. It stands to reason that what is implied here is that her depression will last beyond the confines of the page itself. But, whatever meaning we might detect in these final words, it is easy to see that the heroine is no longer the same.

As pointed out at the beginning of this chapter, illness always entails a metamorphosis—the extent of Phillis's transformation has been so radical that, as in the case of Kafka's Gregor Samsa, only death can free her mind from the ghost of her past. Although she does not die, the future can belong only to another Phillis, possibly with the same body as Phillis Holman, but certainly with another mind, and another soul. Ultimately, the reader is left with the illusion that "her wish for change of thought and scene"[42] will restore the unity between her mind and body. But, concluded as it may be, Phillis's voyage in the dark has already written on her body words so hard and painful that no future love or affection can cancel or modify them. The text of her malady is, in many respects, the text of a culture that is not ready to accept the forces of change, especially if they involve an open-minded and progressive approach to the sphere of femininity.

4

The Cursed Hearth:
Desire and Deceit in the
Short Stories of Elizabeth Gaskell

FOR ELIZABETH GASKELL THE DESTABILIZING EFFECTS OF CHANGE were most evident in the context of the family group. In particular, her imagination was highly sensitive to the physical and psychological metamorphoses of the individual, whose behavioral codes were profoundly modified by the social transformations of Victorian England. Her fiction reflects a keen receptivity to such situations in which centrifugal historical forces were exerting a disruptive influence on the family, often portrayed on the point of falling apart or disintegrating. For Gaskell, the family represents a weak link in the social chain, since it is invariably undermined, pathologized, and, more often than not, destroyed by the whirlwind of a new economic order. Her exploration of this destructive change entails above all a narrativization of the way the family nucleus is modified in its patriarchal structure, inner organization, and values. Involving as well a more general investigation of the complexities and mysteries of human life, this particular aspect constitutes the main impulse behind Gaskell's most significant and complex works. It is by no means accidental that, in Gaskell's masterpiece *Wives and Daughters* (1865), the heroine's muted psychological crisis is induced by the arrival of a stepmother, Mrs. Hyacinth Kirkpatrick, whose social pretensions configure a disjunctive element in the loving father-daughter relationship.[1] *Wives and Daughters* narrates the story of a young girl, Molly Gibson, who is forced to live with an egotistical and vapid stepmother, whose only aim seems to be the fulfillment of her own desires. In this case, Dr. Gibson's decision to remarry does not give his family a new equilibrium but introduces instead a further factor of psychological dissatisfaction and social discrepancy. Notwithstanding every effort to offer his daughter a good education, Dr. Gibson paradoxically transforms his domestic space into a stage on which sincerity is ousted by hypocrisy, honest dialogue by word mincing and ambiguity, simple everyday gestures by scheming intricacies. In Gaskell's imagination, family groups are always a locus of instability.

This idea of a changing society, often too ready to destroy the values of the domestic hearth, gives the impetus to Gaskell's tales, which, as representations of the family unit, tend to dramatize the predominance of negative centrifugal forces over those of solidarity and altruism. With her Gothic tales, Gaskell reacts not so much in terms of "disillusionment with ideals of historical progress,"[2] as Rosemary Jackson has suggested, as in response to her literary imaginary, which is strongly drawn toward mystery. Her approach is essentially metahistorical since her main intention is always to go beyond the surface of things, and thus deliberately overlook the immediate effects brought about by change.

In spite of her philanthropic commitment and her sensitive response to the theme of the "two nations," and in spite of her strong concern for the plight of the masses, which were daily being swallowed up by such a monstrous metropolis as Manchester, Gaskell adopted the fantastic mode of writing in a conscious artistic effort of achieving a full dramatization of the mysterious and indecipherable pathways of the human soul. In her tales the trope of the crowd as a dangerous class does not open up a historic vision but is often merely a background to accentuate the solitude of characters who are exposed to the temptations of Evil. Unsurprisingly, as a consequence of their wicked actions, such characters meet the zero degree of their social dimension, while they discover that an empty space has taken the place of the community and, more dramatically, that their destinies are anchored to lies and deceit rather than to truth and harmony.

The story that, perhaps more than any other, lays bare the inability of society to impose any values is *Lois the Witch* (1859). By focusing her attention on a lonely girl who decides to leave her home in Warwickshire to live with her relatives in New England, Gaskell traces a journey culminating in isolation, falsity, and self-destruction.[3] In fact, when Lois disembarks at Boston she finds no member of her uncle's family waiting to greet her: "And Lois was left alone in New England."[4] Her whole story is already inscribed in this phrase, for, contrary to the bright and pristine New World she has expected, Lois Barclay encounters at Salem a world of malign spirits, sullen voices, and spectral visions, where darkness prevails over light and the "eldritch scream" drowns out any words of solidarity.

When she arrives at Salem, Lois's relatives are anything but ready to greet her. All she finds is the cold hearth of a house in which deception, dishonesty, and death lay down the law. Subsequently, when her cousin Manasseh realizes that Lois is willing to accept his proposal of marriage, he can only, in conformity with his puritanical approach to sexuality, cry out that the girl is a devil: "Take her away, Mother! Lead me not into temptation. She brings me evil and sinful thoughts. She overshadows me, even in the presence of my God. She is no angel of light, or she would not do this. She troubles me with the sound of her voice bidding me marry her, even when I am at my prayers. Avaunt! Take her away!"[5] To the enchanted eyes of her cousin, Lois's beauty represents the very incarnation of evil and her body becomes such an object of temptation to him that he accuses her of being a witch. The apocalyptic tone of Manasseh's outburst, far from being an isolated expression, epitomizes the need for a scapegoat of a society that, while negating sexuality and making purity its dogma, in reality negates the very essence of life. While Dr. Cotton Mather thunders, "Satan is among you!"[6] while the scaffold on which Lois the Witch meets her death is being prepared, the girl's refusal to confess sins she has never committed—the refusal, that is, to recognize *her* world in that hallucinating and disconnected world—must be interpreted as the most rebellious act in the whole story.

The elements of fantasy and the supernatural dimension of *Lois the Witch* are not merely parts of a functional background to a tragic and absurd human event. They also serve to underline the impossibility of a mediation between a real world—partly derived from the typical rationalism of the Unitarian Church—and a world of mystery that, once recognized and focused, the writer aims to render in realistic terms. Consequently, everything from Manasseh's hallucinations to his sexual repression, from the shadows in the forest to the mass hysteria, finds an explanation in the closing pages: "The stillness and silence were broken by one crazed and mad, who came rushing up the steps of the ladder, and caught Lois's body in his arms, and kissed her lips with wild passion. And then, as if it were true what the people believed, that he was possessed by a demon, he sprang down, and rushed through the crowd, out of the bounds of the city, and into the dark dense forest, and Manasseh Hickson was no more seen of Christian man."[7] The reality of Lois's innocence is thus restored before the whole community. The emptiness and silence around Lois the Witch, as she hangs on the scaffold, become filled with an awareness that, along with divine justice, human justice is paradoxically reaffirmed, for Manasseh pays the just price for his crime, and the darkness toward which he escapes is the darkness of his own self and not that of the population of Salem. Thus, although another victim has been sacrificed, the disrupted harmony is at the same time recomposed. There remains no mystery, no common condition of darkness, and, above all, no guilt.

The events narrated in the intense Gothic atmosphere of *The Old Nurse's Story,* in which evil is seen as a mysterious and unexplainable phenomenon, are developed along very analogous lines. *The Old Nurse's Story* can be regarded, that is, as a tale of the supernatural, a ghost story, and a tale of mystery. But it is, of course, much more than this. As in *Lois the Witch,* at least five thematic units may be detected: 1) disintegration of the family: Rosamond, a child of about five, finds herself alone in the world after the deaths of her parents; 2) spatial displacement: Rosamond goes to live in a house that she discovers to be full of deceit and treachery; 3) moral passiveness of relatives: Rosamond does not receive the protection that her nurse hopes she will be given in her new dwelling; 4) the destructive and self-destructive nature of female beauty; 5) resolution of the mystery: the epilogue finally resolves the contradictions in terms of an order that punishes the guilty and restores dignity to the innocent.

Unlike *Lois the Witch, The Old Nurse's Story* does not represent corruption in terms of the environment but through a *specter child.* With her insistent lamentations, she seeks to lure Rosamond outside the villa and to drag her through the dark, barren heath in which, many years previously, she and her mother, maddened by sorrow, had found their death on a cold winter's night. What is the link between the *specter child* and the aristocratic Furnivall family who host Rosamond and her nurse? What secret lurks within the icy atmosphere of the Furnivall household and within the grave silence that enshrouds old Grace Furnivall, the present owner of the villa? What is the origin of the organ music that, while actualizing a locus of a total disharmony, invades the rooms like a soul in torment on windy winter nights?

These questions derive from an initial dramatic event that refuses to recede into the past and continues despite the lapse of decades to assert its presence until the truth is disclosed. The main characters of the antecedent episode, Maude and Grace Furnivall, the beautiful daughters of an old lord, both fall madly in love with a foreign musician, whom the music-loving Lord Furnivall has invited to the house. There follows a series of tragic events: the sisters' rivalry culminating in Maude's elopement with the musician, the birth of the child out of wedlock, Maude's return to Furnivall Manor House with her child, Lord Furnivall's decision to cast both daughter and granddaughter out of the house on a "wild and fearful night,"[8] and the death of Maude and the child on the heath from frostbite at the foot of a holly bush.

At the center of the story is a thirst for revenge. After Maude's flight with her lover, Grace puts all her energy into accomplishing destructive plans: "she was heard to say many a time that sooner or later she would have her revenge."[9] But Grace Furnivall underestimates the effect this will have on her conscience—for the dramatic scene on the heath exceeds her desires and leaves a terrible and painful mark in her soul. Far from being liberated, she bears from this moment onward the burden of a guilt that even time is unable to eradicate.

The very music that is at the origin of the tragedy invariably triggers the furious reactions of Lord Furnivall on stormy nights, until he finally repudiates both daughter and granddaughter before the whole household, including the servants:

> he prayed that they might never enter Heaven. And all the while, Miss Grace stood by him, white and still as any stone; and when he had ended she heaved a sigh, as much as to say her work was done, and her end was accomplished. But the old lord never touched his organ again, and he died within a year; and no wonder! for, on the morrow of that wild and fearful night, the shepherds, coming down the Fell-side, found Miss Maude sitting, all crazy and smiling, under the holly-tree, nursing a dead child,—with a terrible mark on its right shoulder.[10]

The father of the rival sisters dies, but the organ—abandoned to dust and falling to pieces—persists in giving voice to the uncontrollable fury of the old man on dark winter days, thus reenacting both the scene of the curse and its fatal consequences. Against Grace's revenge there is also the eternal revenge of Maude, who never ceases to haunt the conscience of her sister, who, now in her eighties, seems to be waiting for a final confrontation with evil in order finally to be liberated from the phantoms of her past.

At this point it is useful to stress the importance of a particular narratological feature. The actual story of the two sisters is narrated by the old nurse, Hester, who is entrusted with the little Rosamond. The opening scene presents a group of children who are the sons and daughters of Rosamond, the girl whom the old nurse, as a young woman, managed to save from the *specter child*. Thanks to the strategy of having the story narrated so long after the events, the whole diegesis acquires a tone of common sense that, while weakening its Gothic effects, highlights its clear-cut moral development. This reassuring tone is evident from the very beginning: "You know, my dears, that your mother was an orphan, and an only child; and I dare say you have heard that your grandfather was a clergyman up in Westmoreland where I come from."[11] It goes without saying that the first-person narrator exhibits a much stronger control over the events than she evidently had while actually experiencing them. This explains why, for example, in describing the gloomy notes of the organ booming throughout the house, Hester declares that, for her, such a supernatural element was essentially one of fun.[12] Similarly, the fact that all access to the eastern wing of the house has been forbidden, rather than inciting fear in the nurse, who is aware that the prohibition applies to an event that no one has the courage to disclose, only stimulates her curiosity.

The isotopy of interdiction has a peculiar relevance to a portrait of Maude, hidden from other people's gaze, metaphorically abandoned to a destiny of obscurity and death. After showing her Miss Grace Furnivall's portrait, regularly hung on the wall, in one of the less frequented rooms ("Such a beauty she must have been! But with such a set, proud look, and such scorn looking out of handsome eyes"),[13] Dorothy, the old servant, secretly informs her of the portrait of Maude Furnivall. And this dusty picture is among the objects that may be neither looked upon nor mentioned: "and then I helped Dorothy to turn a great picture that leaned with its face towards the wall, and was not hung up as the others were. To be sure, it beat Miss Grace for beauty; and, I think, for scornful pride."[14]

The significant syntagm here is *scornful pride*, in which the juxtaposition of the two negative words gives full expression to the inhumanity that characterizes the Furnivall family. It is no accident that *pride* and *proud*[15] are recurrent terms in the descriptions of Lord Furnivall and his beautiful daughters. Indeed, Grace Furnivall exists in a world of rigidity, severity, and obstinate cruelty that has a petrifying effect on her. Hester eventually learns the secret behind the hard, impenetrable features of the old owner from Dorothy, who tells her the true story—a story within the story—of the *specter child* and of Grace's terrible guilt. Consequently, the situation of stasis made up of prohibitions, silence, dust-covered objects, and rooms that have been locked for decades becomes the visible evidence of the essentially internal struggle of Grace. Her unresolved and unavoidable inner conflict emerges in Dorothy's tale with all the memories and phantoms that have continued to haunt the cursed place. In his tragic immobility, Lord Furnivall seems to be waiting in this tale for his own moment of final atonement. Nevertheless, the crystallized grayness of the house, the uncontested dominion of a decay of dust and death, the worn curtains and the stifling air of the locked rooms conceal a struggle that principally concerns the internal world of Grace, its present owner, who is continually haunted by tempestuous winds and restless ghosts.

With respect to Rosamond, the power of the spectral presence exerts itself in all its destruction only when, lured by the painful cries of the child, she vanishes into the cold heath on a dark snowy afternoon. When a shepherd accidentally discovers her, he saves her from dying of frostbite. In her innocence the victim of the spell describes the spectral vision as something that has really happened, ignorant of the fact that only a lucky accident has prevented the repetition of the cursed scene of a child's death after so many years. In Rosamond's own account of her encounter with the child, "I never looked at her feet, but she held my hand fast and tight in her little one, and it was very, very cold. She took me up the Fell-path, up to the holly trees; and there I saw a lady weeping and crying; but when she saw me, she hushed her weeping, and smiled very proud and grand, and she took me on her knee, and began to lull me to sleep; and that's all, Hester—but that is true; and my dear mamma knows it is,' said she, crying."[16] The tension gradually mounts until the whole sequence of the misdeed is revealed, as if in a one-act play. The four main characters—Miss Maude and her child, old Lord Furnivall and the young Grace—dramatically reenact in the same setting, the great hall of the house, the same events that have occurred sixty years previously.

While the raging elements give expression to their tormented souls, the scene is identically repeated by the four actors, who, unlike the characters of the past, are now similar to ghosts reciting their roles for the benefit of a particular public: old Grace Furnivall together with her servant, Hester, and the little Rosamond, who, in this imaginary climax, undergo yet another time the temptation of saving the *specter child.*

Once again, the nurse succeeds in fighting back evil, while Grace Furnivall is unable to bear the vision. The old woman falls into a swoon, never to regain consciousness. Her final words before she dies: "Alas! Alas! What is done in youth cannot be undone in age! What is done in youth cannot be undone in age!"[17] In the reenactment of the crime, time closes up like a fan, annulling the gap between present and past, which unite to converge around a single frightening epiphany. Thus, Grace Furnivall, as a young woman comes face to face with her decrepit self in old age and hears the desperate words of her old self uttering the unutterable and laying bare a guilt that can only be atoned for by death.

In conformity with the tradition of the Gothic novel, Gaskell's tales assign a special topological privilege to castles, large country mansions, and ancestral palaces—all those places in which time has left stories and the stories themselves are full of mysteries, phantoms, restless nights, and unspeakable secrets.[18] It is no accident, for example, that in *The Old Nurse's Story*, it is Furnivall Manor House itself that, proleptically, reveals to Hester the ghostly tensions and cold relationships governing that closed community: "When we drove up to the great front entrance, and went into the hall I thought we should be lost—it was so large, and vast and grand. . . . The afternoon was closing in and the hall, which had no fire lighted in it, looked dark and gloomy, but we did not stay there a moment."[19] Hester immediately realizes that the house is cursed: the sense of forlornness is further heightened as she explores its rooms. There is no fire in the great fireplace: cold prevails over warmth, darkness over light, inhumanity over humanity, mortal silence over speech, which is nevertheless characterized by the reassuring tones of the narrative voice. Significantly, Hester declares, "I began to think I should *be lost in that wilderness of a house.*"[20] Here the repetition of the term *lost* not only anticipates the attempt by the phantoms to force Hester to become lost on the vast desolate heath, but also refers to the lost state of the fallen soul.[21] The desolate land of the heath, where the overgrown plants surround the villa almost as if to strangle it, recalls the transition from a state of innocence to a "paradise lost," to a wilderness reminiscent of Milton and Bunyan. Since the hearth of the house is cursed, it is finally only through humble servants, such as Dorothy and her old husband, James, that Hester and Rosamond find the warmth and kindness reviving their struggle to keep the petrifying coldness of Grace Furnivall at bay.

In *Morton Hall* (1853) the main character is the house itself. The story can be divided into three thematic sequences: usurpation, mystery, and death. First, usurpation occurs during the reign of the Puritans. A Scotsman, Richard Carr, receives Morton Hall as a gift for his loyalty to Cromwell, and the owner is forced to flee to Bruges together with his court. During the years of the Restoration, the beautiful daughter of the usurper, Alice Carr, manages to keep hold of the property, because of her family bond with General Monck.[22] As in *The Old Nurse's Story*, beauty is again associated with hardness, a quality of which Alice Carr, as a faithful representative of puritanical ideology, is a destructive example: "She was taller than most women, and a great beauty, I have heard. But, for all her beauty, she was a stern, hard woman."[23]

The disruptive moment in the story begins when Alice Carr agrees to marry Sir John Morton, the last descendant of the usurped family, who very soon realizes that he prefers the pomp and revelry of the nobility in London to the severity and harshness of his new family environment. With the failure of their marriage, Alice Carr's religious convictions become all the more stoical and she soon transforms Morton Hall into a den of fanatical Puritans and conspirators against the Crown. In her religious zeal, the woman decides to organize a great banquet in honor of the preachers—a banquet that concludes with the dramatic entrance of John Morton, who breaks into the house and forces everyone to flee: "The man shut and locked the great house-door, and the echoes of the clang went through the empty Hall with an ominous sound."[24]

At this point the mystery begins. With its tables still richly laid, its candelabras glowing in the halls, its polished furniture and all other signs of luxury, the house is locked up and transformed into a territory that no one is allowed to enter, above all, Alice Carr, the usurper: "Somehow, the Hall got an ugly name; the roast and boiled meats, the ducks, the chickens had time *to drop into dust*, before any human being now dared to enter in; or, indeed, had any right to enter in, for Sir John never came back to Morton; as for my lady, some said she was dead, and some said she was mad, and shut up in London, and some said Sir John had taken her to a convent abroad."[25] Thus, Morton Hall is suddenly transformed into a place of death—and the villagers themselves refer to it as "the Devil's House." The spiders' webs and dust that gather in the rooms tell a tale of pride and mortality, and the feast prepared for the Puritans gradually decays and endures as a symbol of their vanity and fanaticism. Time devours and reduces everything to nothing. What remains is the mystery of a frozen scene. And together with the disturbing presence of the puritanical phantoms, who are unable to forget the wrong inflicted on them, there is only a space that is itself a ghostly memory of a historical and human catastrophe.

Alice becomes mad, and before dying she puts a terrible curse on Morton Hall. All subsequent attempts to restore the place to life ultimately fail, and, many years later, Miss Phillis, the heir of Morton, and her nephew are forced through poverty to renounce their claim to the evil place. The curse falls not only on the Hall, but also on Morton's descendants, for Miss Phillis and her nephew, John Marmaduke Morton, are unable to find redemption even in a modest little house: "We durst not to be left only one alone; yet, at the cottage where Miss Phillis had lived, there was neither fire nor fuel. So we sat and shivered and shook till morning. The squire never came that night nor all next day."[26] The reader is left with the complicated story of Morton Hall, narrated by one of the witnesses of its last phase, as a place of death and decadence: "After the squire, John Marmaduke Morton, had been found dead in that sad way, on the dreary moors, the creditors seemed to lose all hold on the property. . . . The old house fell out of repair; the chimneys were full of starlings' nests; the flags in the terrace in front were hidden by long grass; the panes in the windows were broken, no one knew how or why, for the children of the village got up a tale that the house was haunted."[27] Alice's madness, the interruption of the great banquet, the gloomy and dusty rooms in which the phantoms of the puritanical preachers scream for eternal vengeance are the main ingredients of the drama. Years pass, various owners come and go, while Morton Hall remains not only an abandoned house but also a place haunted by the mystery of words and gestures so heartless that no redeeming light can reach them. As a result of its tragic history, Morton Hall seems to embody a final condemnation of human beings to incomprehension and silence. No one can boast possession of the place simply because no one wants to possess it any longer.

Spatial representation also assumes a particular relevance in *The Grey Woman* (1861). In this story, the psychological instability of the main character leads to her eventual physical metamorphosis in the melo-dramatic context of her escape and search for refuge. The story, set during the early years of the French Revolution, concerns the misad-ventures of a young girl from Heidelberg (Anna Scherer) who reluc-tantly agrees to marry a French nobleman (Monsieur de la Tourelle). On her first meeting with him she only notes "the affected softness and effeminacy of his manners."[28] This initial image contrasts violently with the character's real personality, for his soft manners actually con-ceal an extremely evil and bloody nature. Monsieur de la Tourelle is the leader of the Chauffeurs, a cruel band of criminals who wreak terrifying and deathly havoc along the left bank of the Rhine.

From a semantic and structural viewpoint, *The Grey Woman* again presents the fivefold paradigm of Gaskell's Gothic stories: 1) family disintegration: Anna Scherer finds herself alone in the world after abandoning her father, an old mill owner; 2) spatial displacement: Anna goes to live in Monsieur de la Tourelle's castle, which she dis-covers to be a place full of deceit and treachery; 3) moral passivity of the community: in spite of the fact that her husband turns out to be a criminal, Anna will benefit from the protection of society only at the very end of the narration; 4) the self-destructive metamorphosis of beauty; 5) final resolution: the guilty are punished, the truth is disclosed, all contradictions are explained, and the social order and family unity are finally reaffirmed.

The first sequence in Anna's story shows her attempt to be inde-pendent of her father, who wants her to marry the first of his ap-prentices. After her refusal, the second sequence involves her escape together with her faithful servant, Amante, and installs her in the castle called Les Rochers, which she immediately perceives in a to-tally negative light: "So it was in no cheerful frame of mind that we approached Les Rochers, and I thought that perhaps it was because I was so unhappy that the place looked so dreary."[29] Here Anna learns that she can exercise her authority only in the restricted number of rooms that have been specifically assigned to her. The third sequence begins with her discovery of her husband's double life and follows an existential development that concludes only when Anna Scherer is no longer Anna Scherer. In fact, the girl can retrieve her inner harmony only through her social death since, in wanting to follow her youthful romantic dreams, she has been deaf to the voice of reason. The final page confirms the metamorphoses of both her physical and legal identity. The rebel girl no longer exists and in her place there is now another woman: "The few people I saw knew me only as Madame Voss; a widow much older than himself, whom Dr Voss had secretly married. They called me the Grey Woman."[30]

For her final happiness she has had to pay a heavy price, the loss of her beauty, which had such an overpowering effect on Monsieur de la Tourelle. Thus, Anna becomes the Grey Woman—she has lost "her complexion of lilies and roses, lost her colour so entirely through fright, that she was known by the name of the Grey Woman."[31] Not only are her face, hair, and complexion grey, but her very soul has gradually adopted the same color. Such a dominant grayness is the result of the passivity that from the first scene to the last has been the unifying trait of her character.

As regards the topological organization of the story, a castle figures here too as a negative feature of reality, a life-negating place that offers no protection or sense of certainty. Made up, as it is, of two parts, a new and an old one, in stark contrast with each other, the castle's disturbing doubleness, with its unexplored and prohibited rooms, expresses its owner's heinous duplicity and moral darkness. Anna Scherer's entrance into Les Rochers may be equated to an encounter with a sinister underworld in which evil is always lying in wait: "Incongruous as the two parts were, they were joined into a whole by means of intricate passages and unexpected doors, the exact positions of which I never fully understood. . . . I trembled in silence at the fantastic figures and shapes which my imagination called up as peopling the back-ground of those gloomy mirrors."[32] Trapped in the castle with its long ill-lit corridors, cold and somber atmosphere, locked doors, whispering voices, and incomprehensible signs, Anna Scherer finds that "this grand isolation of mine was very formidable."[33] Although what most frightens her about the castle are its mirrors, in which she imagines terrifying scenes, everything about it is cold and inhuman. This inhumanity finds its fitting stage when, after entering Monsieur de la Tourelle's secret chamber unseen, Anna discovers the truth of his secret activity. Characterized by a total respect for the conventions of the Gothic genre, the scene also includes a corpse beside which Anna is forced to lie as she hides under the table: "I drew myself to the side of the table farthest from the corpse, with as much slow caution as if I really could have feared the clutch of that poor dead arm, power-less for evermore."[34]

The castle, with its cold corpse, its burned out candles, blocked doors, and chilling darkness, has all the air of a deathly labyrinth. In Gaskell's view, given the meanness and callousness of the great wealthy aristocracy, it is appropriate that Anna Scherer manages to flee from the fury of her husband thanks to the help of a character from the lower orders. It is her maid Amante who, disguising herself as a tailor, succeeds in safely taking her mistress far from the area around the cursed castle. Thus, the heroine and her maid become— "a travelling pedlar and his wife,"[35] whose behavior, language, and movement do not seem to arouse suspicion. But, when they are discovered, Anna Scherer's maid (i.e. her false husband) is ready to give her life to save her mistress. Once again salvation is through the lower orders of the social scale, from those people who face daily life with a practical spirit and sense of duty. However, it is clear that the role of such characters as Amante is diegetically marginal and does not substantially modify the portrayal of a society besieged by moral anarchy and psychological disharmony.

In Gaskell's short stories, curses are more than a mere plot device.[36] Indeed, they always have a thematic function, which, as in *The Poor Clare* (1856) and *The Doom of the Griffiths* (1858), relates to the primordial struggle between good and evil, and the clash between contrasting sentiments and passions. In *The Poor Clare*, the character whose terrible words set in motion the ensuing tragic events is Bridget Fitzgerald, a Catholic widow of Irish origins. She puts a curse on Squire Gisborne, who is guilty of having killed her little dog, Mignon, out of sheer cruelty. Exaggerated as it may seem, her reaction is justifiable from a psychological and emotional point of view. The animal not only has been her sole companion in life but had also belonged to her rebellious and restless daughter, Mary, who had run away from home years previously "[to] go forth into the wide world."[37]

But to explain who Bridget Fitzgerald is we need to turn back to *Lois the Witch* and to the theme of witchcraft:

> She looked as if she had been scorched in the flames of hell, so brown and scared, and fierce a creature did she seem. By-and-by many saw her; and those who met her eye once cared not to be caught look-

ing at her again. She had got into the habit of perpetually talking to herself; nay, more answering herself, and varying her tones according to the side she took at the moment. It was no wonder that those who dared to listen outside her door at night believed that she had converse with some spirit; in short, she was consciously earning for herself the reputation of a witch.[38]

In Gaskell's concern to present matters from a strongly sociological perspective, accusations of witchcraft are invariably launched by the dominant group as a means of excluding and obliterating the individual whose behavior upsets the social order. A reputation for witchcraft is therefore projected onto whoever does not conform with the normal codes of behavior—and in this sense, as has been seen in *Lois the Witch*, even beauty can seem to be a configuration of evil when it is not supported by an elevated social status. However, even if Bridget Fitzgerald is a witch only in the eyes of the superstitious people of the village, her curse produces devastating and irreparable effects. In an incredible series of events and coincidences, Gisborne happens to be no less than the husband of Bridget's rebellious daughter, and her curse obtains the opposite result from the one she intended, for Mary is deceived and treated so spitefully by her husband that, in a fit of depression, she throws herself into the river and drowns.

The sense of mystery is further heightened by an unexplainable event: Lucy, the child of Gisborne and Mary, lives in perpetual terror because she is haunted by her double: "In the great mirror opposite I saw myself, and right behind, another wicked, fearful self."[39] As in *The Grey Woman*, mirrors are the surface upon which evil is revealed. They become not only a vehicle of deceit but also the space in which curses become visible. Before such a supernatural phenomenon, Gisborne can only cry, "The curse—the curse!" thus recognizing its continuing destructive influence on his daughter as well. The terrible truth behind the beautiful girl is presented to the eyes of the narrator as "a ghastly resemblance, complete in likeness, so far as form and feature and minutest touch of dress could go, but with loathsome demon soul looking out of the grey eyes, that were in turn mocking and voluptuous. My heart stood still within me; every hair rose up erect; my flesh crept with horror. I could not see the grave and tender Lucy—my eyes were fascinated by the creature beyond."[40] Once again there are broken families; feminine beauty, in the form of Mary and her daughter, Lucy; and mystery behind every gesture and event, together with the sense of an order that is impossible to establish.

In this essentially negative landscape, the curse continues to exert its pernicious influence in every predictable and unpredictable way until eventually reality is once more restored to its natural dimension. The sexual connotation of the lexical choices *voluptuous* and *fascinated* in the preceding description implicitly exposes an essentially destructive attitude toward the language of sexuality.[41] Thus, sexuality and cursing become superimposed and confused and ultimately relegated to that area of linguistic rejection upon which society has always grounded its methods of isolating and excluding those who stand outside the norm.

Significantly, the curse can only be undone with the spatial displacement of the main protagonist as well as of the events. Determined to do penance for the rest of her life, Bridget goes to Antwerp, where she is taken in by the Convent of Poor Clares under the name of *Magdalen*.[42] In the epilogue, in which she struggles with evil ("I defy the demon I have called up. Leave me to wrestle with it!"),[43] the old woman confesses her guilt and thus frees her niece, Lucy, from the double demon and the curse. Despite the melodramatic tone of the conclusion of *The Poor Clare*, the thematic coherence of the exploration of the evil potential of language in Gaskell's stories must be underlined. It is through such an exploration that the writer's literary imagination draws its ideas and themes from the rich oral tradition of popular legends.

This is also the case with *The Doom of the Griffiths,* in which Owen Glendower, a national hero from the north of Wales, puts a curse on the best friend who has betrayed him: "Thou shalt live on to see all of thy house, except the weakling in arms, perish by sword. Thy race shall be accursed. Each generation shall see their lands melt away like snow; yea, their wealth shall vanish, though they may labour night and day to heap gold."[44] The culminating moment of the curse occurs after nine generations, with a terrible act against nature: "The son shall slay the father."[45] It is important to stress that here not only is prophecy itself fulfilled, but that also in this case revenge falls on the family as an effect of language. The hatred, or the evil, persists over such a long span of time precisely in the form of words. The cursed words even triumph over the delaying strategies that Owen, the last of the Griffiths, implements in order to prevent the ancient prophecy from coming true. He keeps as far away as possible from the cold and inhospitable palace of Bodowen, in which his father and stepmother live: "Bodowen was no longer a place where, if Owen was not loved or attended to, he could at least find peace, and care for himself: he was thwarted at every step, and in every wish."[46] After fleeing from the palace in search of a new family among the humble people along the coast, he meets Nest Pritchard, the beautiful daughter of a fisherman, at Ty Glas. Their secret marriage with the subsequent birth of their son provokes the indignant reaction of Squire Griffiths, who sees in his son's choice a betrayal of the ideals of his family, whereas the accidental death of the newborn child at the hands of the squire inevitably leads the story to its melodramatic conclusion. In the end, harmony has been destroyed, any last residue of human sympathy between son and father annihilated, and the inescapable tragedy imposed by the curse accomplished.

From the dark depths of a Welsh landscape described in its most minute details, the reader feels the sense of a zero degree realism. A ghostly world devoid of moral certainty is mirrored against a human world of conflicting desires, which interweaves with the eternal struggle of the elements and is dialogically inscribed in terms of human designs characterized by excess and primitivism.

The dominant aspect of the stories that have been taken into consideration may also be seen in connection with the writer's major novels. Undoubtedly, on a macrotextual plane Gaskell's semantic universe hinges on a search for a new female identity, which, while expressing the need to conserve the essentially feminine quality of gentleness, also expresses the more urgent need to free Victorian women from the limiting roles imposed on them by tradition and to portray them as the real protagonists of change and its contradictions.

Works such as *Mary Barton, North and South,* and *Sylvia's Lovers* emphasize women's new role, their need to have their own say, to narrate and thus *write their own stories.* Gaskell resolves polarities such as gentleness and commerce, femininity and authority, the angel of the hearth and the socially committed woman, partly by downplaying the disruptive impact of the historical context, partly by ideally staging an improbable reconciliation between the classes. There remains, at bottom, a deeply ingrained ideological ambivalence: on the one hand, the powerful transgression that informs almost every page of her narrative discourse; on the other, the need of actualizing a diegetic closure marked by a pacifying sense of order and social harmony. In a sense, Gaskell's preoccupation with making literature redemptive is her response to a humankind that, from her Unitarian perspective, appears more and more exiled from God, and doomed to moral darkness.

In the case of her stories, this crisis of representation lies precisely in Gaskell's wish to offer explanations that deny mystery its impenetrable valence, for in her weltanschauung everything must be justified and settled; semantic obscurities are regularly rejected and never regarded as an integral part of human experience. Therefore, any hermeneutical gaps or situations of deadlock that are determined by a mysterious event are either in some way explained or simply avoided; the initial element of disruption is always eventually cleared up, leaving no room for problems of interpretation. For Gaskell, there is no sense in describing the consequences of a curse that falls on a particular character if she cannot offer a key to transform the mystery, however unexplainable, into a moral lesson to impart to the reader. There ultimately remains a contradiction between the need to face what cannot be controlled and explained by purely rational instruments and the desire to impress on everything the positive signs of a society yearning to fulfill its dream of order.

5

The Whirlpool:
Gissing, Vocation, and Modernity

THE WHIRLPOOL (1897) IS UNDOUBTEDLY ONE OF GEORGE GISSING'S
best novels.[1] Despite Henry James's reservations about its artistic
value, Gissing finally received a gratifying recognition of his talent
from the reading public as well as from the critics.[2] By choosing to
focus upon the emerging classes of British society in *The Whirlpool,* he
confronts the extremely complex thematics of a redefinition of fin-
de-siècle sociocultural and axiological coordinates, with particular
emphasis on the turmoil produced in interpersonal relationships by
the world of finance. Gissing's "study" of the jubilant race toward modernity appears precisely when Victorian society seems euphorically
projected into the new century. Thus, adopting the realistic stance
of a detached observer, he registers and reflects on the changes that
have occurred to the fabric of society, while trying to understand
to what extent the new way of life is infecting and jeopardizing the
Victorian family and its values. Matrimony is not, however, one of
the dominant motifs of *The Whirlpool.* To assert that such is the case
would limit the framework of references with respect to the diverse
semantic directions that the novel actually takes. Gissing is not interested so much in illustrating the way matrimonies are made and
unmade, nor, it seems in dramatizing—as James does in *What Maisy*
Knew (1897)—the disastrous consequences that failed unions can
have upon children. His intention is rather to narrate the contrast
between the respectable face of the middle classes at the end of the
century and the moral decadence of society.

Along the lines of this narrative program, Gissing explores new
territories with equally new expressive techniques. Once he had concluded his work, the author must have felt, in this respect, rather

gratified, and, in a letter to his editor, Bullen, he makes no effort
to conceal his own satisfaction: "I must confess that I rather count
upon this book. It is doubtful whether I shall do anything better, or
anything again so good."[3] What was it about the writer's last work,
one may ask, that made him hold it in such high esteem? And can
such a judgment be ascribed to mere self-exaltation or, as rather
seems the case, to other good reasons for being so happy with *The
Whirlpool*? Gissing was well aware that the novel contained new elements that mainly concerned a more ironic and less involved narrative voice. This detachment allowed him to avoid, in H. G. Wells's
words, "the idealising touch, the partiality, the inevitable taint of justification."[4] At the same time, his narratological strategy was crucial
in achieving more refined and artistic effects, especially with regard
to characterization.

Even until recently, some critics have underlined that the basis of
his imaginative vision in *The Whirlpool* draws inspiration, at various
points, from autobiographical experience. In my opinion, tracing
eventual parallels between the fictional text and the personal events
of the author's life is pertinent only to the extent to which they contribute to disambiguating certain textual knots. A narrowly biographical
approach is otherwise methodologically alien to an analysis of the
artistic text and its semiotic dynamic. Unfortunately, Gissing is too
often the object of biographical criticism. As a result, much remains
to be done in an investigation of his fiction as an epistemic response
to the late Victorian debate on culture and the changing ethos of
British society. In this regard, *The Whirlpool* is a novel of great importance. Significantly, in a letter to his friend Eduard Bertz, the writer
had anticipated the main argument of his new novel which, after having written the first three chapters, he provisionally titled "Benedict's
Household": "I have got to work again and quite seriously. . . . The
theme is the decay of domestic life among certain classes of people,
& much stress is laid upon the question of *children*."[5] Contrary to his
original intentions, the theme of childhood was not developed to the
extent Gissing perhaps had in mind. In the end, his decision was to
give priority to the narrative nuclei that were more congenial to his
literary imagination. In other words, even in the case of *The Whirlpool*, Gissing continues his textualization of the phenomenology of
irresolvable conflicts in a context in which sociology and pathology
are inextricably interwoven. Time and again, the writer is attracted
by situations in which the hero or the heroine has no choice but to

accept the laws of a ruthless and evil society or to abandon himself or herself to the blackest despair.[6]

Thus, within the economy of the novel, the theme of education in relation to the family (or rather the tie between parents and children) is of slight significance. Even the idea of the "decay of domestic life" understood as the loss of an ethical center is relevant, not so much to the family group (which actually, from a narrative angle, is never conceived in terms of a dialogue between parents and children), as to the main characters. These figures are always imprisoned within their own egoistic fantasizing and oscillate constantly between conformity and rebellion. Centrifugal and centripetal forces spark off the destructive dynamic that is concealed behind the apparently solid and compact surface of Victorian society, a dynamic that, homologically, creates tensions, dilemmas, and contradictions in the individual, who naturally succumbs to a state of permanent uncertainty. The moral collapse of the microcosm of domestic space is qualified in sociological terms: Gissing explains that this collapse results from the decadence "among certain classes of people," that is, the upper-middle classes, who in the 1890s were recklessly and freely entering unexplored territories of the modern age. Inspired by an overarching idea of moral independence, exalted by unprecedented forms of socioeconomic power, they were confusing values and disvalues, body and spirit, egoism and altruism, and their own interests with the interests of others. If, as Peter Keating has noted, "to be modern is to experience lost positives and to have no idea what can possibly replace them,"[7] then we can unquestionably define Gissing as a writer of modernity.

The Whirlpool is a novel that dramatizes axiological emptiness and moral decadence. The world in which its characters move is qualitatively poor, incapable of offering an alternative that is not one of disharmony. However important the motif of matrimony may be on a diegetic level, it is easy to see that it is only a pretext to present a far broader theme—the individual's search for self-realization and, by contrast, the destructive feeling of frustration after defeat and failure. Indeed, *The Whirlpool* is also a novel about vocation and antivocation, in the sense that values always entail their corresponding contraries. Everything is played out on a stage dominated by chaos and conflict, a stage on which harmony and humaneness are banished. Thus, while the novel's protagonists pursue their all-consuming vocational trajectories in order to fulfill their inner wishes, only too late do they discover that, observed from a realistic standpoint, the routes of their lives are directed toward an existential wasteland. What they experience is a persistent whirlpool in which everything is swallowed up and destroyed. Through its fundamental metaphor, *the whirlpool,*[8] the text primarily actualizes the London of the new commerce and finance, whose bold games of speculation dominate the collective imaginary. However, Gissing's intention is not to write a novel about finance: he is not attracted to the fictional possibilities offered by the astuteness and mystifications of speculators. In fact, it is no accident, as Colin Partridge notes, that "the central metaphor of the whirlpool was obvious to contemporary reviewers but its implications about the destructive force of speculation are varied, subtle and not immediately discernible even to a present-day reader. Gissing's association of financial speculation . . . is simple and unoriginal."[9] Yet Gissing's vision is not in fact naïve and simplistic even though he lacks a direct knowledge of the world of London finance. From a narratological perspective, the problem does not concern his subject matter as such, but the narrative voice. It is the narrator's visual angle that gives the novelistic text its thematic coherence and functionality. In this sense, the writer is not interested in a detailed representation of the frenetic vortex of financial speculations, which is not part of his narrative program. More precisely, what Gissing wants to convey to the reader is a thematization of the repercussions that the mad race of the economic world have on individual destinies. These consequences can be catastrophic when it is the lives of those totally immersed in their pursuit of a vocational project that are affected. In this respect, a conversation between the novel's main character, Harvey Rolfe, and his friend Mrs. Abbott provides an important interpretative key. She has been a victim of the giddy London cityscape, since her husband has committed suicide after making a bad speculation:

> "Presently there will be huge establishments for the young children of middle-class people. Naturally, children are a nuisance; especially so if *you live in a whirlpool.*"
> "Yes, I know it too well, *the whirlpool way of life,*" said Mrs. Abbott, her eyes on the far mountains. "I know how easily one is drawn into it. It isn't only idle people."
> "Of course not. *There's the whirlpool of the furiously busy.* Round and round they go; brains humming till they melt or explode. Of course, they can't bother with children."
> "One loses all sense of responsibility."

"Rather, they have never had it, and it has no chance of developing . . . When there's no leisure, no meditation, no peace and quietness,—when, instead of conversing, people just nod or shout to each other as they spin round and round the gulf,—men and women practically return to the state of savages in all that concerns their offspring."[10]

The abyss and barbarism are the two dysphoric paradigms Harvey Rolfe seeks to combat as an intellectual with a strong humanistic and philanthropic faith. For her part, almost in the attempt to defend herself from sinking into a darkness devoid of human hope, Mrs. Abbott turns her gaze to the mountains, which, besides indicating a spiritual elevation and a euphoric self-individuation, stand out as an authentic warning from nature. The whirling movement that drags everything down is seen against the immobility of the Welsh hilltops. These configure, metaphorically, an ontological anchorage and fulcrum as well as a sort of affectionate and protective embrace. The triple occurrence of the lexeme *whirlpool* enacts, moreover, the obsessive circular thoughts of people who would rather be elsewhere: the society Harvey Rolfe has in mind is one in which parents are warmly enagaged in the education of their own children and to instill in them the edifying precepts of tradition. But in a society that denies the individual the possibility to stop and think and to enjoy time as something preciously at the service of man (*no leisure, no meditation, no peace and quietness*), there emerges only one option: a race toward barbarity. And it is a barbarity that, in a context of selfishness and hypocrisy, appears all the more insidious and persistent because it wears the attractive mask of modernity. Carried along this pathway by the maelstrom of competition, weak and sensitive individuals are finally overcome and destroyed. One of the most effective images in the novel is precisely that of *brains humming, till they melt or explode.* This image of explosion alludes to the giddiness of those who succumb to its centripetal movement, as well as to the recurring manifestation of a monstrous entity named *Finance.*

Essentially, the semantic field represented by the destructive vorticosity is the result, on a topological level, of a clash between internal and external space. On the one hand, there are the secrets of finance and the exclusive circles of the capital; on the other, there is the great mass of all those who, encouraged by the popular myth of easy money, strive toward the center (i.e., the locus of high finance). This binary division involves the notion of boundaries that, in this case, can be regarded as the point of friction and destructiveness. Indeed, between the resistance of the center and the pressure of the periphery lies a border region, a large area in which conflicting forces produce a vertiginous rotation.

The definition of the sociocultural coordinates of outside and inside remains a factor dependent on individual responses. Thus, if for Rolfe internal space (London, the business world, the desperate search for success) is absolutely negative, for his wife, Alma Frothingham, it is exactly the opposite. Her dream is to make her name in the world of music, to be at the center of attention and to become an object of veneration of a male public. For Alma, the countryside means boredom, existential discomfort, lack of society and self-expression; her self-individuation can occur only in a world in which she feels alive and admired. By proposing a return to nature (i.e., a move from the center to the periphery), Harvey Rolfe shows the necessity of fighting against the depersonalizing chaos of the metropolis, whose noisy animation overwhelms individual voices and obscures spiritual values. The alternative he imagines is a landscape that is far removed from the polluted vapors of London and that, romantically, exalts the soul and restores integrity to the body. For Harvey Rolfe the need to conquer a sort of healing space in which the relationship between man and nature has not yet lost its dialogical dimension is urgent:

> The great silence had nothing of that awesomeness which broods in the mountain calm of wilder solitudes. Upon their ear fell the long low hushing of the wood, broken suddenly from time to time by a fitful wind, which flapped with hollow note around the great heap of stones, *whirled as if in sport*, and was gone. Below, in leafy hollows, sounded the cry of a jay, the laugh of a woodpecker; from far heath and meadow trembled the bleat of lambs. Nowhere could be discovered a human form; but man's dwellings, and the results of his labour, painted the wide landscape in every direction. On mountain sides, and across the undulating lowland, wall or hedge mapped his conquests of nature, little plots won by the toil of successive generations for pasture or for tillage, won from the reluctant wilderness, which loves its fern and gorse, its mosses and heather. Near and far were scattered the little white cottages, each a gleaming speck, lonely, humble; set by the side of some long-winding, unfrequented road, or high on the green upland, trackless save for the feet of those who dwelt there.[11]

This is the mental space that the protagonist's imagination opposes to the din of the metropolis toward which, on the contrary, his wife aspires in her totalizing desire to see her own musical vocation wholly realized. The harmony that Rolfe seeks is produced by "a fitful wind" that blows through the vegetation in the woods, creating a series of twists and whirls whose designs and sounds seem to enjoy their own extravagant course (*whirled as if in sport*). Not only is the whistling of the wind relevant to Rolfe's romantic sensibility, but also the cry of a jay, the song of a woodpecker, and the bleating of lambs paint a pastoral scene that, from his perspective, dramatizes a perfect dialogism between man and nature. This descriptive scene is completed by the reverent attention of the farmer for "the reluctant wilderness," still dominated by the colors of the gorse and the fern, heather and moss.

To what extent can man's respect for the natural landscape be regarded as a redeeming force stemming from fin-de-siècle British society? What is the difference between the behavior of those who live in the city and those who live on its outskirts, or beyond in the open countryside? How can man's perception of space and time be modified by a return to nature and its peaceful rhythms? The salient aspect of the descriptive passage quoted lies precisely in the transformation of spatiality into temporality: the eye can perceive on that blessed scenery of perfect harmony how "the toil of successive generations" has slowly conquered and tamed its wilderness: hence, a contrast between the long and quasi-archaic temporality belonging to this "periphery" and the devastating frenzy of the hectic center (London as a place of barrenness and pathology). In this sense, the scene not only speaks of a world that is now lost forever, but also emphasizes human labor that, in this faultless and healing context, implies obscure genealogies whose actions are not recorded by the chronicles of history. In other words, what Harvey Rolfe sees before him is not the landscape of an illustrated postcard, in the style of a mannerist oleograph, but, on the contrary, the painting of a landscape in which realistic observation and idealistic desire seem combined in a very nostalgic manner.

Rolfe interprets his mental "periphery" as an example of a harmonious relationship between man and nature and, implicitly, as a polemical response to the velocity of the center where the experience of modernity is characterized by the obsessive search for novelty. While Wales is the alternative offered to the protagonist in imaginary post-Wordsworthian terms, he perceives, on the level of his personal options, his birth town Greystone as the only pivot around which he can raise a defense against barbarism: "the midland town which was missed by the steam highroad, and so preserves much of the beauty and tranquility of days gone by."[12] This location is the natural refuge of tranquility and moral purity toward which he eagerly turns every time he feels too close to the brink of the abyss: "I shall be off tomorrow to Greystone for a few days. I feel as if we were all being swept into a ghastly whirlpool which roars over the bottomless pit."[13] These are the words Rolfe writes to his friend Hugh Carnaby, who has just lost all of his belongings after having made a bad speculation. It goes without saying that society has no intention of forgiving those who make mistakes, above all when financial interests are at stake. The way out for Hugh Carnaby and his wife, Sibyl, is not the protective space of childhood, which, however far away and hidden, would not be able to protect them from financial disaster. As an almost inevitable choice, they are compelled to follow the road to the colonies, where, under the flag of the British empire, they can hope to make a fortune and eventually return to the country, restored to respectability and moral dignity.

Before considering the character of Alma Frothingham, it may be useful to consider Jenny Calder's brief but effective description of the figure of the New Woman: "The New Woman wanted to walk the streets of London and travel on the railway unchaperoned. . . . She wanted a more practical education, more experience of life before having to make major decisions—and she wanted to make her own. She wanted to do more in the open air, take more exercise, ride a bicycle, climb mountains and swim."[14] In many ways, this is the female model to which Alma wishes to conform, totally absorbed as she is by her vocation to make her mark in the world of music as a professional violinist. However, she has neither the psychic temperament nor the ideological clarity to act in an unorthodox and unconventional way. In her personal attempt to conquer a space of independence, she seems to forget that, despite the vanguard proclamations of the feminist movement, society can only see women as being at the service of their husbands and families.

From a thematic viewpoint, Alma is the character who most completely embodies the destructiveness of the vortex. Her life illustrates a parable that, on an ontological level, subsumes the destinies of all those who, once on the edge of an abyss, are unable to withdraw because of ethical-social blindness, weakness of character, or lack of courage. The whirlpool is a metaphor that relates to cultural conformity and social orthodoxy. A vulnerable woman like Alma is driven by her hunger for the "whirl of fashion."[15] But, while she cannot resist the intoxicating changeability of fashions, her health is unable to cope with the obligations and taxing rhythms of modern life. A victim of her vocation as well as of her naïve idea of dominating the world (including the whirlpool), Alma Frothingham is the natural heir of the typology of heroine who tends more toward pathological collapse than triumph over others. In many respects, she is the unconscious slave of her own beauty rather than the clever administrator of her femininity.[16]

From a semantic-structural angle, the heroine's story is divided into three fundamental moments that approximately correspond to the three parts into which *The Whirlpool* is subdivided:

PHASE ONE: Alma's father, Bennet Frothingham, commits suicide after the bankruptcy of the Britannia financial enterprise: "There was a strain of melancholy in the man, legible in his countenance."[17]

Vocation: "Alma Frothingham, not quite twenty-one, was studying at the Royal Academy of Music, and, according to her friends, promised to excel alike on the piano and the violin."[18]

Obstacle: "The disaster that had befallen her life, the dishonour darkening upon her name, seemed for the moment merely a price paid for liberty."[19]

Solution: Her marriage to Harvey Rolfe, who has inherited money (two inheritances, to be precise, which help to give him an easy life). Escape from the whirlpool of London and life in North Wales.

Theme: The physiognomic readability of the (pathological) melancholy of Bennet Frothingham; money, speculation, and death.

PHASE TWO: The birth of her son, Hughie, is not enough to enlighten Alma's life. In her isolated existence in Wales she continually complains of headaches.

Vocation: "She had ceased to play upon her violin, save for entertainment and admiration of friends."[20] Shift toward the center: resumption of vocation, sacrifice and desire for success, affirmation: "Her fellow-musicians declared that she was 'wonderful.'"[21]

Obstacle: "Nervous collapse; care and quiet; excitement of any kind to be avoided. . . . Avoidance of excitement was the most difficult of all things for Alma at present."[22]

Solution: Interruption of her career as concert violinist.

Theme: Alma Frothingham's neurasthenia; the end of her vocation; the heroine's life becomes an expression of inanity.

PHASE THREE: Transfer to Gunnersbury: "Into this ambition Alma had thrown herself with no less fervour than that which carried her off to wild Wales five years ago."[23] New beginning and postabortion trauma.

Vocation: "Using your freedom, you chose to live the life of an artist—that is to say, you troubled yourself, as little as possible about home and family . . . the failure of our experiment is simple and natural enough."[24] Forced to abandon her career, Alma succumbs to her husband's appeal to return to a "normal" life, which fills her with even more guilt as both mother and wife.

Obstacle: Alma senses her life's becoming increasingly closed in by a circle that threatens to suffocate her: the clandestine maneuvers and encounters to which she has been subjected during the months of her London adventure are exposed in the open daylight. Alma is incapable of facing reality and unable to sleep without the use of morphine.

Solution: Alma dies after an overdose of morphine. Harvey Rolfe and the little Hughie retire to Greystone.

Theme: Survival of the fittest and those who live furthest away from the whirlpool: Alma's death frees Rolfe from matrimony and a new world begins. The *explicit* marks the moral and social supremacy of masculinity.

Ultimately, Anna Frothingham's story is a perfect illustration of the existential pattern of those who are drawn by the charm of the metropolitan vortex. Thus, partly duplicating the tragedy of her melancholic father, who was unable to endure the shame of financial ruin, the heroine chooses self-immolation in order to avoid any sort of confrontation with a reality that suddenly becomes complicated and indecipherable. A crucial watershed in her self-fashioning is represented by her debut as violinist, at once a musical triumph and a physical breakdown: "She could speak no more of her musical triumph. With the colour of her cheeks she had lost all animation, all energy."[25] What she gradually discovers is that her blood contains all the seeds of physical and nervous degeneration. Before discovering her hereditary weakness, she is convinced that the people who could help her to achieve success are wholly in her power. She is also convinced that, thanks to her gifts (musical talent and beauty), she will conquer the center of the "whirlpool" and eventually impose her artistic personality over everyone else's: "Her battle had to be fought alone; she was going forth to conquer the world by her mere talents, and can a woman disregard the auxiliary weapons of beauty?"[26] Behind the apparently casual tone of the final question lie the traps that lead to the disintegration of her own self: The "auxiliary weapons" turn against her because Alma is physically and psychically too weak to vie for the first place in good society, too naïve to understand the intricacies of the world. Thus, despite her initial iconoclastic attitudes, the heroine is forced to submit and accept those very rules against which she had previously fought.

In Gissing's pathologized view, physically weak individuals are mere sites of nervous degeneration. Alma's extreme psychic fragility, along with her more general vulnerability, seems to indicate that femininity and vocation will never meet in a proper and healthy way. Thus, after her neurasthenic collapse, and given her inability to break with her morphia habit, Alma feels that her voice has become an empty shell in a somber landscape. She can only take refuge in silence and self-confinement, never breaking with "the familiar draught of oblivion."[27] The emerging portrait is that of an ontologically unstable woman with no power to react against the difficulties and complications of life—not for nothing, indeed, is Alma always configured as a paradigm of negativity from her very first appearance in the diegesis: "Her features suggested neither force of intellect or originality of character."[28] From Gissing's perspective, the association between hysteria and the New Woman becomes a deliberate strategic choice to exhibit his total aversion to female emancipation. For him, such an aspiration to a full independence not only leads to the disintegration of the family as a social unit, but is also antithetic to the natural inclination of women to cultivate such values as kindness, prudence, and innocence, which have very little in common with an aggressive society and the hunger for experience typified by the new women.[29]

Educated in the vortex of high finance, Alma is the product of a mistaken marriage—"Bennet Frothingham spoke of his first marriage as a piece of folly."[30] She is deprived of affection by her mother from the age of five and, consequently, constructs her world without a maternal model and, more importantly, without possessing what in Freud's psychoanalytic theory is called the reality principle—a principle through which one is able to defer immediate gratification. Still, not having a clear idea of the difference between reality and appearance, she turns to the practices of financial speculation and builds her ego upon the priority of her own pleasures, always ready to use her imagination at the expense of a realistic approach toward people and events: hence her decision to pursue a path that leads to failure, while inducing her to view Harvey Rolfe solely as an object of matrimony to help her to reach her own objectives.

If love pertains to being, matrimony pertains to appearance. Alma, who is born and educated in close contact with the fictional world of finance and speculation, only knows matrimony. As W. Francis Browne has observed, the relationship of the couples in the novel— and here the reference is equally applicable to Hugh Carnaby and his wife, Sibyl—always functionalizes the individual's desire for assertion rather than the romantic notion of an encounter between kindred spirits: "Each relationship epitomizes the disruptive contemporary trends that Gissing observed in his era. The almost total absence of romance, or love, reflects the barrenness of a society that reduces emotions to sexual liaisons and the struggle for dominance of one sex over the other."[31] The first case of ambivalence in the dichotomy *being/appearance* regards Alma's musical vocation, which, far from configuring an inner need, seems in many ways to be the fictional response to a certain fashion that is widespread among the new middle-class families. Music therefore becomes a form of disharmony and self-deception:

> For Alma had no profound love of the art. Nothing more natural than her laying it completely aside when, at home in Wales, she missed her sufficient audience. To her, music was not an end in itself. Like numberless girls, she had, to begin with, a certain mechanical aptitude, which encouraged her through the earlier stages, until vanity stepped in and urged her to considerable attainments. Her father's genuine delight in music of the higher kind served as an encouragement whenever her own energies began to fail; and when at length, with advancing social prospects, the thought took hold of her that, by means of her violin, she might maintain a place of distinction above ordinary handsome girls and heiresses, it sufficed to overcome her indolence and lack of the true temper. . . . Alma had an emotional nature, but her emotions responded to almost any kind of excitement sooner than to the musical. *So much had she pretended*

*and posed, so much had she struggled with mere manual difficulties, so much
lofty cant and sounding hollowness had she talked, that the name of her art
was grown a weariness, a disgust.*[32]

Apparently, in Alma's world, only fiction counts. Fiction is first and
foremost. She does not possess the great musical talent that would
seem to be at the origin of her successful debut; her art is that of
dissimulation and duplicity. If her vocation has been the result of a
pondered choice, conditioned by social competence rather than a
burning inner desire, it is easy to conclude that the professional coldness with which the girl manages to face the public and convince it
of her ability is the result of a supreme effort. What is dominant in
her ego is an almost inhuman emotional investment, combined with
a paroxysmal and hysterical will to impose herself on others. The key
word in the passage quoted previously is *vanity*, which, as is explicitly
stated, functions as a counterweight to a series of negative elements
(*no profound love, indolence, lack of true temper, weariness, disgust*) used
to characterize an essentially superficial person, incapable of going
beyond appearances. This is also why she can only emulate the behavioral traits of all the other young women of her class who, thanks
to their self-imposed musical vocation, hope to raise their price in
the market of matrimonial transactions. From this perspective, as
has been mentioned, Alma Frothingham's main strategical options
are those of deception and self-deception. In her frenetic search for
motivational drives, in her effort to fabricate psychological resources
for a vocation that is always on the point of failing her, the only justification she can find is in success, and in a lifestyle based on constant
self-affirmation.

Significantly, the anaphoric parallelism with which the quotation
concludes sufficiently emphasizes how her talent is merely pseudotal-
ent, her eagerness a desire to stand out, and her passion for the violin
only boundless disgust: *So much had she pretended and posed —> so much
had she struggled —> so much lofty cant and sounding —> a disgust.* All this
confirms the pathological structuring of her efforts to assert herself
in a world to which, ontologically, she does not belong, while suggesting the opening of a scenario that leads to self-destruction and death.
It is not so much a question of deceit, as a complex and articulated
fictional construction around her own person seen as the locus for
a narcissistic self-veneration. It must also be noted that the lexeme
vanity is associated with the heroine from her very first appearance

in the novel. For Alma, vanity is an existential vector that seems to give a meaning to her life:

> A moment's perfect stillness, and the quartet began. There were two ladies, two men. Miss Frothingham played the first violin, Mr. Æneas Piper the second; the 'cello was in the hands of Herr Gassner, and the viola yielded its tones to Miss Dora Leach. Harvey knew them all, but had eyes only for one; in truth, only one rewarded observation. Miss Leach was a meagre blonde, whose form, face, and attitude enhanced by contrast the graces of the First Violin. Alma's countenance shone—*possibly with the joy of the artist, perhaps only with gratified vanity.*[33]

Her vocation is already visibly presented through a less euphoric perspective in this scene with the quartet. If the first image romantically conveys a sense of joy in the pleasure of creativity, this almost immediately gives way to the less positive definition of a vanity that is easily appeased by the transitory gratification of circumstances. In the antitethical lexemes *joy* and *vanity*, in their overlapping, and in the way they are morphologically and syntactically intertwined, we may recognize one of the peculiar traits of the heroine: she experiences a progression of contradictions stemming from an impossible reconciliation between the insensitivity of the whirlpool and the vulnerable sensitivity of her own soul. Alma's vanity appears again (this time associated with deceit) in the letter she sends to her musician friend during her sojourn in Germany: "She wrote briefly to Doris Leach, giving an account of herself, which, though essentially misleading, was not composed in a spirit of conscious falsehood. For all her *vanity*, Alma had never aimed at effect by practice of deliberate insincerities."[34] While she is still in Germany, her reaction to the marriage proposal of the wealthy forty-year-old Cyrus Redgrave—a proposal that is both cold and antisentimental—is marked by vanity. She convinces herself that no form of economic limitation will be able to deprive her person of those resources of social charm and beauty that belong to her by right. Redgrave's audacious proposal, however, dismantles the fictional world Alma has constructed, so that she is soon forced to realize that her value, in the market of matrimony, is much lower now that she is no longer the daughter of a powerful man of London finance: "Childish vanity and ignorance had forbidden her to dream of such an issue. She had not for a moment grasped the significance to a man of the world of the ruin and disgrace fallen upon her family. In theory she might call herself an exile from the polite world; none the less did she imagine herself still illumined by the social halo, guarded by the divinity which doth hedge a member of the upper-middle class."[35] Immediately afterward, Alma's self-deceit is put to the service of others. Thus, as she energetically defends her personality in the attempt to conceal the harm Cyrus Redgrave has caused her through his behavior, her only solution is to lie: "Irritated by self-consciousness, revolting against a misinterpretation which would injure her vanity, though it was not likely to aim at her honor, Alma had recourse to fiction."[36] Clearly, in Alma Frothingham's world, fiction and vanity go hand in hand: one is functional to the other in a circularity of thought that, as negative circumstances thicken, assumes the configuration of an intricate and entrapping web. Confronted with her social and moral responsibilities, her pathologized mind is unprepared to fight against the adversities of life and assert her own independence. Her only possible escape is into self-oblivion.

What is the material object that gives visibility to the *whirlpool* metaphor? What is the dominant icon of the vortex? In what way does Victorian society, wrapped up in its maddening metropolitan tourbillion, represent itself and its sensibilities? Where precisely is the privileged locus of the dialogical exchanges between individuals in a world that is moving too fast to allow room for reflection and self-characterization? Apparently, the object embodying the dynamics of existential fragmentation is the letter.

The Whirlpool is not an epistolary novel, and yet letters play a fundamental role both in the interpersonal relationships and in the diegetic structure. Letter writing is a structuring paradigm of *The Whirlpool*: long letters, short letters, messages carried over the ocean or sent a few houses away, letters that answer other letters, letters that do not wait for a reply, and replies that arrive too late. Letters that serve as clues or quotations. Covert letters and formal letters, well-considered letters and letters written in haste. Notes and cards, messages written with malice and treachery and letters written in all naivete, crucial messages and insignificant messages. In other words, the novel contains an incredible number of letters that crisscross, as words seem to chase each other in an epistolary whirlwind. This ceaseless activity of letter writing establishes a network of meanings that merge and separate—distant communications and more or less enigmatic strategies in which one person's words try to better those of another. Still, what actually links all this epistolary correspondence, however long, short, official, or unofficial it may be, is the need always to channel the receiver's mind into a certain direction, for the greater profit of the writer—letter writing belongs to a society in which everything is interpreted according to the gain-and-loss law. Central to the epistolary strategy is the will to transform the other (the reader of the letter) into a pawn in one's own hands. Anodyne and inoffensive as it may appear, a missive always sets the ground for a negotiation that includes, in Darwinian terms, a winner and a loser. A letter is the verbal site of a fictitious dialogue. Only the writer has a total ideological control over the epistolary words, while the recipient plays the role of a silent ghost. All this, from an ideological viewpoint, means that letter writing is not simply a form of communication but also a modality of self-definition—that is why epistolary activity seems to be central to Alma Frothingham's daily life.

The Whirlpool creates indeed its conflictual tensions and yet holds itself together through a dense network of letters. The epistolary modeling of *The Whirlpool* defines the psychological context in which the multiple tensions that inspire the protagonists are configured. More than the real contexts, each character expresses his/her essential aspirations through letter writing that becomes a fruitful territory for fantasizing personalities. In this sense, *The Whirlpool* may be defined as a narrative text in which characters live as writers/readers of letters. The decisive moments of the story always present an intricate web of voices in which spoken words and written words communicate and compare their respective aims. A significant example occurs in the epistolary exchange between Alma and Sibyl Carnaby, after the bankruptcy of the Britannia financial enterprise:

> Among a number of notes and letters which she wrote next day was one to Miss Frothingham. "Dear Alma," it began, and it ended with "Yours affectionately"—just as usual.
>
> "Could you possibly come here some day this week? I haven't written before, and haven't tried to see you, because I felt sure you would rather be left alone. At the same time I feel sure that what has happened, though for a time it will sadden us both, cannot affect our friendship. I want to see you, as we are going away very soon, first of all to *Honolulu*. Appoint your own time; I will be here."
>
> By return of post came the black-edged answer, which began with "Dearest Sibyl," and closed with "Ever affectionately."

"I cannot tell you how relieved I am to get your kind letter. These dreadful days have made me ill, and one thing that increased my misery was the fear that I should never hear from you again. I should not have dared to write. How noble you are!—but then I always knew that. I cannot come tomorrow—you know why—but the next day I will be with you at three o'clock, if you don't tell me that the hour is inconvenient."[37]

The friendship between the two women can no longer be the same because of the economic situation that forces the Carnabys to emigrate: Sibyl knows very well that Alma can no longer be her best friend, not only because of what has happened to the Britannia but also because of Alma's disappointment over her marriage to Carnaby: "Sibyl's choice of a husband had secretly surprised and disappointed her, for Hugh Carnaby was not the type of man for whom she felt an interest."[38] This is a world of secrets confided and secrets deeply buried. Nevertheless, rivalry is evident while they are totally absorbed in their respective imaginary worlds. Indeed, both recite the roles of superior aristocrats who put to one side questions of money and matrimonial choices. From Alma's point of view, moreover, the tie has always presupposed a certain sincerity. Previously it had proven to be fundamental in reinforcing her conviction that "in Sibyl, and in Sibyl alone, she found genuine appreciation of her musical talent."[39] Still, we understand clearly that Alma's vanity lies behind their friendship, since she needs someone always ready to praise her for her musical talent. This is why she continues to regard Sibyl as a friend, in spite of her marriage to a man who does not deserve female attention.

Alma Frothingham experiences more than any other of the characters the frenetic rhythm of a correspondence that occupies every minute of her life, in her continual search for moral and economic support for her vocation. Even when everything seems to be going against her, she has no intention of ceasing to affirm her musical talent. Marriage and the need to have a great sum of money at her disposal, her future projects together with the projects others have designed for her, her life both near and far away from the great pursuit of ambitions and vanity, London and "the vortex of its idle temptations":[40] all of these elements emerge more in the correspondence than in her daily life, which, in contrast, only reveals its signs in fragments and ambiguously discontinuous phrases:

On her table lay Redgrave's note; a very civil line or two, request-
ing permission to call. There was another letter, black-bordered,
which came from her step-mother. Mrs. Frothingham said that she
had been about to write for several days, but all sorts of disagreeable
business had hindered her; even now, she could only write hurriedly.
In the last fortnight she had had to go twice to London. "And really
I think I shall be obliged to go and live there again, for a time; so
many things have to be seen to. It might be best, perhaps, if I took a
small flat. I was going to say, however, that the last time I went up, I
met Mr. Redgrave, and we had quite a long talk—about you. He was
most sincerely interested in your future; indeed it quite surprised me,
for I will confess that I had never had a very high opinion of him. I
fancy he suffered no loss. His behaviour to me was that of a gentleman, very different from that of some people I could name. But it was
you he spoke of most. He said he was shortly going to Germany, and
begged me to let him have your address, and really I saw no harm
in it. He may call upon you. If so, let me hear all about it, for it will
interest me very much."

Alma had half a mind to reply at once, but on reflection decided to
wait. After all, Mr. Redgrave might not keep his promise of coming to
see her at Bregenz, and in that event a very brief report of what had
happened would suffice. But she felt sure that he meant to come.

And decidedly she hoped it; why, she was content to leave a rosy
vagueness.[41]

Even after her husband's suicide, Mrs. Frothingham still feels a fascination for the great metropolitan vortex and turns back to it as
soon as she can, while her stepdaughter tries to steer away from the
suspicious glances of others by going on holiday to Germany. But
apart from confirming her desire to move back to London, the letter
contains a specific narrative program that is intended to assure Alma,
who is a burden to her family, an economically prosperous future.
By using a strategy of indirection, Mrs. Frothingham introduces Mr.
Redgrave's ambitions, wisely balancing the segment "we had a long
talk—about you" with the intention of giving sufficient but not particularly enticing evidence of the good intentions of the suitor, of
whom the woman is indirectly the supporter and intermediary. It is
only after she has clearly expressed her conviction that Redgrave is
a true gentleman that she makes the admission (a grave one from
the point of view of the young woman's privacy) of having provided
him with her address in Bregenz (her justification "I saw no harm in

it" betrays her subsequent perplexity about how she has acted, leaving Alma to understand that, although it was not in bad faith, it was nevertheless deliberately superficial). The whole episode takes on an ironic significance in that Redgrave will be at the origin of Alma's tragedy. As a woman married to Rolfe and confiding her trust in Redgrave's protection Alma becomes again the focus of malicious gossip that will also involve her friend Sibyl. It is as a result of this complicated web of interrelations that Hugh Carnaby unintentionally attacks Redgrave, who, consequently, dies on the spot. (In passing I would like to add that Cyrus Redgrave acquires the right to enter the whirlpool of finance by becoming a partner in Carnaby's bicycle factory: "Harvey himself declared his surprise at hearing that Redgrave had entered into partnership with Hugh Carnaby. Had Sibyl anything to do with this?")[42]

Finally, it may be worthwhile here to quote the letter Alma writes to Harvey Rolfe immediately after she realizes that her "admirer" is assuming an attitude that she regards as being abusive toward her. The text may be considered in many ways the best introduction to Alma's character, not only because it lays bare all of her limitations, but also because it reveals how she relates to the written word.

> Dear Mr. Rolfe,
>
> I am sure you will not mind if I use the privilege of a fairly long acquaintance and speak plainly about something that I regard as important. I wish to say that I am quite old enough, and feel quite competent, to direct the course of my own life. It is very kind of you, indeed, to take an interest in what I do and what I hope to do, and I am sure Mamma will be fittingly grateful for any advice you may have offered with regard to me. But I feel obliged to say quite distinctly that I must manage my own affairs. Pray excuse this freedom, and believe me, yours truly,
>
> Alma Florence Frothingham.[43]

In the light of subsequent events, this letter takes on the connotations of a purely fictional text: everything that is stated, on the level of action, must be read in its contrary meanings. Her affirmation of liberty and autonomy with respect to her vocation conceals, in reality, a desire to be guided and oriented. It is no accident that, despite the explicitly antagonistic tone of her letter, she agrees to marry Harvey Rolfe soon after. Furthermore, her choice to write to Rolfe rather than to speak to him—which would have been much simpler and much more natural—exposes her essentially emotional personality. In this sense, letter writing is her favorite strategy precisely because she fears not being able to withstand a physical confrontation. Well aware of the gossip that characterizes the environment surrounding Alma, Harvey Rolfe finds himself writing her a letter to express his feelings. And he assumes the attitude of one who is conducting an operation that is at once dangerous and gratifying, as if passion and reason are battling within him and neither one or the other manages to prevail: "At midnight he was penning a letter. It must not be long; it must not strike the lyrical note; yet assuredly it must not read like a commercial overture. He had great difficulty in writing anything that seemed tolerable. Yet done it must be, and done it was; and before going to bed he had dropped his letter into the post. He durst not leave it for reperusal in the morning light."[44] It is not the letter that the reader sees but the strategic lines of his reasoning before it is written: the aims of the writer are those of brevity combined with a total absence of sentimentality. He wants to project an image of himself that is marked by a sort of pragmatic antiromanticism. But the epistolary text does not produce a clarifying effect on Alma, considering the fact that she hurriedly asks Rolfe a question that, as a comment to his letter, implies a worldview: "There was something you didn't speak of in your letter. What kind of life do you look forward to?"[45] What vocation does he have? What does he, an idle thinker, want to do with his life? What are his plans apart from the time spent at the Metropolitan Club? Harvey Rolfe has no answer to Alma's by no means naïve question, precisely because he is a man without a vocation, a man without an ambition apart from the vague declarations of struggle against the growing barbarity of Victorian society.

Clearly, letters and reality belong to two separate spheres, and, for this reason, their only common ground can be that of interpretation. Both letters and reality ask to be "read" and interpreted by going beyond the surface of their words/signs. Still, the fact remains that letter-writing has always a performative power: in "bring[ing] into existence an appropriate recipient . . . the letter creates the appropriate self to itself."[46] As I observed earlier, the lack of dialogue is the most apparent aspect of a letter, precisely because a recipient is shaped by the letter itself—each epistolary text defines its own recipient-ghost. With regard to the gap between life and letter-writing, there is in *Jude the Obscure* a significant comment by Jude on the nature of his correspondence with Sue Bridehead: "You are often not so nice in your real presence as you are in your letters."[47] In this case, the difference is to Sue's complete disadvantage, because with her anxious and tendentiously hysterical personality, she fills the words she utters with a destructive anguish. By confessing that his cousin's letters are nicer than the words she speaks, Jude, naively, exposes the destabilizing tension of her character which, like Alma's, is incapable of being coherent with her ideas and almost always causes her to act against her own intentions.

Given the paradigm of vorticosity as well as the cogent functionality of epistolary writing in *The Whirlpool*, one may easily conclude that this great mechanism of correspondence constitutes the interface of a subjectivity permanently wavering between centrifugal and centripetal forces. If it is true that in the novel letters are almost always written with the intention of communicating some kind of truth, it is equally true that this never happens and that any theoretical intention of speaking the truth is only the first stage toward self-deception. As Alma's letter clearly shows, an epistolary document is a self-defensive fabrication, a text encoded with the aim of setting others on the wrong path as well as triggering false expectations. In this context, the textualization of *The Whirlpool* could not avoid emphasizing the great mass of correspondence that, within the economy of the novel, establishes a sort of parallel itinerary for all the characters. The longer and richer in details the letters are, the wider and more deeply ingrained the duplicity and dissimulation, and the more pathologized and parlous the state of the writer. There remains the image of an enormous congestion of epistolary words that, in ways that are very similar to the new economy, seem to be written not to communicate or document people's lives, affections, and daily labors, but simply to obstruct interpersonal relationships—or, to put it differently, to obscure the receiver's gaze before the chaos of lives and thoughts that mark the age of modernity.

Significantly enough, the final image of *The Whirlpool* presents Harvey Rolfe and little Hughie as the only pole of authenticity and coherence: "Hand in hand, each thinking his own thoughts, they walked homeward through the evening sunshine."[48] This explicit seems to suggest that the only ones who manage to survive on earth are those who remain at the window, immobile and idle, happy to enjoy the beauties of nature. In Gissing's view, masculinity—romantically invested with an ecological radiance—seems to be the only

solution to the disharmony of the world and, above all, to the pathological drives hidden behind women's self-destructive vocation. Still,
it is not exaggerated to maintain that father and son, physically very
close ("Hand in hand"), but mentally already divorced and on di-
verging paths ("each thinking his own thoughts"), cannot be seen as
an alternative to the world of disharmony; the family group Harvey
Rolfe and Hughie are intended to represent is not an apt response to
social disintegration simply because the final scene is a sort of utopian dream, an improbable construction that can only be interpreted
as an escape from the whirlpool of modernity.

6

Jude the Obscure and the
Spectacle of Disharmony

IT WOULD BE WRONG TO REGARD *JUDE THE OBSCURE* (1895)[1] SIMPLY AS Thomas Hardy's last novel, without taking into account its enormous impact on the fin-de-siècle literary scene. The thirty-three years that separate its publication from the author's death define the cultural coordinates of a choice—that of abandoning the novelistic genre—that is the explicit recognition of a crisis. This crisis must be seen not only on the level of a personal rejection of the novel, but, more importantly, as the awareness of the limits of a literary tradition that, in that particular cultural climate, appears totally inadequate to interpret the intricacies of the real. As the new century is speedily approaching, Hardy writes *Jude the Obscure,* moved, more or less intentionally, by the necessity to look toward the future. At the same time, while narrating the story of Jude Fawley, he purposely lays bare his own uncertainties regarding the artistic results of his endeavor. From this perspective, the words of the preface to the first edition acquire a particular meaning. Here, Hardy declares that "[*Jude the Obscure*] attempts to deal unaffectedly with the fret and fever, derision and disaster, that may press in the wake of the strongest passion known to humanity; to tell, *without a mincing of words,* of a deadly war waged between flesh and spirit; and to point to the tragedy of unfulfilled aims."[2] Besides the foreshadowing of the fundamental themes, it is important to point out the explicit reference to his choice of dealing with the new narrative material "without a mincing of words." As a result, Hardy's choice goes squarely against the genealogy of the Victorian novel, which, in the narrativization of human passions (for example, the conflict between the flesh and the spirit), invariably adheres to a technique of reticence. Instead of exposing the naked truth of certain unpleasant aspects of reality, this technique works toward their occultation. Appealing to the dichotomy spirit/flesh, Hardy announces to the reader a line of diegetic development that, in its anti-Victorian essence, suggests a world where the noblest vocational routes often collide with those equally intense of sexuality—a sexuality reluctant to put itself at the service of reason and intellectual exigencies. The vector of conflict dominates the book from beginning to end, according to a narratological program that aims at moving opposing human motivations into an arena in which the instruments of realism can be tested. Abandoning, moreover, the traditional concept of the beginning and end of the story, the author adopts a problematical stance with respect to the narrated events. He tries to imagine—partially anticipating the modernists—a diverse representation of temporality, which entails a fracture of the cause-and-effect principle.[3]

It is no coincidence that in a letter to Edmund Gosse, dated November 20, 1895, Hardy confesses: "Of course that book is all contrasts—or was meant to be in its original conception. Alas, what a miserable accomplishment it is, when I compare it with what I meant to make it!—e.g. Sue & her heathen gods set against Jude reading the Greek Test[amen]t; Christminster academical, Chr[istminster] in the slums; Jude the saint, Jude the sinner; Sue the Pagan, Sue the saint; marriage, no marriage; &c. &c."[4] Of course, the Hardyan explanation regarding the nature of the dramatized "contrasts" applies only to the superficial surface of the narrative since it does not deal with the prevailing theme of *Jude the Obscure,* which juxtaposes the individual desire for order against the great cosmic disharmony. In subverting the general narratological model (order-disorder-order), and in denying the Victorian reader the pleasure of a morally and socially gratifying closure, *Jude* imprints the diegetic development on the paradigm *disorder-order-disorder.* A transgressive element resides in the author's refusal to make the novel's conclusion coincide with the end of his moral design. In the paradoxical reversal of the tripartite division, the middle term *order* stands for *desire for order,* projecting one's view toward a space in which the harmony of creation may be recognized. This involves a desire for self-knowledge that can be equated with the conquest of a positive relationship with the world in terms of the realization of one's vocation. Since the *quest* does not produce the desired order, we can reduce the tripartite diagram, through a paradoxical exegetic operation, to the simplicity of a tautological and monothematic formula—*disorder-disorder-disorder*. By conveying the certainty of an interpretative horizon, this formula foregrounds a textualizing process designed to model, not only semantically, but also in the actual organization of the diegesis, the disharmony of the cosmos.

In talking "without a mincing of words" in *Jude*, Hardy gives another turn of the screw to those topics and themes little appreciated by the Victorian palate, which, in the case of *Tess of the d'Urbervilles* (1891),[5] had already given him plenty of problems with critics and, more generally, with a plethora of right-minded readers. What does "without a mincing of words" mean but writing courageously, without keeping an eye on the eventual reactions of censors and reviewers, and not allowing oneself to be conditioned by a dominant way of thinking ready to tolerate a discordant voice but never disposed to give space to an iconoclastic one with a precise ideological timbre? Even if it is not possible to say *everything* in *Jude,* the writer assumes the attitude of one who wants to put his ideas into play, with an acute awareness of an autobiographical risk. In the actual execution of the task, his own utterances may be confused with those of his characters: "Like former productions of this pen, *Jude the Obscure* is simply an endeavour to give shape and coherence to a series of seemings, or personal impressions, the question of their consistency or their discordance, of their permanence or their transitoriness, being regarded as not of the first moment."[6] In the concluding paragraph of the preface, even before underlining the "personal" dimension of his impressions, the author refers to "form and coherence" in order to indicate the essential gap between the moment of autobiographical experience and the moment of its being written down. It is more than obvious that the goal of a unitary and artistically coherent vision, besides imposing a strategic distance from the material treated, postulates a narrator whose voice cannot be mistaken with that of the author *Thomas Hardy*, who nevertheless is present behind the scenes acting as occasional prompter and detached observer of the events.

Yet, as Dale Kramer has noted, there has been a persistent literary tendency to read *Jude the Obscure* as an artistic failure on account of Hardy's immoderately direct involvement with the doings and sayings of the eponymous hero: "The customary reaction to *Jude the Obscure* is that while an evaluation may be taking place, it is an evaluation by the storyteller himself, speaking *in propria persona*. Readers with this reaction to the novel believe that Hardy has lost control of his art . . . he has seized upon his story idea of blighted intellectual and emotional aspiration to vent his own feelings of frustration and bitterness."[7] In response to such readers, one might appeal to the ample and intense literary study that went into the composition of *Jude*. But, more importantly, what should be pointed out is the shortsightedness of readers who ignore what should be obvious—the modernist projection and irradiating innovativeness of a novel written at the height of artistic maturity. Hardy is absolutely aware that reality cannot be captured in a single and clear-cut image, but only through a sequence of irreconcilable tensions: hence, his artistic decision to dramatize the primacy of the fragment over the whole, openness over closure, individual incoherence over institutional smugness, the erring spirit over the certainties of the *nómos*, precariousness and existential instability over the deontic paradigms of society.[8] Still, content should not be confused with form. To the content of Jude Fawley's incoherence, the zigzag trajectory of his physical and spiritual migrations, and his unrealistic plans, corresponds the novel's structural unity. In its semantically consistent design, *Jude* therefore marks one of the fundamental moments of nineteenth-century fiction.[9]

Impervious himself to the ideological pressures of late Victorian orthodoxies, in his last novel Hardy fictionally and meticulously constructs a clockwork mechanism that is analogous to a literal "explosive" act. In other words, his work aims at defining new trajectories of meaning in order to stir the sensibilities and critical responses of future readers. In the wake of Lotman's semiotic theory of culture, we can say that *Jude the Obscure*, with the unpredictability of its semantic universe, actualizes "another reality, a kind of landslide and a resemanticization of memory,"[10] in the sense that it is a text against orthodoxy. Though such an interpretative approach is obvious enough, many scholars have read *Jude* disapprovingly as a propaganda piece, thus adopting the narrow perspective of maintaining that a literary text must always keep a distance from ideological thematics. Carl Weber's opinion, which, in many respects, is an exemplary synthesis of the misinterpretations to which *Jude* has been subjected, follows this line of thinking: "If Hardy failed as he did, it was not because the novel, as art-form, is unfitted to bring about social reform; it was because Hardy's aim was too sweeping, his skill too defective, and—it must be admitted—his artistic control too frenzied."[11] Even more astonishing is this opinion if we consider that the drafting of *Jude* was the result of a long and meditated choice: quite different from the artistic frenzy to which Weber's prejudiced attitude alludes.[12] Indeed, each aspect of the novel is organized in a manner that is not at all casual, precisely because Hardy wanted to thematize a more general axiological crisis. In this context, great meaning is laid upon the novel's topological metalanguage, which is marked by a series of displacements whose itineraries lead beyond the borders of Wessex. Such a fragmentary configuration of Jude's movements is an index of the disruptive dynamic of society. In his continual fluctuation between centripetal and centrifugal forces, this system of broken flights culminates in the spatial centrality of Christminster, significantly located at the extreme limit of the northern region.

There is nothing hurried in *Jude the Obscure*. The title itself is the result of a series of attempts and second thoughts that, in some ways, testify to the extent of the difficulties encountered in the drafting of the novel, whose corrections and textual additions can be regarded as a rich and interesting palimpsest for further studies. The first title proposed for the serial publication in *Harper's New Monthly Magazine* was "The Simpletons," but this choice was immediately abandoned because a novel by Charles Reade entitled *A Simpleton* had already appeared in the same magazine in the early 1870s. As an alternative, Hardy thought of "The Recalcitrants," a less ironic title, which, alas, did not reach the editorial office in time. Awaiting a new proposal, the publisher was forced to revert to the initial title, "Hearts Insurgent," which Hardy had already rejected.[13] Judging from the manuscript kept in the Fitzwilliam Museum in Cambridge, among the titles taken into consideration, there was also "The Dreamer."[14] Besides the oscillations between singular and plural—that is, the exclusive centrality of Jude Fawley and the allusion to a broader actantial context—what is concealed behind this question of finding an appropriate title is the difficulty of establishing a point of anchorage capable of implying a decision that fully convinced, above all, the author himself, for whom, as never before, the title was of paramount importance. Why were there so many versions before arriving at *Jude the Obscure*, adopted for the volume edition of November 1895? The titles of Victorian novels follow precise rules, often dictated by the publishers themselves: Hardy tries to bypass this obstacle, and, for this reason, he chooses the provocative syntagm *Jude the Obscure*, which, though following an established tradition of using the name of the protagonist as title, adds the transgressive epithet *Obscure* with the precise intent of arousing, within the horizon of the average reader's expectations, an effect, to say the least, disruptive and alienating.

Jude the Obscure respects the rule that pertains to almost every Hardyan novel: the opening scene always presents someone who is moving, directed toward a destination that should suggest a first stage of a project, the realization of a dream, the pursuit of a long cultivated vocation, the search for a definitive answer to one's desire for change. In Deleuze's words: "To fly is to trace a line, lines, a whole cartography. One only discovers worlds through a long, broken flight."[15] Thus, the incipit shows Richard Phillotson, schoolmaster of the eleven-year-old Jude, who has decided to abandon Marygreen in order to follow his dream: to settle permanently in Christminster, the university city where he intends to graduate and then be ordained. His gaze is directed toward a precise point in northernmost Wessex: Christminster is a place that breathes culture and hosts various institutions of higher learning. Christminster can only signify self-realization that, in Phillotson's euphoric perspective, implies the carrying out of the important and sacred role of the transmitter of knowledge:

> The schoolmaster was leaving the village, and everybody seemed sorry. The miller at Cresscombe lent him the small white tilted cart and horse to carry his goods to the city of his destination, about twenty miles off, such a vehicle proving of quite sufficient size for the departing teacher's effects. For the schoolhouse had been partly furnished by the managers, and the only cumbersome article possessed by the master, in addition to the packing-case of books, was a cottage piano that he had bought at an auction during the year in which he thought of learning instrumental music. But the enthusiasm having waned he had never acquired any skill in playing, and the purchased article had been a perpetual trouble to him ever since in moving house.[16]

The beginning in medias res has the function of actualizing the scene of a departure that means a separation from a place. For a boy like Jude, who had in Phillotson his only friend and affective and cultural reference point, the parting implies an acute suffering and a first warning of the instability of human relationships. In their apparent air of casualty, the first sentences of the novel are inscribed in Jude's imagination as a sort of imprinting from which, in the future, he is never to escape. In relation to the rural environment that surrounds him, the load of books and the piano trigger in Jude a fantasizing movement imbued with restlessness and rebellion against a very unjust and indifferent world. And in line with the symbolic value of the piano, the narrator immediately introduces a series of clues (*But the enthusiasm having waned*) from which we can derive that the enthusiasm of the schoolmaster does not always yield success: the musical instrument becomes both a sign of a failure and an existential "disharmony," as well as a proleptic indicator of future commitments and betrayals in relation to the new enthusiasm (that is, his ecclesiastical career). Furthermore, in the words that conclude the opening paragraph (*the purchased article had been a perpetual trouble to him ever since in moving house*), there is ample evidence of a mobility that mirrors man's inability to put down roots and, thus, to believe in something, to establish lasting relationships between his own being and the surrounding reality. What is presented is a society in which everything is in dizzying transition, while negative conclusions and loss of certainties seem to prevail.

Jude's process of identification is further fostered by the gift of a book that assumes, together with the last recommendations of his mentor, a strictly symbolic valence: "I shan't forget you Jude. . . . Be a good boy, remember; and be kind to animals and birds, and read all you can. And if ever you come to Christminster remember you hunt me out for old acquaintance sake."[17] Paradigmatically constructed around the opposition memory/oblivion, the words of Phillotson are much more than a farewell: they are sculptured in the mind of the young Jude to define, in an indelible manner, the space of a modelization centered on very precise rules of conduct. The recommendations of the schoolmaster lend themselves to segmentation in four semantic nuclei:

1. *Goodness*: during his whole life Jude will act as a good and generous person (his sins and mistakes will have tragic consequences not because he has forgotten his vocation to goodness, but for his pure incapacity regarding self-control and self-analysis).
2. *Kindness toward animals*: in a universe seen through a Darwinian lens, being kind to animals (and in particular birds) connotes Jude as an exception. He always acts contrary to the doctrine postulating the survival of the fittest.[18] Not coincidentally, many years after, Phillotson admits to Jude: "Cruelty is the law pervading all nature and society; we can't get out of it if we would!"[19]

3. *Reading*: in the scheme of cultural growth, reading and books are conducive to the fullness of being. Consequently, Jude is convinced that the book itself as object and the activity of reading are the founding prerequisites for his social redemption and the realization of his dreams.

4. *Christminster*: from the moment he hears Phillotson pronounce the toponym, the university city becomes Jude's obsession, and he is no longer able to imagine his life away from this cultural pole. The young Jude does not possess the interpretative tools to understand that Phillotson is not credible as a model to imitate, both for his discontinuous enthusiasm as well as his social position, which is well below the economic standard required to attend the university at Christminster. However, to the young Jude—"his face wearing the fixity of a thoughtful child's who has felt the pricks of life somewhat before his time"[20]—the words of his schoolmaster suffice and, in addition, the book is more than enough to project him toward a world totally different from the restricted perimeter of Marygreen.

Jude earns his living driving out the rooks from the field seeded by farmer Troutham: the distance between this primordial space and Christminster seems incommensurable. As soon as he reaches his workplace, Jude immediately puts in practice the last teachings of the schoolmaster: instead of scaring the birds with his rattle, he lets them feed on the grain without the least hesitation. Unwanted and chased away by everyone, he identifies with the crows to which humanity reserves the unjust treatment typical of a cruel and insensitive universe: "They stayed and ate, inky spots on the nut-brown soil and Jude enjoyed their appetite. A magic thread of fellow-feeling united his own life with theirs. Puny and sorry as those lives were, they much resembled his own."[21] After Phillotson's departure, he feels that his only friends are now the rooks, "inky spots" that, in their frightful agitation, seem to write in the soil his story of solitude and nonbelonging. However, he soon learns that the goodness and generosity he daily puts into practice are not met by a corresponding feeling on the part of others. Thus, when farmer Troutham discovers that, to the detriment of his interests, the boy shows an absurd prodigality toward the rooks, he grasps Jude and hurls him in the air. While the man is violently striking him with the rattle, the young transgressor becomes a "whirling child, as helpless under the centrifugal tendency of his person as a hooked fish swinging to land, and beholding the hill, the rick, the plantation, the path and the rooks going round and round him in an amazing circular race."[22] From experience, Jude begins to understand that the teachings of Phillotson are not so easy to apply, though, in a very indirect manner, the notion that it is always the heterogenesis of the ends that prevails begins to take shape in his mind.

Nothing is as simple as it seems. The short distance that, from our perspective, seems to separate desire from its realization is often an unbridgeable abyss, a fall into darkness from which it is not always easy to reemerge. Victim of his own generous nature, while the farmer, in his uncontrollable ire, makes him swing and swirl, Jude suffers the painful experience of a vision where hill, rooks, plowed field, rick, and path show him a confused reality lacking a center— the superimposition of objects, the tumult of blurred images, the loss of contact with solid ground, and the sensation of having lost the control of his own body, become a sort of prelude to the existential chaos in which the "transgressor" will conclude his life. And it is no coincidence that, in the scene of the rooks, he is portrayed as a fish, hooked on the fishing line, that is pulled out of his natural element and hurled to the ground: the nonbelonging to a recognizable topography, the "blurred" relationship between the surrounding social milieu and his character are the ontological traits that constantly define the Hardyan hero.

After the terrible experience of farmer Troutham, Jude begins, from his boyhood perspective, to interrogate himself on the contradictions that characterize human behavior: "from the perception of the flaw in the terrestrial scheme," he goes on to ask himself why "what was good for God's birds was bad for God's gardener."[23] Even his aunt, Drusilla Fawley, who regards the child as an intruder and another mouth to feed, talks about a universe where things do not always go the way they should and, establishing a great social divide between her home and the university city, makes her position immediately crystal-clear: "We've never had anything to do with folk in Christminster, nor folk in Christminster with we."[24]

Solitude, injustice, nonbelongingness: these are the dysphoric paradigms that make up Jude's psychological personality, causing in him a reaction that forces him to seek the negated values: community (he imagines himself a member of the intellectual circles of the university city), justice (he aspires to a prestigious cultural position, above all, to do some good), belongingness (his dream is to settle in a place such as Christminster to put down roots and recognize himself as part of that world, sharing with it his projects, ideals, and aspirations). The first chapters of *Jude the Obscure,* culminating in the vision of Christminster, delineate with extreme precision the formative elements of Jude's sensibility, providing the interpretative models for his future conduct and representing proleptically everything that will be confirmed by the successive diegetic development. One of the first perceptible acquisitions of the young Jude is that the disharmony of the world, from a linguistic viewpoint, is rendered by a strategic use of the lexemes *cruel/cruelty* in decisive moments of the narration:

> Jude went out, and, feeling more than ever his existence to be an undemanded one, he lay down upon his back on a heap of litter near the pig-sty. The fog had by this time become more translucent, and the position of the sun could be seen through it. He pulled his straw hat over his face, and peered through the interstices of the plaiting at the white brightness, vaguely reflecting. Growing up brought responsibilities, he found. Events did not rhyme quite as he had thought. Nature's logic was too horrid for him to care for. That *mercy* toward one set of creatures was *cruelty* toward another sickened his sense of *harmony.* As you got older, and felt yourself to be at the center of your time, and not at a point in its circumference, as you had felt when you were little, you were seized with a sort of shuddering, he perceived. All around you there seemed to be something glaring, garish, rattling, and the noises and glares hit upon the little cell called your life, and shook it, and warped it.
>
> If he could only prevent himself growing up! He did not want to be a man.[25]

The isotopy of disharmony, which involves primarily the divarication between thought and facts, becomes the structural core of Jude's imagination. What he apprehends immediately is the difficulty in harmonizing the events that take place around him: the vectors that should carry our desires when assembled to construct the algorithm for success, are seen to be unrelated and dissonant; in their incapacity to "rhyme" we can identify the proairetic matrix of failure. The evident contradiction among the various points of view, the irreconcilability of the individual ideas, the different structures of sentiment, all contribute to establishing the notion that values should never be considered as absolutes, but should be viewed, rather, as the arena of an unsettling relativization of everything: depending on the visual angle, the terms *mercy/cruelty* are interchangeable. Consequently, the reasons for that harmony on which Jude would have liked to build his relationship with the cosmos are invalidated. And we can understand his refusal to see the natural course of his life and the acquisition of maturity as a gain: an increasing awareness invariably entails an increase of suffering.[26] Even though the protagonist has imagined his own individuation in the world as a result of conquering the center of a circle (i.e., high learning), he now prefers to linger on the circumference as a strategy aimed at postponing maturity, suffering, and life's dissonances: hence, the transformation of temporality into a spatial metaphor whereby the wisest option is that of stasis, that is, the immobilization of time. Thanks to this peripheral position, Jude lives in the illusory belief that he will succeed in blotting out the "rattle" of the real and avoid being devastatingly swept away by life. For, what is life if not a sequence of "noises" enclosed within the circle, a great dissonance that would only hurt his sensitivity? (With regard to the dominant isotopy, we may note in passing that the term *rattling* suggests the physical tool [*rattle*], thus establishing a definite semantic and psycholinguistic link between the awkward, disharmonious sounds and Jude's former job in Troutham's fields.)

As already mentioned, *Jude the Obscure* is structured around the contrasting paradigms of immobility and movement. Jude desires to achieve a privileged position from which to survey the ways of the world: a space far from chaos and vulgarity and close to noble and harmonious sentiments of humanity. But the substance of which his soul is made up renders him too sensitive to face the minor and major adversities of life, so much so that his spontaneous self-identification makes him suffer at the idea of trees being cut down or pruned: "This weakness of character, as it may be called, suggested that he was the sort of man who was born to ache a good deal before the fall of the curtain upon his unnecessary life should signify that all was well with him again. He carefully picked his way on tiptoe among the earthworms, without killing a single one."[27] This authorial intrusion, placing the protagonist within the dramatic encoding belonging to tragedy, adds a further element in focalizing his character and motivations: Jude as child contains *in nuce* Jude the man. It follows that the development of the diegesis may only be read as a dramatization of a failure, and the reader is informed of this from the very first pages.

The story of Jude is a story that goes against the grain. The novel is constructed in a way that always reverts to the beginning and does not, according to a recurrent narratological rule, "keep an eye" on the end. Everything that happens, viewed from a wider perspective, is already written in the first pages of the novel. The symbolic vision of Christminster is placed within this context. After the loss of his job and subsequent dejection, Christminster gives Jude's desiring spirit a renewed and radical motivation:

> Some way within the limits of the stretch of landscape, points of light like the topaz gleamed. The air increased in transparency with the lapse of minutes, till the topaz points showed themselves to be the vanes, windows, wet roof slates, and other shining spots upon the spires, domes, freestone-work, and varied outlines that were faintly revealed. It was Christminster, unquestionably; either directly seen, or miraged in the peculiar atmosphere.
>
> The spectator gazed on and on till the windows and vanes lost their shine, going out almost suddenly like extinguished candles. The vague city became veiled in mist. Turning to the west, he saw that the sun had disappeared. The foreground of the scene had grown funereally dark, and near objects put on the hues and shapes of chimaeras.[28]

Christminster is a city immersed in fog. Christminster is a fable on the harmony of the universe. It is a mirage that challenges the present marked by desolation and suffering. After the "brown surface of the field," after the unending horizon of a "bleak open dawn,"[29] the university city appears from the winter haze as a miraculous vision, ready to reveal itself to Jude's epiphanized and epiphanizing gaze. In contrast to the shanty architecture of Marygreen, imposing buildings of a faraway place stand out clearly. As if by magic, they seem so very near: the urban setting is transformed into a fabulous city built with precious materials, mythical, immortal, and resplendent like the Celestial City. But this revelation does not last long: after a few minutes the fog reclaims Christminster; one by one the lights are snuffed out. The sun disappears and the night's deathly shroud envelops the scene: everything is nullified. Only the memory of the vision remains, and that, to the child's eyes, can only mean abandonment, being set adrift, at the mercy of a fantasizing drive that, climactically, reinforces in him the conviction that the veiled image will be, or rather, *is* the place of his life. For this reason, through his ecstatic and visionary gaze, Jude appropriates that world extending beyond the hill. The enchanted city of his dreams seems more and more real with each passing day: delivered from invisibility, Christminster becomes the New Jerusalem that, in his inebriated imagination, will fill the cup of experience with the most noble and elevated knowledge:

> Through the solid barrier of cold cretaceous upland to the northward he was always beholding a gorgeous city—the fancied place he had likened to the New Jerusalem, though there was perhaps more of the painter's imagination and less of the diamond merchant's in his dreams thereof than in those of the Apocalyptic writer. And the city acquired a tangibility, a permanence, a hold on his life, mainly from the one nucleus of fact that the man for whose knowledge and purposes he had so much reverence was actually living there; not only so, but living among the more thoughtful and mentally shining ones therein.
>
> In sad wet seasons, though he knew it must rain at Christminster too, he could hardly believe that it rained so drearily there. Whenever he could get away from the confines of the hamlet for an hour or two, which was not often, he would steal off to the Brown House on the hill and strain his eyes persistently; sometimes to be rewarded by the sight of a dome or spire, at other times by a little smoke, which in his estimate had some of the mysticism of incense.[30]

For Jude, Christminster is no longer an invisible city but the *locus* in which he can realistically pursue his vocation. This is the city of Phillotson, the man who has bequeathed him the fundamental precepts by which to live and who, as wise mentor, has shown him the path to follow. In his fantasizing process, Jude subordinates each received sensation to the service of an image that, from his particular perspective, seems to become more and more tangible and real. As product and creation of his dreaming mind, of his desire to escape from the insignificant and squalid community of his village, Christminster becomes the ethical pivot of the world. The references to *The Pilgrim's Progress*—"Apollyon lying in wait for Christian"[31]—and to the "Apocalyptic writer" undoubtedly place Jude's predicament on a highly symbolic plane: he is portrayed, in his journeyman's tension, as Everyman, preparing to meet a series of terrible trials before attaining that ultimate truth that only death can give.[32] Jude would like to be not only Everyman but also Christian of *The Pilgrim's Progress*, who, on his way toward the Celestial City, tries very hard never to divert his thoughts from the gratifying goal, "the City . . . builded of Pearls and Precious Stone."[33]

As a result of his "weakness of character," however, Jude diverts his thoughts from the radiant vision at the age of nineteen:[34] the encounter with Arabella Donn leads not only to a hurried marriage with a sexually provocative girl, but also to a detour from the great academic projects and finally to the miserable life of a man who has lost his ideals. And after the end of his dreams Jude finds a self-destructive consolation in alcohol.[35] His books become the metaphorical space of his moral downfall, as Hardy makes us notice in a highly dramatic scene: "There lay his book open, just as he had left it, and the capital letters on the title-page regarded him with fixed reproach in the grey starlight, like the unclosed eye of a dead man: H KAINH ΔIAΘHKH."[36] The New Testament projects onto the protagonist the petrifying stare of death, a reproach that anticipates the inglorious end that awaits him. And the contemptuous comments of Arabella sanction the devaluation of the book as a superfluous object, a bothersome nuisance spoiling the daily routine: "'I won't have them books here in the way!' she cried petulantly; and seizing them one by one she began throwing them on the floor."[37] Completely overwhelmed by Arabella's cunning and exuberant practicality, throughout his first marriage, which ends with her departure for Australia, Jude can only play a passive role. Everything has happened: nothing has happened. Jude finds himself alone, and, thanks to his weakness of character, he can fool himself into thinking that he is still at the beginning of his journey. As with Bunyan's hero, from the City of Destruction toward the Celestial City.

After the failed marriage with Arabella Donn and the long interval marked by disaffection and alcohol, Jude literally resumes his journey toward Christminster. The New Jerusalem that, many years before, he had believed to perceive from the top of a hill, once again imposes its language. Of course all his projects are dashed the moment he sets foot in the university city: nothing of all that he had imagined is real; beginning with Richard Phillotson, who, downcast and defeated in his ecclesiastical aspirations, lives in the same conditions in which he had lived at Marygreen. This discovery, which has taken place during Jude's first encounter with his cousin, Sue Bridehead, assumes all the characteristics of an anticipated failure: "He lives a little way out in the country, at Lumsdon. He's a village schoolmaster." Jude's reaction at apprehending the news betrays all his downheartedness: "'Then he couldn't do it!' Jude's countenance fell, for how could he succeed in an enterprise wherein the great Phillotson had failed? He would have had a day of despair if the news had not arrived during his sweet Sue's presence, but even at this moment he had visions of how Phillotson's failure in the grand University scheme would depress him when she had gone."[38] But, even before this disappointment, it has struck him that he does not feel a euphoric relationship with Christminster—that same space to which, for more than ten years, he has directed his gaze and placed his aspirations. Walking the streets of Christminster, Jude immediately perceives his total exclusion, the impossibility of belonging to a microcosm that makes him feel a ghost, invisible and insignificant to the eyes of others:

> The minutes passed, fewer and fewer people were visible, and still he serpentined among the shadows, for had he not imagined these scenes through ten bygone years, and what mattered a night's rest for once? High against the black sky the flash of a lamp would show crocketed pinnacles and indented battlements. Down obscure alleys, apparently never trodden now by the foot of man, and whose very existence seemed to be forgotten, there would jut into the path porticoes, oriels, doorways of enriched and florid middle-age design, their extinct air being accentuated by the rottenness of the stones. It seemed impossible that modern thought could house itself in such decrepit and superseded chambers.
>
> Knowing not a human being here Jude began to be impressed with the isolation of his own personality, as with a self-specter, the sensation being that of one who walked, but could not make himself seen or heard. He drew his breath pensively, and, seeming thus almost his own ghost, gave his thoughts to the other ghostly presences with which the nooks were haunted.[39]

The Gothic architecture of Christminster immediately delineates a physiognomy invested with decrepitude and spectrality: an insinuating doubt makes Jude wonder whether these old buildings host a way of thinking that is as decrepit and spectral as their façades. He ends up feeling as if he is a specter himself. What he experiences is the sensation of solitude that, taking him back in time, is not very dissimilar to what he has felt in the lugubrious field of farmer Troutham. If, on the one hand, Jude still wants to believe in Christminster, on the other hand, he cannot help noticing that the urban setting does not appear to him as the City of Pearls and Precious Stone, but as a place laden with hostility. The sequence of syntagms and lexemes clearly underlines such a negative response: *windy, moonless, ruffled, out of harmony, dark, black, obscure, decrepit, superseded, ghostly*. In his nocturnal solitude, Jude sees himself as a shadow among shadows, and he begins to talk in the middle of the street "like an actor in a melodrama who apostrophizes the audience on the other side of the footlights."[40] The journey toward the grandeur and nobility of human thought turns out to be a failure: the daytime visit, in aggravating further this sense of failure, teaches him that "the spirit of the great men had disappeared."[41] As a stonecutter, also well acquainted with the restoration of churches, Jude observes with a professional eye the Gothic buildings of the city, which, under the sunlight, reveal all their naked fragility, to the point that he is moved by their condition: "Cruelties, insults, had, he perceived, been inflicted on the aged erections. The condition of several moved him as he would have been moved by maimed sentient beings. They were wounded, broken, sloughing off their outer shape in the deadly struggle against years, weather, and man."[42]

The Darwinian outlook of the narrator, partially blended with that of the protagonist, imagines a struggle for life that, also involving inanimate things, manifests itself in a melancholic manner on those very monuments built to resist the ravages of time. Thus, in the city that is the epitome of culture, that mortal conflict is restaged in the same dramatic manner in which it occurs in a forest or ocean bed. This conflict, to the eyes of the newcomer, appears like the daily struggle of men for whom survival is more important than the superrefined philosophical arguments of Christminster's thinkers. In short, Jude begins to revise his perspective, and, after having lived in the city for some time, he cannot but conclude that life is elsewhere. Life is not among those moldy walls where the only thing one can breathe is an atmosphere of mortality: "He began to see that the town life was a book of humanity infinitely more palpitating, varied, and compendious than the gown life. These struggling men and women before him were the reality of Christminster, though they knew little of Christ or Minster. That was one of the humours of things. The floating population of students and teachers, who did know both in a way, were not Christminster in a local sense at all."[43] Jude undergoes a forced transition: from the book received from Phillotson to the book of humanity. From a conviction of an exclusive truth to be sought in the heart of academia to the conquest of its opposite awareness: the only truth to follow is the one from palpitating life, from the external spectacle made up of persons who work and who struggle daily in order to survive. That center to which he was directed and that, according to his mislaid plans, should have given him the fullness of being is only an appearance, a museumlike reality whose ghosts can only transmit their own hollowness, their ritual without substance, their dusty thoughts not based on the altruistic sharing of values but on inhumanity, egotism, on the closure of any sort of dialogue with the world. After receiving the letter from the academic of Biblioll College advising him to forget the idea of a university career—"You will have a much better chance of success in life by remaining in your own sphere and sticking to your trade than by adopting any other course"[44]—Jude understands that there is no possibility of continuity between the decrepitude of the buildings and the decrepitude of the ideology professed within those walls. The utopia of Christminster collapses, and, together with this utopia, the conviction that there are places where it is possible to admire, as a sort of divine message to humanity, the harmony of the world also collapses—the perfection of Christminster is inhuman, cold, and asphyxiating. There is no luminosity on earth; there are no guiding lights to illumine man's progress: Jude becomes more and more convinced that the only way to resist the negative values of the university city, to defy its deafening silence, is to return to his origins: to Marygreen, that is, that peripheral dot of the circle where it is easier to protect oneself from the abuses and injustices of society.[45] The inverse journey toward the circumference (i.e., Marygreen as marginality) expresses Jude's longing for obscurity, away from the false lights of Christminster: "His fixed idea was to get away to some obscure spot, and hide, and perhaps pray; and the only spot that occurred to him was Marygreen . . . he turned his back to the city that had been such a thorn in his side and *struck southward into Wessex.*"[46]

The return to Wessex means, above all, the repossession of a chthonic space that, as does a maternal womb, gives him back a lost innocence together with the vital energies to continue to live. Adopting a polemical stance against the mortality of Christminster—a microcosm placed outside the axiological horizon of his native soil—Jude, without a job, without a clear idea of what to do, without anyone to console him, decides to choose the open road.[47] Once he is at Marygreen, induced by a strong tension to forget, his dominant desire will be to sleep and enter oblivion: "He fell asleep for a short while, and when he awoke it was as if he had awakened in hell. It was *hell*. . . . He thought of that previous abyss into which he had fallen before leaving this part of the country; the deepest deep he had supposed it then; but it was not so deep as this."[48] The triple reference to profundity (*deepest, deep, deep*) confirms the tragic dimension of his sinking, whose immediate result is the transformation of his academic dream into a nightmare, the paradise of knowledge turned into an infernal dejection. After years of suffering and vain battles, Jude finds himself at the point of departure: his is a kind of circularity that, instead of spiraling itself upward, invariably takes a downward direction, toward an abyss where no redemption becomes possible.

Yet despite his failure on all fronts, in returning to the original matrix of his dreams Jude wishes to overcome his desperation and to turn Marygreen into a point zero from which to start all over, as though nothing had happened. At this stage of his self-definition, Jude's overarching intention is that of putting into practice the first lesson of his mentor: to do good to others and to practice self-abnegation, to defeat the meanness of egotism. Jude confesses his limits and faults to the young curate of the village, Mr. Highridge: "a fellow gone to the bad; though I had the best intentions in the world at one time. Now I am melancholy mad, what with drinking and one thing and another."[49] From this confession onward, Jude Fawley reactivates the blocked mechanisms of his wish fulfilment and, once again, starts to imagine a future in which he will be a country curate, always ready to do some good to people. Thanks to his inexhaustible fantasizing capacity, he succeeds in finding in his soul new reasons to believe and to persist in struggling, new energies and new hopes to resume his life's interrupted journey.

In the first diegetic elaboration of *Jude the Obscure,* Sue Bridehead played a centripetal function with respect to Jude's aspirations. In fact, according to Hardy's original plan, Jude's longing movement toward the university city is by no means motivated by the schoolmaster's, but by his cousin Sue, initially conceived as an orphan adopted by the provost of a college at Christminster. As Paterson has noted, "Jude's fatal fascination for Christminster was to have been generated not by Phillotson but by Sue Bridehead."[50] In addition to a series of indirect references at the beginning of the narrative—Aunt Drusilla associates Sue and Jude for their common intellectual leanings[51]—

the heroine enters the scene only in the second part of *Jude*. At first, her entry is in a photograph that Jude requests from his aunt, a picture that, in his infatuation, he puts on a shelf as a psychological anchorage point against solitude and the downheartedness inflicted by Christminster.[52] Eventually, she materializes as a person made of flesh and blood whom, voyeuristically, he observes and follows while she is working as a metal engraver in a shop. In his mental contortionism, Jude prefers not to introduce himself immediately to his cousin, but to watch her from a distance, just as for weeks, he has stared at her picture—an icon that, before actually meeting her, he has cherished and kissed many times in his acritical process of idealization: "He kept watch over her, and liked to feel she was there. The consciousness of her living presence stimulated him. But she remained more or less an ideal character, about whose form he began to weave curious and fantastic daydreams."[53] After Jude's disappointment in not being able to be a part of the academic world, Sue becomes an escape and an alternative: Jude substitutes the desire to appropriate the university city with the desire to possess his cousin, who, in his imagination, assumes the same psychological-cultural dignity as the university city. Sue becomes his new vision, his new ideal "picture" with which he can identify. Thus, after two or three weeks of cautious stalking, their eyes meet and Jude finally begins, though silently, to interact with the young woman: "She looked right into his face with liquid, untranslatable eyes, that combined, or seemed to him to combine, keenness with tenderness, and mystery with both, their expression, as well as that of her lips, taking its life from some words just spoken to a companion, and being carried on into his face quite unconsciously. She no more observed his presence than that of the dust-motes which his manipulations raised into the sunbeams."[54] Perspicacity, tenderness, and mystery: on his cousin's face Jude reads the salient features of his own character, but, at the same time, it is her eyes that define the enigma of a woman who stakes her existence on unpredictability. The eyes are "untranslatable" in the sense that they reveal nothing of her interior world; eyes that suggest tenderness but that hide destructiveness as well; eyes equated to an enigma not presaging anything positive. The syntagm *untranslatable eyes* establishes a direct link with the naïve illusion of Jude the child who strives to translate languages (ancient and modern) by using a simple mathematical model—"He learnt for the first time that there was no law of transmutation as in his innocence he had supposed . . . but that every word both in Latin and Greek was to be individually committed to memory at the cost of years of plodding."[55] This discovery produces in him the effect of a betrayal: the acquisition of knowledge is something much more complex than a simple act of will.

Observing her face and, above all, fixing his eyes on Sue's, Jude realizes that they resist any possible "translation"; they do not let themselves be interpreted: even in this case he becomes aware that he does not possess the formula capable of allowing him to cross the threshold of those eyes to decipher the signs of the soul. Yet, believing that a physiognomy should convey the *invisible* through the *visible*, Jude aspires to read Sue's countenance by applying the same ingenuous grammatical principles that many years before had already deceived Jude the boy. His cousin's life is, however, very much a labyrinth, crisscrossed by many paths, and, only in time may he be able, in some way, to make sense of those meandering ramifications. Besides the photograph on the shelf, besides his aunt's letter beseeching him to keep away from his cousin, Jude knows nothing about her, and, seen simply from an exterior perspective, she appears in all her restless beauty: "There was nothing statuesque about her; all was nervous motion. She was mobile, living, yet a painter might have called her handsome or beautiful."[56] In his ardor of unaware lover, Jude cannot decipher the signs of that face: only afterward will he discover that, when she was eighteen, Sue had had a relationship with an academic and lived with him in London but, as she insisted, only as a trusted friend.

> "He asked me to live with him, and I agreed to by letter. But when I joined him in London I found he meant a different thing from what I meant. He wanted me to be his mistress, in fact, but I wasn't in love with him—and on my saying I should go away if he didn't agree to *my* plan, he did so. We shared a sitting-room for fifteen months; and he became a leader-writer for one of the great London dailies; till he was taken ill, and had to go abroad. He said I was breaking his heart by holding out against him so long at such close quarters; he could never have believed it of woman. I might play that game once too often, he said. He came home merely to die. His death caused a terrible remorse in me for my cruelty—though I hope he died of consumption and not of me entirely."[57]

What sort of a person hides behind Sue's words? What kind of rapport may a young woman, who professes herself to be a follower of J. S. Mill, have with the external world and its institutions? What were the original motivations for choosing to live as "mistress," even if the man had promised to maintain a chaste relationship? The first element that emerges is the manner in which Sue narrates her London story: the linguistic structure of its enunciation (made up mainly of *and* and *but*) suggests a peculiar coldness pertaining to the parataxis, which, psychologically, is an index of the indifference and detachment of the speaker from those same narrated events. Her words do not evince the slightest sentiment, not even a touch of sympathy or liking for the person with whom, for better or for worse, she has shared a part of her life. This type of attitude lays bare a cipher of "explosiveness" in the character implying an element of unpredictability in both her actions and her words.[58]

The entire discourse has, however, a very precise semantic progression marked by a chiasmatic disposition of verbal subjects that ultimately leads to the death of the "friend": *He asked me to live with him* (ostensible sociability/acceptance of the other) —> *I wasn't in love with him* (coldness/negation and refusal of sexuality)—> *I was breaking his heart* (cruelty/lack of sensibility/egoism) —> *He came home merely to die* (destructiveness/death): hence, the circularity of Sue's reasoning, which culminates in death. The heroine, in her desire to put into practice her liberal and "explosive" readings, carries out audacious experiments at the expense of the feelings of the other characters. For Jude, his cousin's tale should be more than a simple warning, but he allows himself to be captivated by her words and beauty without reflecting on the nature of her actions.[59] Unpredictable, glacial as her temperament may be, Jude is dazzled by her transgressive ways. There is something in Sue that likens her to Eustacia Vye in *The Return of the Native* (1878), but she has neither her passion nor her sensuality.[60] Though they are both restless and perennially unsatisfied, Sue incarnates much more convincingly than Eustacia what Hardy calls "the modern vice of unrest."[61] Ironically enough, as soon as he arrives at Christminster, Jude associates his cousin with the idea of a gratifying harmony, a musical harmony that, penetrating body and soul, produces "a sustaining atmosphere of ecstasy."[62]

Sue is a character constructed upon the contradictions and complexity of the marriage theme. In line with the dynamic of the diegesis, she undergoes a deep transformation that leads from her initial, absolute affirmation of her individuality to a total submission to the *nómos* and institutions. Much more pronouncedly than Jude's existential quest, the heroine's development has the essential function of

giving narrative substance to the novel's epigraph: "The letter killeth."
A first important comment on this theme is found, not coincidentally,
in the words of Sue when, while making wedding preparations, she
suddenly refuses to marry Jude: "How hopelessly vulgar to me an institution legal marriage is—a sort of trap to catch a man—I can't bear
to think of it. I wish I hadn't promised to let you put the banns this
morning."[63] But let us go back to the epigraph taken from the second
letter of Paul to the Corinthians: "The letter killeth, but the spirit
giveth life" (3:6). As if wanting almost to stimulate the reader, Hardy
only quotes the first half of the verse, thereby postponing his definitive exegesis. Indeed, Jude's complete interpretation of the Scripture
occurs after he has married Arabella Donn for the second time, that
is, when he is one step away from his total physical and spiritual disintegration. Thus, in meeting Sue after his remarriage with Arabella, he
reminds her that *the letter* (i.e., the marriage contract) causes the death
of feelings, and life itself becomes death for those who bind their love
to the laws of society:

> "Don't go—don't go!" he implored. "This is my last time! I thought
> it would be less intrusive than to enter your house. And I shall never
> come again. Don't then be unmerciful. Sue, Sue: we are acting by the
> letter; and 'the letter killeth.'"
> "I'll stay—I won't be unkind!" she said, her mouth quivering and
> her tears flowing as she allowed him to come closer. "But why did you
> come, and do this wrong thing, after doing such a right thing as you
> have done?"
> "What right thing?"
> "Marrying Arabella again. It was in the Alfredston paper. She—
> has never been other than yours, Jude—in a proper sense. And there-
> fore you did so well —O so well!— in recognizing it—and taking her
> to you again."[64]

"The letter killeth" was the motto of Sue, who, in her search for self-
realization, had refused marriage from the time she was eighteen,
manifesting all her contempt toward those whose "philosophy only
recognizes relations based on animal desire."[65] "The letter killeth"
reaffirms Jude. And, significantly, even in this case, Hardy omits the
second half of the verse, the part that implies redemption. However,
by the end of the novel, Sue's position regarding marriage is totally
changed. The just thing to do is no longer to transgress or to affirm
the primacy of the spirit over the letter, of the self over society. Now,

for her, the exact opposite is true: to yield to conventional thinking and ethical orthodoxy, to banish from one's life all hedonistic
tendencies, to kneel before society and demonstrate the meaning of
suffering and her willingness to expiate her sins. During the psychological-behavioral transition between the first phase, Hellenistically
Arnoldian, and the second, following a more rigorous Hebraic im-
print, there is an episode that Sue interprets as a divine punishment
decreed by a severe, austere God: the killing of her children (two sons
fathered by Jude) by Little Father Time (son of Jude and Arabella),
who, in turn, hangs himself. At this point, afflicted by an agonizing
remorse, Sue realizes that the Pauline verse *the letter killeth* cannot be
applied to everyday affairs. Rather, the opposite is true, considering
that the transgressive condition as an unmarried couple is at the origin of all domestic tragedies (loss of employment, the impossibility of
finding a house or shelter, the death of the children, a state of forced
wandering and social marginalization).

In short, the biblical text becomes the space of negativity that,
excluding the spirit, axiologically recognizes the victory of social
conventions and beliefs (that is, the preeminence of appearances)
over ontological principles that promised not only self-realization
but also the union of two halves ready to "edify" a euphoric totality,
romantically saturated with high ethical values. The narrator, in one
of the first encounters between Sue and Jude, clearly highlights the
incapacity of the couple to bring about a fusion of their yearning
souls. In this specific context, space becomes a representation of a
convergence only partially realized, of an incomplete "edification":

> The broad street was silent, and almost deserted, although it was
> not late. He saw a figure on the other side, which turned out to be
> hers, and they both converged toward the cross-mark at the same
> moment. Before either had reached it, she called out to him:
> "I am not going to meet you just there, for the first time in my life!
> Come further on."
> The voice, though positive and silvery, had been tremulous. *They*
> *walked on in parallel lines*, and, waiting her pleasure, Jude watched till
> she showed signs of closing in, when he did likewise, the place being
> where the carriers' carts stood in the daytime, though there was none
> on the spot then.[66]

Lives that never completely meet, parallel paths that visibly validate
the measure of their respective egotisms: even if desiring to belong

to one another, even if moved by an urge to put down roots in a given place, Sue and Jude aspire, in their innermost hearts, to incarnate antithetical paradigms: mobility, nonbelongingness, the impossibility of a union of the two halves male and female. From this point of view, it may be interesting to note that the same segment—*They walked on in parallel lines*—with just a slight variation, spatially defines the first encounter with Arabella Donn as well:

> He set down his basket of tools, picked up the scrap of offal, beat a pathway for himself with his stick, and got over the hedge. *They walked in parallel lines*, one on each bank of the stream, toward the small plank bridge. . . .
>
> They met in the middle of the plank, and Jude, tossing back her missile, seemed to expect her to explain why she had audaciously stopped him by this novel artillery instead of by hailing him.[67]

It is clear that, on the plane of their respective psychobehavioral codes, Sue and Arabella are antithetical characters—intellectual sensibility against sexualized animality: "[Arabella] was a complete and substantial female animal."[68] It is not a matter of establishing psychological analogies; rather, what should be emphasized is the repetition, by Jude, of the same behavior, regardless of the person who is by his side. Like Sue, Jude is incapable of establishing dialogical bridges, of transforming his ideas into facts, of transferring from the interior to the exterior his ardent desire for harmony. His passion for the open road becomes, for Jude, an end in itself: as is the case with his intransitive and tautological thoughts, the roads inevitably lead only to themselves, negating progress, negating change. And, even more importantly, negating all possibility of authentic connection with other human beings and other destinies.

"[Father Time] was Age masquerading as Juvenility, and doing it so badly that his real self showed through crevices."[69] With the appearance of Little Father Time (actually his real name is Jude, the same as his father's), another thread of dissymmetry and fragmentation is ingrained in the weaving of the narrative, whose lines of development are invested with a mainly tragic connotation: "'His face is like the tragic mask of Melpomene,' said Sue, 'What is your name, dear? Did you tell us?'"[70]

For the new parents, the name of the little boy from Sydney is not important. He is basically the dysphoric proof of Jude's first marriage.

No one seems to care about the real name of the new arrival simply because his face speaks on his behalf, rendering visible temporality as the guise of mortality. It seems as though the long voyage from Australia to England has engraved in the boy's mind a voyage in time, a cartographic network in which, under the terrible insignia of death, all the epochs of man were scrupulously transcribed.[71] His view of the world categorically excludes the present. Incapable of laughter, silent and pensive in his unbelief, yet ready to emit judgments sculptured on marble, Father Time always sees, at the end of every itinerary, the ephemeral valence of all things: he is neither at the center nor at the periphery of the circle; he simply places himself outside society. As though not belonging among the living or the dead, he notes the cruelty that reigns in the universe, incarnating a modelization of the world dominated by the vanity of everything. Convinced that men never learn from experience, Father Time experiences his new family ties with a fatalism that renders him very touching in Sue's eyes. She does her best to help him regain his lost innocence: "The cloud upon his young mind makes him so pathetic to me; I do hope to lift it someday. And he loves me so."[72] The muse of tragedy, Melpomene, has taken possession of the character whose words and actions have already been written once and for all: Sue's motherly proposals are not enough to save him from the malefic cloud that follows him. On the contrary, this cloud, with the passing of time, becomes ever more insidious and pervasive, exercising its ill-omened dominion over the entire Fawley family.

As William E. Buckley has noted, "[Father Time] shatters the textuality of both *Jude* and the canon by the very violence of his metaphoric eruption."[73] In fact, defying the conventions of realism, Hardy introduces with Father Time an *erupting* character that becomes a strong confounding factor within the novelistic genre, precisely because the average Victorian reader is not prepared to accept the portrait of such an unorthodox child. In addition, his introduction provokes an effect of disorder that, destabilizing the textualization itself, offers the necessary instruments to reread and revise the Hardyan narrative macrotext. To put it differently, *Jude the Obscure* aspires to place itself outside the tradition of the Victorian novel in order to create a literary space whose antirealism implies the transition toward new modalities of representation. In this sense, Father Time epitomizes a further step forward in literary experimentation with regard to the tragic dimension of modern life. His function accords with strategic lines that rely exclusively on the bewilderment of the reader, who, from a metanarrative angle, questions the text and its seeming formal disorganization.

In fact, Father Time actualizes the reality that does not lend itself to any kind of modelization, the staging of an eternity that ridicules every human effort to interpret the world and to possess its mystery. The face of the child, resembling the lineaments of an old man, has already registered everything as if it were the great book of time. His sad eyes have seen everything and can only imagine epilogue scenes, places where reality, instead of catastrophically revealing itself, implodes in a great void:

> "I feel that we have returned to Greek joyousness, and have blinded ourselves to sickness and sorrow, and have forgotten what twenty-five centuries have taught the race since their time, as one of your Christminster luminaries says. . . . There is one immediate shadow, however—only one." And she looked at the aged child, whom, though they had taken him to everything likely to attract a young intelligence, they had utterly failed to interest.
>
> He knew what they were saying and thinking. "I am very, very sorry, Father and Mother," he said. "But please don't mind!—I can't help it. I should like the flowers very very much, if I didn't keep on thinking they'd be all withered in a few days!"[74]

Each word of Father Time is imbued with a resigned sense of the end. While Sue lives a few moments of joy in the pavilion of flowers, rediscovering a zest for life (a Hellenic trait that seemed forever buried) and an exaltation that places her beyond temporality, the young Jude delivers his sentence on the ineluctable destiny of all things. The natural inclination of his thoughts is toward a simple observation: the time allowed to human beings to taste happiness is always too short, and it is always a time besieged by the shadow of death. For this reason, he sees himself as a burden for his parents: "'I ought not be born, ought I?' said the boy with misgiving."[75] For Father Time, the end is not just a theoretical fact, the last detail that exclusively regards his manner of interpreting the world. Death is something concrete; it is always very close to every human being—the end is an option readily realized. Accordingly, he awaits the last day and tries to anticipate it in order to shorten that span of suffering that is human life. Sue is not aware of the boy's self-destructive intentions, and thus, in all her honesty and straightforwardness, she explains to him the difficulties of family life:

"Can I do anything?"

"No! All is trouble, adversity and suffering!"

"Father went away to give us children room, didn't he?"

"Partly."

"It would be better to be out o' the world than in it, wouldn't it?"

"It would almost, dear."

"'Tis because of us children, too, isn't it, that you can't get a good lodging."

"Well—people do object to children sometimes."

"Then if children make so much trouble, why do people have 'em?"

"O—because it is a law of nature."

"But we don't ask to be born?"

"No indeed."[76]

The daily realities confirm what Father Time has always known: Sue's double negation (*No! All is trouble. . . . No indeed*), in addition to revealing her incapacity to perceive the dialogical gap between herself and the boy, is a direct invitation to put an end to an existence that is always interpreted according to a most pessimistic ontological code: "trouble, adversity, suffering." In its dense entanglement of themes (marriage and offspring, the law of nature and vital space, the world's hatred of children), the dialogue gives an explicit verbal expression to what Father Time has been nurturing in his innermost self since the encounter with his new family: that is, everything considered, the best thing to do is to exit from the world's scene. What gradually takes shape in the boy's mind is the notion that, in order to solve any problem, it is enough to remove the obstacle that is the cause of all the ills of the Fawleys, that is, himself and Sue and Jude's other children.

After countless vicissitudes, after a series of moves within and outside Wessex, Christminster offers the ironically appropriate scenario for the epilogue: the corpses of the children, three livid little bodies hanging from hooks in the wall, present themselves to Sue as an emblem of her failed marriage. "*Done because we are too menny*"[77] is the message left by Father Time on a piece of paper that Sue finds on the floor. These words are linked directly to the epigraph, completing its sense and interpretation: the second part of the Pauline verse (the words missing from the epigraph—"but the spirit giveth life") are substituted by the words of Father Time, which, implicitly, want to demonstrate that the spirit does not give life but, on the contrary, brings death. Sue has refused the "letter"; she has refused the legality of marriage for a romantic ideal exalting the spirituality of the union against every kind of "contractual" vulgarity—the price paid is the death of the children. Hence, her drastic and sudden change of course and the return to Phillotson's orthodox protection, with the spirit of one eager to conform to the laws of society: "'We must conform!' she said mournfully. 'All the ancient wrath of the Power above us has been vented upon us, His poor creatures, and we must submit. There is no choice. We must. It is no use fighting against God!'"[78] In the end, Sue is forced to abandon her Hellenism and forced to recognize that God is above all: one must submit to his laws. The acceptance of religion also implies the acceptance of the rules of society—but only after negating herself, negating her self-aspirations, and, ultimately, negating any assertion of her individuality. In the words scribbled in pencil by Father Time, the couple recognize not only the reasons that have led the boy to the extreme gesture: they also read a sort of death sentence against their idealistic plans as well as against their own selves. Their narratives terminate in social and cultural marginalization, and not only the words but the corpse of Father Time represent a macabre and painful symbol of their complete failure: "The boy's face expressed the whole tale of their situation. On that little shape had converged all the inauspiciousness and shadow which had darkened the first union of Jude, and all the accidents, mistakes, fears, errors of the last. *He was their nodal point, their focus, their expression in a single term.* For the rashness of those parents he had groaned, for their ill-assortment he had quaked, and for the misfortunes of these he had died."[79] The narrator's voice intervenes in the climactic moment of the tragedy to give his own interpretation of the story. Hardy, in a most explicit manner, wants to show the reader that the words he is reading (that is, the novelistic text) were all written, in a prodigious spatial-temporal synthesis, on the visage of Father Time. His physiognomic traits are read as a tragic book, as a written space that, emblematically, renders visible the invisible ontological abyss into which Jude and Sue have fallen.

The death of the boy is also an act of disclosure, a sort of apocalyptic vision of everything that should never have happened. It is a point of distortion of the order of things, which his corpse shows, not in the gratifying sequentiality of the dominant idea, but in a dramatic scene that demystifies social harmony as a fiction.[80] It is also a point of intersection of the destinies of Jude and Sue, who, in the end, realize that the coordinates within which to seek their harmonious convergences no longer exist: what exists is solely a void from which voices arise declaring their condemnation without appeal. Finally, it is a point of explosiveness in which an unforeseen and absurd event has specific functional consequences, not only toward the epilogue (where Jude's death is expected), but in the staging of horror itself. To be sure, it is a horror that pertains to society and its institutions, the narrow-mindedness of the Victorian mentality and the moldy cultural environment of academia, toward which Hardy himself had aspired with some ambition. In its absolute essentiality, the mask of Father Time is the icon of a drama, the only image that, from a theatrical perspective, exposes completely the reasons for the homicide-suicide. From an anaphoric parallelism that lexically presents Father Time's reaction (*For the rashness . . . for their ill-assortment . . . and for the misfortunes . . .*) emerges the suggestion that, at this point, Jude and Sue can only choose to disappear, to hide with their misdeeds for the rest of their lives.

Even before the death of the children, Jude had become aware that all his cultural baggage, all his migrations from one place to another, had led him only to a chaotic vision that, in the light of experience, constituted an ironic counterpoint to the initially inspired vision of the New Jerusalem: "I am in a chaos of principles—groping in the dark—acting by instinct and not after example. Eight or nine years ago . . . I had a neat stock of fixed opinions but they dropped away one by one, and the further I get the less sure I am."[81] Light has become darkness; messianic *claritas* has degenerated into an all-pervading chaos. The movement from the periphery toward the center of culture has meant the progressive loss of certainties: dilemmas have compounded other dilemmas; obstacles have engendered other obstacles to the point of paradoxically revealing that the attainment of the goal may be equated to the attainment of the center of paralysis. Nevertheless, it is true that at the beginning of *Jude the Obscure*, the first definition of Christminster is that of a humble carter whose words, without many preambles, give the boy Jude an image of the city antithetical to the utopian vision of his fervid imagination: "'On'y foreign tongues used in the days of the Tower of Babel, when no two families spoke alike.'"[82] Jude is obviously unable to read the words behind the words: he cannot grasp the fact that the representation of Christminster as Babel is not a hyperbole; it is not the fruit of typical popular exaggeration, but the naked truth. Once in the city, he sees the dialogical closure of the academic world, whose linguistic Babel acts as a social barrier against the outside world, against the variegated and multiform expressions of experience. On the one hand, there is the unfolding of daily life, with its different languages and the suggestiveness of individual words that, in practical contexts, testify to the presence of flesh and blood speakers in a reality made up of work, of authentic gestures, of conflicts and harmonies. On the other, there are the stifling and oppressive rooms of the university where languages are spoken that nobody understands, where problems with not the faintest relevance to daily life are endlessly discussed. Jude becomes aware of these things too late. And, even when he has understood that a New Jerusalem does not exist, he continues for some perverse reason to fix his gaze toward Christminster. To seal his dissonant journey, Jude dies at the wrong time, during the collective festivities of the Remembrance ("To think he should die just now! Why did he die just now!,"[83] shouts an irritated Arabella) a few paces from those ancient buildings in which Jude would have liked to live in the illusion of his intellectual adventure. It is no surprise that his death takes place on a desolate stage, in the extreme solitude of a man desiring only oblivion.

Notes

INTRODUCTION

1. It is significant that, from a linguistic perspective, the Victorians were profoundly aware of the historical and economic hegemony of English. In this sense, Goodwyn Barmby (1820–81), a radical writer and a utopian socialist with no formal education, expressed very clearly the idea of English as the best medium to surmount linguistic and cultural barriers among the nations: "Let us, however, add to these intrinsic advantages of the English tongue the power of the external position of that language, and we shall not be at a loss to decide in favour of its being the probable universal speech of humanity. Let us recollect that it is spoken by the largest population of any western civilized language. Let us not forget that it is the expression of the two most influential commercial, and, therefore, international and progressive countries of the globe—Great Britain and the United States. Let us remember that these countries are the most advanced in political reform and mechanical discovery, and that they certainly together form the most influential power in the world. Let us recollect the intrinsic advantages of the Anglo-Saxon, and we shall be justified in deciding that the English tongue has the preferability and probability for becoming, above all other varieties of speech, the common language of mankind, the universal tongue of the world, and the unitary speech of the future of progress" (Goodwyn Barmby, "Universal Language and Phonography," *Howitt's Journal of Literature and Popular Progress*, 1 [February 1847]: 96).

2. E. M. Forster, *Howards End*, ed. Oliver Stallybrass (Harmondsworth, England: Penguin, 1976). The epigraph can be regarded as a self-quotation since Forster is citing words taken from the novel itself. It is the protagonist of *Howards End* who embodies the ideals of a full sociocultural integration intended as harmonic totality: "Only connect! That was the whole of her sermon. Only connect the prose and the passion, and both will be exalted, and human love will be seen at its highest. Live in fragment no longer. Only connect, and the beast and the monk, robbed of the isolation that is life to either, will die" (188). In many respects, *Howards End* can be interpreted as the last Victorian attempt to offer a worldview that postulates a demise of materialism and money worship. In Forster's view, the hard task of giving meaning and order to the chaos of modernity: this is the role played by Margaret Schlegel, whose objective is to elaborate and compose a unique orderly design from the conflicting fragments of distant individual lives and experiences.

189

3. For an analysis of the semantic and structural functionality of the poem, see Francesco Marroni, "Thomas Hardy e l' 'esplorazione della realtà': Una lettura di *The Darkling Thrush*," *Strumenti critici* 8, no. 1 (January 1993): 87–111. See also Francesco Marroni, *La poesia di Thomas Hardy* (Bari: Adriatica, 1987), 73–101.

4. Thomas Carlyle, *The French Revolution: A History*, ed. K. J. Fielding and David Sorensen, 2 vols. (Oxford: Oxford University Press, 1991), 1:8.

5. With respect to Carlyle's attitude toward contemporary historians, K. J. Fielding has acutely noted: "[Carlyle] provokes and bewilders; his language jostles the reader with irony and allusion. . . . Stylistically his targets are admired historians who have adopted its established, superior, measured tone, such as Hallam, James Mill, Archibald Alison, Gibbon, Hume, and Bolingbroke. As a result, the work [*The French Revolution*] can appear mannered and eccentric, as he strives to achieve a way of writing that will suit his subject, with methods which may still seem disturbing" (Introduction to Carlyle, *French Revolution*, vii).

6. Here it may be interesting to quote what Alan Shelston writes on the significance the French Revolution had in the making of Carlylean thought: "It was part of Carlyle's creed that the cataclysmic events of history were both predestined and an inevitable consequence of human self-deception, hence his lifelong obsession with the French Revolution as the archetypal historical exemplum" (Introduction to Thomas Carlyle, *Selected Writings*, ed. Alan Shelston [Harmondsworth, England: Penguin, 1987], 18).

7. Carlyle, *French Revolution*, 221–22.

8. Carlyle, *Chartism*, in *Selected Writings*, 154–55 (italics mine).

9. In the introductory pages of *Chartism*, Carlyle underlines the urgency "to interpret and articulate the dumb deep want of the people!" and, immediately afterward, "that great dumb toiling class" (154).

10. Carlyle, *Chartism*, 157.

11. Ibid., 191.

12. Joseph W. Childers, "Industrial Culture and the Victorian Novel," in *The Cambridge Companion to the Victorian Novel*, ed. Deirdre David (Cambridge: Cambridge University Press, 2004), 83, has aptly underlined the significant role played by the Chartist newspaper *Northern Star*, especially in the late thirties, when reforming hopes were still more deep seated than political disappointments: "In its early years, however, it demonstrated the vigor with which many members of the industrial working classes were willing to work for political reform. It had its own newspaper, *The Northern Star*, which was owned and operated by Feargus O'Connor. First published in 1837, it specialized in the details of local struggles and catered to the interests of the more militant Chartist flange. By the end of 1838, the *Northern Star* was selling 50,000 copies a week, and it was soon evident to the working and middle classes alike that Chartism was a force to be reckoned with."

13. A. L. Morton and George Tate, *The British Labor Movement, 1770–1920: A Political History* (New York: International, 1957), 78. It is well known that the Chartist leaders presented their petition to Parliament in 1839 and again in 1848. The petition consisted in a six-point program: universal manhood suffrage, equal electoral districts, vote by secret ballot, annual parliaments, pay-

ment of and abolition of property qualifications of member of Parliament. The petition was rejected by the Parliament both in May 1839 and, again, in April 1848. After the second rejection, Chartism gradually dissolved and never again appeared as a revolutionary threat for the national security and the hegemonic role of the industrial bourgeoisie.

14. George Gissing, "The Salt of the Earth," in *The House of Cobwebs*, with an introduction by Thomas Seccombe (London: Constable, 1931), 265.

15. Charlotte Brontë, *Shirley*, ed. Andrew Hook and Judith Hook (Harmondsworth, England: Penguin, 1978), 335.

16. Ibid., 336–37.

17. Paradoxically enough, female mill workers were much more independent than such middle-class girls as Shirley and Caroline, whose major fear was that of becoming a spinster. The impact of the industrial revolution on cultural and behavioral codes was very strong, and, primarily, it involved a growing awareness among females of their social role along with a gradual abandonment of some recurring stereotypes of femininity. Maura Ives, "Housework, Mill Work, Women's Work: The Function of Cloth in Charlotte Brontë's *Shirley*," in *Keeping the Victorian House: A Collection of Essays*, ed. Vanessa D. Dickerson (New York and London: Garland, 1995): 267, has perceptively underlined this significant change in the definition of new boundaries as regards a more active and autonomous function of women in Victorian society: "Contemporary mill girls contrasted sharply with Brontë's main female characters. Though mill workers earned low wages, factory work paid better than other forms of work, and the simple fact that they earned a wage, rather than depending upon a male wage earner, made them independent in a way that middle-class women could not be. The earning power of mill girls gave them access to personal and social freedoms of a kind that middle-class women, confined to the home and to a network of family members and female friends, could not attain."

18. On this point see John Plotz, *The Crowd: British Literature and Public Politics* (Berkeley: University of California Press, 2000), 168–70. In particular, commenting on the assault scene, Plotz observes: "The role of the two women who observe the onslaught is to confirm the existence of connection—love, solidarity, and comprehension across barriers—but only between those already united by class and by emotional similarity" (169). In his analysis of the roles played by the two girls, Plotz regards the pair Shirley/Caroline as a paradigm of the imaginative observant woman, prone to dramatize in her own mind what is happening far from her shelter: "To be an observant woman means to witness but not to replicate, to admire but not to join, the well-structured heroism of the citadelled male" (170).

19. With regard to the relevance of Gaskell's point of view, it may be useful to read what she writes in a letter: " 'John Barton' was the original title of the book. Round the character of John Barton all the others formed themselves; he was my hero, *the* person with whom all my sympathies went, with whom I tried to identify myself at the time, because I believed from personal observation that such men were not uncommon, and would well reward such sympathy and love as should throw light down upon their groping search after the causes of suffering, and the reason why suffering is sent, and what they can do to lighten

it" (*The Letters of Mrs. Gaskell*, ed. J. A. V. Chapple and Arthur Pollard [Manchester: Manchester University Press, 1966], 73).

20. Elizabeth Gaskell, *Mary Barton*, ed. Edgar Wright (Oxford: Oxford University Press, 1987), 70–71.

21. Admittedly, Gaskell's attitude toward metropolitan proletarians is imbued with a feeling of sympathy that reveals her intention of voicing the most squalid aspects of such a manufacturing city as Manchester. Compared with Gaskell's, Dickens's way of textualizing the life and culture of urban masses is imaginatively more powerful, even though his interpretation of the phenomenon is less true to life and impressive. His outlook is well exemplified by a most anthologized passage from chapter 47 of *Dombey and Son* (1847–48): "Oh for a good spirit who would take the house-tops off, with a more potent and benignant hand than the lame demon in the tale, and show a Christian people what dark shapes issue from amidst their homes, to swell the retinue of the Destroying Angel as he moves forth among them. For only one night's view of the pale phantoms rising from the scenes of our too-long neglect; and from the thick and sullen air where Vice and Fever propagate together, raining the tremendous social retributions which are ever pouring down, and ever coming thicker!" (Charles Dickens, *Dombey and Son*, ed. Peter Fairclough, with an introduction by Raymond Williams [Harmondsworth, England: Penguin, 1970], 738). On the different ways Gaskell and Dickens responded to the working-class life and the new urban culture, Simon Dentith, *Society and Cultural Forms in Nineteenth-Century England* (Basingstoke and London: Macmillan, 1998), 110, after focusing his attention on *Mary Barton* and *Dombey and Son*, has aptly written: "Where Dickens imagines a good spirit taking the house-tops off, and thus revealing myriad private stories to sympathetic gaze, Elizabeth Gaskell takes her readers on a voyage of discovery to the working-class districts of Manchester, and reveals the lives lived in court and cellar."

22. Wilkie Collins, *The Woman in White*, ed. John Sutherland (Oxford: Oxford University Press, 1996), 20. It is very significant what Collins writes in the following page: "We set our faces toward London, and walked on together in the first still hour of the new day—I, and this woman, whose name, whose character, whose story, whose objects in life, whose very presence by my side, at the moment, were fathomless mysteries to me" (23).

23. *The Life and the Work of Thomas Hardy*, ed. Michael Millgate (Basingstoke: Macmillan, 1989), 134. In another passage of his autobiography, Hardy observes: "Democratic government may be justice to man, but it will probably merge in proletarian, and when these people are our masters it will lead to more of this contempt, and possibly be the utter ruin of art and literature" (247). Henceforth, Hardy's biography will be cited simply as *Life*.

24. *Life*, 134.

25. *Life*, 141.

26. Here it may be worthwhile to recall the novel *After London* (1885) by Richard Jefferies, who, significantly, entitles the first part "Relapse into Barbarism." As to the mass migration to the east, Jefferies offers an audacious pseudoscientific explanation. In fact, according to the narrating voice, this migration was the effect of magnetism produced by a celestial body on the mentality of every

human being: "All that seems certain is, that when the event took place, *the immense crowds collected in cities* were most affected, and that the richer and upper classes made use of their money to escape. Those left behind were mainly the lower and most ignorant, so far as the arts were concerned; those that dwelt in distant and outlying places; and those who lived by agriculture" (Richard Jefferies, *After London*, ed. John Fowles [Oxford: Oxford University Press, 1988], 16, italics mine).

27. George Eliot, *Felix Holt, the Radical*, ed. Peter Coveney (Harmondsworth, England: Penguin, 1975), 399. As far as the thematics of culture and working-class education is concerned, Coveney perceptively focuses Eliot's fear in his ample introduction to the novel: "*Felix Holt* is in a sense part of a mid-Victorian dialogue between culture, in George Eliot's and Matthew Arnold's definition, and the rising democracy; and there is no doubt that they both thought that in that particular dialogue culture was in danger of being shouted down" (64).

28. John Carey, *The Intellectuals and the Masses* (London: Faber and Faber, 1982): 110. In a chapter significantly entitled "Gissing and the Ineducable Masses," Carey comments on Gissing's decision to live in the poorest area of London: "The gulf between himself and the squalid paupers he lived among was a vital component of the ordeal he had chosen to undergo" (102). Here it may be not exaggerated to say that Gissing's way of living the traumatic contrast between his classical formation and the brutish and mean metropolitan underworld was strategically part of his own growth in social awareness as well as a precise personal plan for a romantic and novelistic making of his own biography.

29. George Gissing, *Demos: A Story of English Socialism*, ed. Pierre Coustillas (Brighton, England: Harvester Press, 1972), 281–82.

30. Ibid., 48.

31. *Demos* was written not only under the influence of William Morris's idea of socialism, but also as an emotional response to his own experience of some socialist meetings and rallies that culminated in violence and window smashing: "Socialist agitation in 1885—the year of the founding of the Fabian Society, and the year after the founding of Morris's Socialist League—arose primarily out of unemployment problems resulting from the end of agricultural prosperity and attendant economic recession. The government was blamed, and demonstrations went on throughout the year, climaxed by the scuffle between police and socialist sympathizers and arrest of William Morris in September. Gissing saw this as an opportunity to write something of popular interest, and for the next few months he worked on *Demos* with single-minded intensity" (John Halpering, *Gissing: A Life in Books* [Oxford: Oxford University Press, 1987], 2–63). In particular, the figure of Mr. Westlake is modeled on William Morris, whose conception of socialism aimed at exalting the artistic dimension of craftsmanship as well as offering educational opportunities and cultural growth to the working classes. On the many contradictions that Gissing incurred while portraying socialist leaders and expounding their political ideas, see John Goode, "Gissing, Morris, and English Socialism," *Victorian Studies* 12 (December 1968): 206–26.

32. Gissing, *Demos*, 282.

33. George Gissing, *The Nether World*, Introduction by Walter Allen (London: J. M. Dent and New York: Dutton, 1973), 10.

34. P. F. Mattheisen, A. C. Young, and Pierre Coustillas, eds., *The Collected Letters of George Gissing*, 9 vols. (Athens: Ohio University Press, 1992), 3:47.

35. Cf. J. A. Secord, *Victorian Sensation. The Extraordinary Publication, Reception, and Secret Authorship of "Vestiges of the Natural History of Creation"* (Chicago: University of Chicago Press, 2000), 9–40. The anonymity of the author officially terminated only forty years afterward, when it was disclosed that the book had been written by the geologist and journalist Robert Chambers. On this point see the chapter "Anonymity" (364–400). Regarding the role played by Chambers in contemporary scientific debates, see J. A. V. Chapple, *Science and Literature in the Nineteenth Century* (Basingstoke: Macmillan, 1986), 68–73.

36. Secord, *Victorian Sensations*, 9–10.

37. Robert Chambers, *Vestiges of the Natural History of Creation*, ed. G. de Beer (Leicester, England: Leicester University Press, 1969), 276.

38. See Barbara Dennis and David Skilton, eds., *Reform and Intellectual Debate in Victorian England* (London: Croom Helm, 1987), 8–10. Here it may be interesting to see what the editors write in the introduction: "To the conservative believer the discoveries of men like Robert Chambers (*Vestiges of Creation*, 1844), and Charles Lyell (*Principles of Geology*, 1830) seemed to question the biblical account of the Creation. A science which provoked more real alarm, though, was the historical criticism of Scripture, which demonstrated, by supplying scientific criteria, the inaccuracy of dating and the confusion of authorship in the Bible. They concluded that the New Testament was by and about ordinary men writing in specific historical circumstances, and not, after all, the inspired and literal word of God" (9).

39. See what Chambers, *Vestiges*, 276, observes: "The present race, rude and impulsive as it is, is perhaps the best adapted to the present state of the things in the world."

40. See John Ruskin, *Sesame and Lilies*, in *The Works of John Ruskin*, ed. E. T. Cook and A. Wedderburn, 39 vols. (London: George Allen, 1903–12); 18:108–9. In particular, Ruskin notes: "A highly-bred and trained English, French, Austrian or Italian gentleman (much more a lady), is a great production,—a better production than most statues; being beautifully coloured as well as shaped, and plus all the brains; a glorious thing to look at, a wonderful thing to talk to; and you cannot have it, any more than a pyramid or a church, but by sacrifice of much contributed life" (108).

41. Raymond Chapman, *The Sense of the Past in Victorian Literature* (London: Croom Helm, 1986), 47.

42. For an analysis of the relationship between *Felix Holt* and *Address to Working Men*, see Francesco Marroni, *Spettri senza nome: Modelli epistemici e narrativa vittoriana* (Roma: Carocci, 2007), 41–66.

43. Trollope devoted to the history of the Pallisers the following novels: *Can You Forgive Her?* (1864–65), *Phineas Finn* (1867–69), *The Eustace Diamonds* (1871–73), *Phineas Redux* (1873–74), *The Prime Minister* (1875–76), *The Duke's Children* (1879–80).

44. Anthony Trollope, *Can You Forgive Her?* ed. Stephen Wall (Harmondsworth, England: Penguin, 1972), 267.

45. In the same chapter, Trollope gives a fuller explanation of the public sphere of Plantagenet Palliser, laying stress on his industry, which is never separated from his wish of conquering a crowning role as statesman: "He had already held *laborious* office under the Crown, but had never set in the Cabinet. He had *worked* much harder than Cabinet Ministers generally *work*, —but hitherto had *worked* without any reward that was worth his having. For the stipend which he had received had been nothing to him, —as the great stipend which he would receive, if his hopes were true, would also be nothing to him. To have ascendancy over other men, to be known by his countrymen as one of their real rulers, to have an actual and acknowledged voice in the management of nations, —those were the rewards for which he looked; and now in truth it seemed as though they were coming to him" (Trollope, *Can You Forgive Her?* 271, italics mine).

46. Anthony Trollope, *An Autobiography*, ed. Michael Sadleir and Frederick Page (Oxford: Oxford University Press, 1989), 361.

47. See S. Robin Letwin, *The Gentleman in Trollope: Individuality and Moral Conduct* (Basingstoke: Macmillan, 1988): 81–91. Regarding the functionality of the gentleman in Trollope's fiction, this monograph limits its critical sphere to a scrupulous description of the plots. However, it is interesting to read what, at the end of the book, the author writes on the role of the gentleman in British society: "The gentleman's world does not require a choice between rebellion and submission, violence and reason, alienation and unity, struggle and apathy, certainty and nihilism. It is a world full of nuances. Everything depends on fine distinctions—between wilfulness and originality, rigidity and discipline, distortion and disagreement. Nothing stands still but there is no sign of chaos. Order rests on proportion, harmony and continuity, not uniformity or changelessness. Men are not bound together by domination or submission but by affections, habits, duties and aspirations, as well as friendship, love, loyalty, obedience, respect, and admiration. They can alter and remain consistent. They can be amiable without being dishonest. Deference is no bar to independence nor respectability to originality. Firmness does not exclude sensitivity and moral clarity is one with compassion" (268). For a brilliant and detailed presentation of the nineteenth-century gentleman, see Robin Gilmour, *The Idea of the Gentleman in the Victorian Novel* (London: Allen and Unwin, 1981).

48. Elizabeth Gaskell, *North and South*, ed. Angus Easson (Oxford: Oxford University Press, 1987), 64 (italics mine.)

49. Ibid., 432.

50. Ibid., 429 (italics mine).

51. Ibid., 430.

52. In my view, the interpretation that Arlene Young proposes of John Thornton's role is rather misleading, since it simplifies too much his psychological development and social growth as a real gentleman: "Having been tried and proven true, Thornton is finally recognized as a middle-class gentleman, despite the loss of status that his financial setbacks would entail" (Arlene Young, *Culture, Class, and Gender in the Victorian Novel: Gentlemen, Gents and Working Women* [Basingstoke: Macmillan, 1999]: 85).

53. Elias Canetti, *Crowds and Power*, trans. Carol Stewart (Harmondsworth, England: Penguin, 1981), 33.

54. Gaskell, *North and South*, 59.

55. Regarding some Dantean allusions in *North and South*, see Francesco Marroni, "The Shadow of Dante: Elizabeth Gaskell and *The Divine Comedy*," *Gaskell Society Journal* 10 (1996): 9–13.

56. See Gary S. Messinger, *Manchester in the Victorian Age: The Half-Unknown City* (Manchester: Manchester University Press, 1985), 89–126. With respect to the density and diffusion of factories in Manchester, it may be worthwhile to observe here what Messinger writes: "By 1841, there were 125 cotton factories and thirty silk factories in the parish of Manchester. Proximity to the central city was desirable because it minimised time and costs of hauling raw materials and goods, and because factory offices would be closer to banks, professional services, government offices and the community" (117).

57. Christina Rossetti, *The Complete Poems*, Text by R. W. Crump, Notes and Introduction by B. S. Flowers (Harmondsworth, England, London: Penguin, 2001), 302.

58. Charles Dickens, *Hard Times*, ed. David Craig (Harmondsworth, England: Penguin, 1984), 65.

59. Ibid.

60. Charles Dickens, *Our Mutual Friend*, ed. Michael Cotsell (Oxford: Oxford University Press, 1991), 420, (italics mine.)

61. Humphrey House, ed., *The Journals and Papers of Gerard Manley Hopkins* (London: Oxford University Press, 1959), 256.

62. Ibid., 260.

63. C. Colleer Abbott, ed., *The Letters of Gerard Manley Hopkins to Robert Bridges* (London: Oxford University Press, 1935), 299. The letter is dated February 23, 1889.

64. *Journals and Papers of Gerard Manley Hopkins*, 66.

65. Ibid., 142.

66. Ibid., 205.

67. The kind of landscape that Hopkins bears in mind is that of the romantic poetry, in which clouds—in their different morphological aspects, in their celestial migrations—seem to be a link with a Creator who, showing his presence in nature, consigns his messages to all the elements that compose its fabric. Primarily, in Wordsworth it is possible to find a clear definition of what clouds are. His poetic imagination sees them as a euphoric and privileged instrument of God's message to humanity: "Not in entire forgetfulness, / And not in utter nakedness, / But trailing *clouds of glory* do we come / From God, who is our home: / Heaven lies about us in our infancy!" (William Wordsworth, *Ode: Intimation of Immortality*, in *The Poems*, ed. John O. Hayden, 2 vols. [Harmondsworth, England: Penguin, 1977]: 525, lines 62–66; [italics mine]). Many are the testimonies from Wordsworth's poems. Here it may be interesting to cite the three lines that constitute the beginning of *The 1850 Prelude*: "I look about; and should the chosen guide / Be nothing better than *a wandering cloud*, / I cannot miss my way" (William Wordsworth, *The Prelude 1799, 1805, 1850*, ed. Jonathan Wordsworth, M. H. Adams, and Stephen Gill [New York and London: W. W.

Norton, 1979]: 29, lines 16–18 [italics mine]; apart from a variant in line 16, the 1805 text is here similar to that revised in 1850). Regarding the study of clouds and cloud morphology, at the beginning of the nineteenth century, Goethe paid much attention to nephelometric investigations, above all stimulated by a reading of the work by the English meteorologist Luke Howard, *On the Modification of Clouds* (1803), focused on cloud classification. As a response to his enthusiasm for a systematic study of cloud systems, Goethe published in 1820 *Wolkengestalt Nach Howard*, whose main section consists of a journal taken while directly observing and studying masses of clouds during his stay in Karlsbad (April 23 –May 28, 1820).

68. John D. Rosenberg, *The Darkening Glass: A Portrait of Ruskin's Genius* (New York: Columbia University Press, 1962), 100.

69. The two lectures were delivered at the London Institution, respectively on February 4 and 11, 1884. Considering the importance of the lecturer and the unusual topic of his lectures, the London press featured the cultural event in some detail: "Lecturing at the London Institution last evening on the plague-cloud, Mr. Ruskin said he was desirous of drawing attention to a series of cloud phenomena which, so far as he could weigh existing evidences, were peculiar to our own time, and had not hitherto received any special notice from meteorologists. Neither ancient nor modern poets referred to these storm or plague clouds, and, so far as he could ascertain, they had not been seen in the skies of England, France, or Italy prior to 1870." This is the beginning of an anonymous article, "Ruskin on Plague-Cloud," which appeared in the *London Daily Telegraph* on February 5, 1884.

70. John Ruskin, *The Storm-Cloud of the Nineteenth Century*, in *Works of John Ruskin*, 34:10.

71. Ibid., 39.

72. Ibid., 78.

73. T. E. Kebbel, ed., *Selected Speeches of the Late Right Honourable The Earl of Beaconsfield* (London: Longmans, Green, and Co., 1882): 534.

74. See Phillip Mallett, "Carlyle and Ruskin: Work and Art," in *Victorian Keats and Romantic Carlyle: The Fusion and Confusions of Literary Periods*, ed. Cedric C. Barfoot (Amsterdam: Rodopi, 1999): 223–34.

75. Trollope, *Autobiography*, 354.

76. Matthew Arnold, *Culture and Anarchy*, ed. J. Dover Wilson (Cambridge: Cambridge University Press, 1990), 44–45 (italics in the text). It is well known that one of the salient aspects of the book is the attention paid to a classification of the word *culture*, in its historical and social complexity. As well as analyzing the crucial dualism *culture* vs. *anarchy*, the third chapter presents a revisitation of the social classes of the British nation, founding its argument on the way classes responded to the binomy "sweetness and light": hence Arnold's definition of the triad "Barbarians, Philistines, Populaces," corresponding to "the three great classes into which our society is divided" (105), i.e., the new industrial bourgeoisie, the rising middle classes, and the proletariat. In the fourth chapter, in his attempt to define the values on whose foundations to build society, Arnold takes into account the paradigms of Hebraism and Hellenism as repositories of fundamental values for humanity: "The uppermost idea with

Hellenism is *to see things as they really are*; the uppermost idea with Hebraism is *conduct and obedience*" (131, italics mine). Most clearly, Arnold underlines that, although different and conflicting at a superficial level, Hebraism and Hellenism both unflinchingly aim at "man's perfection or salvation" (130).

77. Arnold, *Culture and Anarchy*, 69.

78. Ibid., 44.

79. See Edward W. Said, *Culture and Imperialism* (London: Vintage, 1993): 50–52 and 157–59. In particular, after placing *Culture and Anarchy* in the historical context of British imperialism, Said notes: "Most readers of Matthew Arnold's anguished poetry, or of his celebrated theory in praise of culture, do not also know that Arnold connected the 'administrative massacre' ordered by Eyre with tough British policies toward colonial *Eire* and strongly approved both; *Culture and Anarchy* is set plumb in the middle of Hyde Park Riots of 1867, and what Arnold had to say about culture was specifically believed to be a deterrent to rampant disorder—colonial, Irish, domestic. Jamaicans, Irishmen, and women, and some historians bring up these massacres at 'inappropriate' moments, but most Anglo-American readers of Arnold remain oblivious, see them—if they look at them at all—as irrelevant to the more important cultural theory that Arnold appears to be promoting for all the ages" (157–58). Here I wish to add that Mr Eyre to whom Said is referring is E. J. Eyre, the British governor of Jamaica who in 1865, as a retaliation to the killing of some whites, initiated a ruthless massacre of the whole black population. It is well known that Carlyle, Ruskin, and Arnold sided with the governor Eyre, while against his brutish methods reacted vibrantly both J. S. Mill and Thomas Huxley.

80. Matthew Arnold, *Selected Prose*, ed. P. J. Keating (Harmondsworth, England: Penguin, 1970), 340. A most felicitous definition of Matthew Arnold is that proposed by John D. Rosenberg, *Elegy for an Age. The Presence of the Past in Victorian Literature* (London: Anthem Press, 2005), 148: "A nostalgia-haunted sensibility in a mind of startling modernity." Most aptly, Rosenberg highlights Arnold's ambivalent attitude toward the main issues of Victorian society: "Beneath his Oxonian urbanity he writes with all our own anxiety, self-consciousness, self-doubt" (148). And, with respect to Arnold's stress of the crucial role poetry may play in the modern world, Rosenberg underlines his inherent contradiction: "His most moving poetry is, paradoxically, about failure—the failure of poetry to sustain itself in a post-Romantic world, and the failure of his own powers as a poet" (149).

81. For an account of the prevailing mental attitude that pervades "Dover Beach," see Peter Allan Dale, *The Victorian Critic and the Idea of History: Carlyle, Arnold, Pater* (Cambridge, MA: Harvard University Press, 1977), 95: "Dr. Arnold's pessimism about modern age is . . . like Carlyle's, but at the same time it is very different. It is in its way far deeper primarily because Arnold tended to doubt the one firm belief, which more than any other sustained Carlyle, the belief in the transcendent power of the human will. In Arnold there is a distinct strain to fatalism, a stoical willingness to acquiesce in the ineluctable course of events."

82. Matthew Arnold, *Poetical Works*, ed. C. B. Tinker and H. F. Lowry (London: Macmillan, 1969), 211–12.

83. Considering that line 18 of "Dover Beach" refers to "human misery," it may be useful to add here that the same syntagm is present in *Culture and Anarchy* (44). At any rate, I would reduce this terminological coincidence only to mere critical curiosity and linguistic statistics.

84. With regard to Arnold's contradictory religious attitude, it may be interesting to see what Jerome H. Buckley, *The Victorian Temper: A Study in Literary Culture* (London: Frank Cass, 1966): 11, notes: "The desperate unbelief that permeates so much of Arnold's verse and wracks so little of his prose arises from distinctly Victorian cultural conditions, a sad contemplation of withering faith and an unprecedented fear of encroaching materialism."

85. As far as the many interpretative readings of "Dover Beach" are concerned, it is interesting to see, from a sociosanitary angle, what Allan Conrad Christensen, *Nineteenth-Century Narratives of Contagion: "Our Feverish Contact"* (Abington: Routledge, 2005), 277, perceptively observes: "Far from the moments of silent communication, the noisy surface of history speaks to Matthew Arnold at Dover in the 'grating roar / Of pebbles'. . . . Historical movements resemble ebbing and flowing tides, and with respect to the ideological sea Bulwer and Kingsley differ from Arnold . . . in detecting signs of a turn of the tide. The tides may also refer to periods of health and disease that naturally alternate in the life of the body politic as in the life of individuals."

86. Elizabeth Gaskell, *Sylvia's Lovers*, ed. Andrew Sanders (Oxford: Oxford University Press, 1986), 502.

87. Ibid., 68.

88. Robert W. Hill Jr., ed., *Tennyson's Poetry* (New York: W. W. Norton, 1999), 283 (123, lines 1–4). In this section, as many Tennyson scholars have underlined, it is evident the way *Principles of Geology* by Charles Lyell influenced the writing of the text.

89. In 1876, such an influential literary critic as Leslie Stephen, *An Agnostic's Apology and Other Essays* (London: John Murray, 1908): 36 and 39–40, in his deep-rooted agnosticism, was prepared publicly, and honestly, to show all his hesitations and aporias with respect to the role and teleological destiny of humankind: "There is a deep sadness in the world. Turn and twist the thought as you may, there is no escape. . . . We are a company of ignorant beings, feeling our way through mists and darkness, learning only by incessantly-repeated blunders, obtaining a glimmering of truth by falling into every conceivable error, dimly discerning light enough for our daily needs, but hopelessly differing whenever we attempt to describe the ultimate origin or end of our paths." Regarding his position in the Victorian panorama, it must be said that Stephen has been often placed in the same wake of thought belonging to Carlyle, Ruskin, and Arnold. On this complex thematics see B. E. Lippincott, *Victorian Critics of Democracy* (New York: Octagon Books, 1964).

CHAPTER 1. *A TALE OF TWO CITIES*

1. Charles Dickens, *A Tale of Two Cities*, ed. Andrew Sanders (Oxford and New York: Oxford University Press, 1988). I have also consulted the following edi-

tions: *A Tale of Two Cities*, ed. G. K. Chesterton (London: Dent, 1970), and *A Tale of Two Cities*, ed. Richard Maxwell (Harmondsworth, England: Penguin, 2000).

2. Barbara Hardy, *The Moral Art of Dickens* (London: Athlone Press, 1985), 11, has rightly pointed out that Dickens's awareness of the complexity of the real, not separated by a strong subscription to the Victorian moral codes, does not mean that his fictional works, by analogy, aim at an ethical linearity and a socio-economic simplification: "A sense of moral order and economic cause does not guarantee harmony or integrity in art, and it could be argued that where the appreciation of the social whole is clearest and most complex, as in *Bleak House*, the art is more strongly divided." In my view, the same applies to *A Tale of Two Cities*.

3. Sonia Orwell and Ian Angus, eds., *Charles Dickens*, in *The Collected Essays, Journalism and Letters of George Orwell*, 4 vols. (Harmondsworth, England: Penguin, 1971): 1:457. In passing, here it may be worthwhile to read what Milan Kundera, *The Art of the Novel*, trans. Linda Asher (London: Faber and Faber, 1990), 42–43, writes regarding the significance of the novelistic genre in its relationship with phenomenic reality: "A novel examines not reality but existence. And existence is not what has occurred, existence is the realm of human possibilities, everything that man can become, everything he's capable of. Novelist draw up *the map of existence* by discovering this or that human possibility. But again, to exist means: 'being-in-the-world'. Thus, *both* the character *and* his world must be understood as *possibilities*."

4. Orwell, *Charles Dickens*, 462–63.

5. Georg Lukács, *The Historical Novel*, trans. Hannah and Stanley Mitchell (London: Merlin Press, 1989), 243.

6. I prefer to use *privatization of history* to *modern privateness in regard to history* (Lukács, *Historical Novel*, 244), as we can read in the cited translation.

7. Lukács, *Historical Novel*, 243.

8. On the complex and meaning-generating relation between an artistic text and its afterlife, Yuri M. Lotman, *Universe of the Mind: A Semiotic Theory of Culture*, trans. by Ann Shukman (Bloomington: Indiana University Press, 1990), 18–19, perceptively observes: "A text, like a grain of wheat which contains within itself the programme of its future development, is not something given once and for all and never changing. The inner and as yet unfinalized determinacy of its structures provides a reservoir of dynamism when influenced by contacts with new contexts. . . . One might expect a text as it lives through the centuries to become faded and to lose the information contained in it. Yet texts that preserve their cultural activity reveal a capacity to accumulate information, i.e. capacity for memory. Nowadays *Hamlet* is not just a play by Shakespeare, but it is also the memory of all its interpretations, and what is more, it is also the memory of all those historical events which occurred outside the text but with which Shakespeare's text can evoke associations. We may have forgotten what Shakespeare and his spectators knew, but we cannot forget what we have learnt since their time. And this is what gives the text new meanings."

9. Andrew Sanders, *The Victorian Historical Novel 1840–1880* (London: Macmillan, 1978), 71. Sanders underlines again his conviction in regard to Dickens's historical awareness in his introduction to *A Tale of Two Cities*: "The novel provides us with a historical context, but with only a limited view of how a par-

ticular Revolutionary process evolved. This has seemed to many commentators to be a straightforward eschewal of analysis, a series of vivid impressions rather than a serious investigation. This is to underrate Dickens's intelligence as an artist" (Sanders, "Introduction," *A Tale of Two Cities*, xii).

10. David D. Marcus, "The Carlylean Vision of *A Tale of Two Cities*," *Studies in the Novel* 8, no. 1 (Spring 1986): 66.

11. Many and different are the suggestions that cooperate in feeding Dickens's literary imagination. We cannot help mentioning the influence of the play *The Frozen Deep* by Wilkie Collins, to whom Dickens pays a tribute in the preface to the novel: "When I was acting, with my children and friends, in Mr. Wilkie Collins's drama of *The Frozen Deep*, I first conceived the main idea of this story. A strong desire was upon me then, to embody it in my own person; and I traced out in my fancy, the state of mind of which it would necessitate the presentation to an observant spectator, with particular care and interest" ("Preface," in *Tale of Two Cities*, xxvii). For a detailed analysis, see Leonard Manheim, "A Tale of Two Characters: A Study in Multiple Projection," *Dickens Studies Annual* 1 (1970): 225–37. With respect to the link of *A Tale* with Collins's play, Manheim observes: "The whole work [*A Tale of Two Cities*] is impregnated with the spirit of the theatre. Its structure is dramatic and Dickens is reported to have sent proof sheets to Henri Regnier with a view toward immediate dramatization for the French theatre" (229). Very useful is also the article by Jean Ruer, "Charles Dickens, Wilkie Collins et *The Frozen Deep*," *Études Anglaises* 23, no. 2 (April-June 1970): 183–89.

12. With respect to Carlyle's influence on Dickens, see Michael Goldberg, *Dickens and Carlyle* (Athens: University of Georgia Press, 1972); William Oddie, *Dickens and Carlyle: The Question of Influence* (London: Centenary Press, 1972). These monographs irrefutably demonstrate that Dickens had a very deep knowledge of Carlyle's writings. Regarding *The French Revolution*, Dickens was highly impressed by this work, from which he drew passages whose artistic reinvention and functional adaptation were part of his creative genius. In particular, Goldberg gives a detailed list of the passages of *A Tale of Two Cities* taken from *The French Revolution* (100–128). For a very scrupulous presentation of the historical sources of *A Tale*, see Ruth Glancy, *A Tale of Two Cities: An Annotated Bibliography* (New York: Garland, 1993): 176–99. Very useful is also the material presented in "Appendix III: Dickens and His Sources," in *A Tale of Two Cities*, edited by R. Maxwell.

13. Robert Alter, "The Demon of History in Dickens' *Tale*," *Novel* 2, no. 2 (Winter 1969): 141.

14. Dickens, *Tale of Two Cities*, 1.

15. On the beginning of *A Tale* see E. L. Gilbert, " 'To Awake from History': Carlyle, Thackeray, and *A Tale of Two Cities*," *Dickens Studies Annual* 12 (1983): 258–59: "In this dramatic and unexpected telescoping of two historical periods into one, Dickens adapts Carlylean anachronism to his own study of the confluence of past and present, past and present being just two more of the many contrasting but interdependent "cities" about which his own tale is to be written."

16. See Briggs, *Victorian People*, 306–7.

17. Dickens, *Tale of Two Cities*, 6.

18. Ibid., 6–7.

19. Ibid., 12–13 (italics mine). Regarding this passage, J. M. Rignall, "Dickens and the Catastrophic Continuum of History in *A Tale of Two Cities*," *English Literary History* 51, no. 1 (Spring 1984): 577, has observed that it is pervaded by a metaphysical dimension that is only in part justified by the description of the sequence: "The passage is only awkwardly related to the scene on the Dover road which it punctuates, since its insistence on the essential, metaphysical mystery of individuality is out of proportion to the condition of the passengers in the coach. Their mutual suspicion and ignorance are occasioned simply by the hazards of the journey." Of course, Rignall's observation finds a confirmation in the peculiar context of the journey, but it is only too evident that Dickens's digression is structurally part of the novel's narrative economy.

20. Dickens, *Tale of Two Cities*, 13.

21. Ibid., 10.

22. Here it must be underlined that in chapter 3 ("The Night Shadows"), it is explicitly narrated that behind Mr. Lorry's silence lies a muted conversation with the person who has benefited from a resurrection: "Now, which of the multitude of faces that showed themselves before him was the true face of the buried person, the shadows of the night did not indicate; but they were all the faces of a man of five-and-forty by years, and they differed principally in the passions they expressed, and in the ghastliness of their worn and wasted state. Pride, contempt, defiance, stubbornness, submission, lamentation, succeeded one another; so did varieties of sunken cheek, cadaverous color, emaciated hands and figures. But the face was in the main one face, and every head was prematurely white. A hundred times the dozing passenger inquired of this spectre: 'Buried how long?' The answer was always the same: 'Almost eighteen years'" (15).

23. Ibid., 410.

24. Ibid., 16.

25. Ibid., 21–22.

26. Ibid., 30.

27. Ibid., 56.

28. Ibid., 49 and passim. In my view, as is written in his memories, behind Dr. Alexandre Manette's request of transforming himself into a shoemaker lies an urgent need to occupy his time (and thereby distract his mind from suffering) as well as—and more sophistically—a way of preserving an actual contact with the real. In sum, as a physician, he adopts a sort of therapy against madness, against an entire disintegration of his self. Still, it is only too evident that, once he is freed from the prison, the very complex psychological development of his personality automatically connects "shoemaking" to *that* particular form of salvation that he found in the North Tower of the Bastille, to that intimate space and circumscribed world that, after many years of physical and psychic confinement, he seems by no means prepared to leave simply because he still believes in the functionality of the "shoemaking" therapy.

29. Ibid., p. 46, italics mine.

30. Leaving aside the motif of the golden hair (or golden curls) belonging to the folktale tradition, it may be interesting to refer to *Silas Marner* (1861) by George Eliot with respect to the memory/forgetfulness dichotomy. In Eliot's

novel, the discovery by the eponymous hero of a baby girl and her golden curls activates in his mind a recovery of his lost past, since Eppie (the baby girl playing before his humble fireplace) makes Silas see the image of her dead sister, who was golden haired just as Eppie is. Silas Marner's social resurrection begins exactly at the moment he decides to offer shelter, food, and human affection to the orphan girl. He abandons his loom, at which he has almost ceaselessly been working for fifteen years, after being banished from the religious community of Lanter Yard because he was unjustly found guilty of stealing the community money. In this case, it is very tempting to draw a parallelism between Silas's work at the loom and Manette's shoemaking. In my view, Silas Marner and Alexandre Manette embody two forms of psychic disharmony.

31. Ibid., 52.

32. Ibid., 164.

33. Ibid., 53.

34. At the beginning of chapter 6 ("Hundreds of People") of the second book, the description of Manette's house, focused on a number of euphoric lexical items (*quiet* and *sunny*, in particular), conveys to the reader a moral definition of its residents: "The quiet lodgings of Doctor Manette were in a quiet street-corner not far from Soho-square. On the afternoon of a certain fine Sunday when the waves of four months had rolled over the trial for treason, and carried it, as to the public interest and memory, far out to sea, Mr. Jarvis Lorry walked along the sunny streets from Clerkenwell where he lived, on his way to dine with the Doctor. After several relapses into business-absorption, Mr. Lorry had become the Doctor's friend, and the quiet street-corner was the sunny part of his life" (ibid., 108).

35. Jams Eli Adams, *Dandies and Desert Saints: Styles of Victorian Manhood* (Ithaca, NY: Cornell University Press, 1995): 54–55, suggests that Carton embodies a kind of Carlylean hero derived from the model exemplified in *Sartor Resartus* (1833–34): "Carton's disregard for decorum intimates his affinities with the Carlylean hero, in whom such disregard likewise affirms a tenacious integrity and self-sufficiency, which will of course support Carton in his crowning self-sacrifice. For Carton as for Carlyle, one's approach to redemption depends importantly on one's power to contempt—including self-loathing."

36. Dickens, *Tale of Two Cities*, 96–97.

37. Ibid., 96.

38. Ibid., 98.

39. Ibid.,. 71.

40. Ibid., 181.

41. Ibid.

42. Ibid., 181–82, italics mine.

43. Ibid., 183–84.

44. The story of the document surfacing from the ruin is textualized as an authentic disinterment: "I knew that this prisoner, of whom I speak, had been confined in a cell known as One Hundred and Five, North Tower. I knew it from himself. He knew himself by no other name than One Hundred and Five, North Tower, when he made shoes under my care. As I serve my gun that day, I resolve, when the place shall fall, to examine that cell. It falls. I mount to the

cell, with a fellow-citizen who is one of the Jury, directed by a gaoler. I examine it, very closely. In a hole in the chimney, where a stone has been worked out and replaced, I find a written paper. This is that written paper. I have made it my business to examine some specimens of the writing of Doctor Manette. This is the writing of Doctor Manette. I confide this paper, in the writing of Doctor Manette, to the hands of the President" (ibid., 392–93).

45. Ibid., 349.

46. Ibid., 410.

47. Ibid., 465–66.

48. Ibid., 343.

49. John Lucas, *The Melancholy Man: A Study of Dickens's Novels* (Brighton, England: Harvester Press, 1980), 287–88, regards Carton's final words as an authorial severe admonition to the Victorian ruling class: "It is hardly possible that Dickens wants us to see in the Paris of 1860s the beautiful city and brilliant people which Carton envisage. But nor can the vision be meant ironically. More likely, Carton is being wrenched from his role to become Dickens's spokesman about—but about what? Well, about violence in England and its outcome perhaps. But really it is fruitless speculation, because at best *A Tale of Two Cities* provides a near desperate warning to the society Dickens had so deeply investigated in *Little Dorrit*. If it does not mend its ways then the revolution will come, and a good thing too. . . . But Dickens knows that no such revolutions will actually come. Hence the weary perfunctoriness that so marks and mars the book."

50. Dickens, *Tale of Two Cities*, 462.

51. Ibid., 464.

52. Thomas Carlyle, *Sartor Resartus*, ed. K. McSweeney and P. Sabor (Oxford and New York: Oxford University Press, 1999), 100. It may be worthwhile to quote the entirety of the phrase from which the syntagm is drawn: "The mystery of a Person, indeed, is ever divine, to him that has a sense for the Godlike." As far as the link between Carton and mystery is concerned, I concur with Rignall, "Dickens and the Catastrophic Continuum of History in *A Tale of Two Cities*," 583, who observes that "with Carton, indeed, Dickens comes closest to creating something like the mystery and opacity of individuality that he refers to in the *Night Shadows* meditation, but only up to a point, since in the final scenes the character's transformation there is a movement back toward conventional coherence and transparency."

53. Regarding the thematics of the double, producing a psychoanalytic reading of *A Tale*, partly derived from the theories elaborated by Otto Rank, Lawrence Frank, "Dickens' *A Tale of Two Cities*: The Poetics of Impasse," *American Imago* 36, no. 3 (Fall 1979): 240, notes that the ending of the novel marks the survival of the immortal self of the twin Darnay/Carton: "The twin who dies stands for the mortal self; the surviving twin, freed from his mortal part, becomes immortal, no longer subject to time and death."

54. See John Bunyan, *The Pilgrim's Progress*, ed. N. H. Keeble (Oxford: Oxford University Press, 1990), 8–9 and passim. On the other hand, it is interesting to note the structural importance of the family paradigm in *The Pilgrim's Progress*: 9–10: "So I saw in my Dream, that the Man began to run; Now he had not run far from his own door, but his Wife and Children perceiving it, began to cry

after him to return: but the Man put his fingers in his Ears, and ran on crying, Life, Life, Eternal Life: so he looked not behind him, but fled toward the middle of the Plain."

55. Dickens, *Tale of Two Cities*, 464.

56. As to my use of the term *ideologeme*, see Fredric Jameson, *The Political Unconscious: Narrative as a Socially Symbolic Act* (London: Methuen, 1986), 87–88: "The ideologeme is an amphibious formation, whose essential structural characteristic may be described as its possibility to manifest itself either as a pseudoidea—a conceptual or belief system, an abstract value, an opinion or prejudice—or as a protonarrative, a kind of ultimate class fantasy about the 'collective characters' which are the classes in opposition. . . . The analyst's work is thus first that of the identification of the ideologeme, and, in many cases, of its initial naming in instances where for whatever reason it had not yet been registered as such."

57. Dickens, *Tale of Two Cities*, p. 34.

58. The narrative centrality of the suburb of Saint Antoine derives from a simple fact: it was here that was lit the spark that led to the conquest of the Bastille and the beginning of the revolution. All this is clearly illustrated by Carlyle in *The French Revolution*, in which, among other things, this poor suburb is defined "Sooty Saint-Antoine" (*The French Revolution*, 1:215). As far as the image of the French Revolution as a big cloud, I cannot help quoting the 304 lines from *The French Revolution* (1791) by William Blake. It may be useful to read the very incipit of the poem: "The dead brood over Europe, the cloud and vision descends over cheerful France. / O cloud well appointed! Sick, sick, the Prince on his couch, wreathed in dim / And appalling mist, his strong hand outstretched, from his shoulder down to bone, / Runs aching cold into the sceptre, too heavy for mortal grasp. No more / To be swayed by visible hand, nor in cruelty bruise the mild flourishing mountains" (William Blake, *The Complete Poems*, ed. W. H. Stevenson [London and New York: Longman, 1989]:125, lines 1–5). William Halloran has noted the functionality of clouds in Blakes's revolutionary poetics: "Throughout *The French Revolution* the clouds are closely associated with war. Dark clouds and clouds of fire are linked with nobles and King; while higher and lighter clouds represent the revolutionaries" (*"The French Revolution": Revelation's New Form*, in *Blake's Visionary Forms Dramatic*, ed. D. V. Erdman and J. E. Grant [Princeton, NJ: Princeton University Press, 1970]: 52).

59. Dickens, *Tale of Two Cities*, 34.

60. Ibid., 34–35, italics mine.

61. Needless to say, here I am citing from the very beginning of *The Communist Manifesto* (1848) by Karl Marx and Friedrich Engels. There are many editions– my quotation is from the one edited by David McLellan (Oxford: Oxford University Press, 1998), 2.

62. See Taylor Stoehr, *Dickens: The Dreamer's Stance* (Ithaca, NY: Cornell University Press, 1965), 13–17. On the anaphoric iteration of the lexeme *Hunger*, after having detected a "method of ordering his imagined world" (15), Stoehr points out, 17: "The cumulative process by which the word-idea *Hunger* becomes a distinctive figure against the background of the street scene, a whole to which all the parts contribute and cling, is analogous to the mechanism of visual perception: a series of ocular fixations (with corresponding eye movements) is

essential to the perception of even the simplest figure, and, within limits, the vividness of the image depends on the number as well as the 'intensity' of fixations and movements."

63. Dickens, *Tale of Two Cities*, 260.

64. Ibid., 262.

65. Ibid., 264. An early presentation of the sea intended as a destructive entity takes place at the beginning of the novel, precisely in chapter 4 ("The Preparation"), when Mr. Lorry decides to take a stroll on the beach of Dover: "The beach was a desert of heaps of sea and stones tumbling wildly about, and the sea did what it liked, and what it liked was destruction. It thundered at the town, and thundered at the cliffs, and brought the coast down, madly" (21). It is interesting here to underline some analogies between Dickens's description and "Dover Beach" by Matthew Arnold, which I have reported in the introductory pages.

66. Ibid., 265.

67. Ibid., 268–69.

68. Ibid., 272.

69. Ibid., 273.

70. Ibid., 286.

71. Canetti, *Crowds and Power*, 94.

72. Dickens, *Tale of Two Cities*, 338.

73. Regarding the connection between Darney and Carton, I concur with what has been rightly noted by Alexander Welsh, *The City of Dickens* (Cambridge, MA: Harvard University Press, 1986): 130: "By dividing the heroic prerogatives between a pair of identical but unrelated twins in *A Tales of Two Cities*, for example, Dickens makes it possible both to live and die for love. The impossibility of a single hero both living and dying for love is obvious, and Dickens goes about the task of making it possible in fiction with full deliberation. Some potential contradictions within a single hero, however, would be improper, and Dickens accommodates them in fiction only unconsciously. He divides the contradictory impulses between two characters but conceals, even from himself it appears, their original connection. These are the contradictions that seem to us most modern. The resulting psychological complexity of the novel taken as a whole undermines the strict division of characters good and bad, blessed and unblessed. In a few novels Cain and Abel are strangely allied."

74. On the ideological meaning of Carton's final speech, Jeremy Tambling, *Dickens, Violence and the Modern State: Dreams of the Scaffold* (Basingstoke: Macmillan/New York: St. Martin's Press, 1995), 152, observes that "the Dickens who assumes that the individual is unknowable, absolutely other, has slipped through another position: that Carton can make some assessment of his life's value and of Darnay's and Darnay's family's value and can act accordingly. At the end Carton substantiates a bourgeois ideology centred round the family."

Chapter 2. Wilkie Collins

1. Wilkie Collins, *The Dead Secret*, ed. Ira B. Nadel (Oxford: Oxford University Press, 1997). Henceforth all references will be to this edition. *The Dead Secret*

originally appeared in twenty-three parts in *Household Words* from January 3 to June 13, 1857. Simultaneously, the novel was published in the United States, in *Harper's Weekly* from January 24 to June 27, 1857. *The Dead Secret* was adapted for theater in 1877 by E. J. Bramwell; the first performance was on August 29, 1877 at the Royal Lyceum Theatre of London; the play was directed by Henry Irving. As to the contemporary reception of *The Dead Secret*, it may be worthwhile to cite what Robert Ashley, *Wilkie Collins* (Brooklyn, NY: Haskell House, 1976): 53–54, writes: "The Victorian reviewers liked the novel, but were disappointed that Collins had not shown a more marked advance over *Hide and Seek*. Despite his relative failure on the latter score, *The Dead Secret* is on the whole the best of the early novels. Its significance in Collins's development is twofold: first, in the portrait of Sarah Leeson there is evidence of a profounder note in characterisation, and, second, for the first time Collins had subordinated everything to mystery. What is still lacking is a plot complex enough, a secret mysterious enough to give full scope to his ability."

2. Wilkie Collins, "Letter of Dedication," in *Basil*, ed. Dorothy Goldman (Oxford: Oxford University Press, 1990): xxvi. In his "Letter of Dedication," Collins lays emphasis on the fact that, following his realistic attitude ("the lights of Reality"), he did not hesitate "to violate some of the conventionalities of sentimental fiction" (xxvi).

3. George Eliot, *Adam Bede*, ed. Valentine Cunningham (Oxford: Oxford University Press, 1996); 176–79.

4. Of course, sensation fiction was marked by what I would define as epistemic nondisjunction between a realistic technique of representation and a fantastic and *unheimliche* dimension, partly derived from the Gothic tradition. From a narratological angle, the combination of realism and melodrama, together with plot intricacies, is the result of a hybridity that cannot be rightly interpreted if we forget the scientific and pseudoscientific contexts of mid- and late- Victorian England. It must also be underlined that in those decades the market was beginning to dictate its cash rules to publishers, whose editorial choices were often depending more on popularity and quantity than on artistic innovation and quality. In any case, it is undeniable that mystery was intrinsically one of the dominant aspects of Victorian society, whose literary paradigm can be considered a reaction to social mobility and a more general transformation of class organization, not to mention an unmapped social phenomenon that was known as the Victorian underworld. On this last point, see Kellow Chesney, *The Victorian Underworld* (Harmondsworth, England: Penguin, 1970); and, more recently, Donald Thomas, *The Victorian Underworld* (New York: New York University Press, 1998).

5. See Winifred Hughes, *The Maniac in the Cellar: Sensation Novels of the 1860s* (Princeton, NJ: Princeton University Press, 1980): 3–37. For its insightful analysis of Collins's fiction, see also Anthea Trodd, *Domestic Crime in the Victorian Novel* (Basingstoke: Macmillan, 1989).

6. According to Tamar Heller, *Dead Secrets: Wilkie Collins and the Female Gothic* (New Haven, CT: Yale University Press, 1992): 2, the main motif of *The Dead Secret* is directly linked with the female gothic: "If the image of buried writing in Collins' novels is affiliated with thematics of secrecy, transgression, and ille-

gitimacy, *The Dead Secret* is an especially clear instance of how his work embodies these thematics generically. The genre *The Dead Secret* recalls is the Gothic,
which has long been concerned with such themes, and particularly in this case
the tradition of Gothic writing by women known as the female Gothic. As developed by such figures as Ann Radcliffe, who popularized the genre in the 1790s,
the female Gothic maps a plot of domestic victimization." Convincing and doc-
umented though it may be, Heller's definition seems partly reductive and misleading when confronted with the semantic complexities of Collins's novel.

7. Collins, *Dead Secret*, 13.

8. Ibid., 15.

9. Ibid., 17–18.

10. Ibid., 15.

11. Ibid., 18 (italics mine).

12. Ibid., 18.

13. Ibid., 19.

14. Ibid., 15.

15. Ibid., 14.

16. Ibid., 30.

17. Ibid., 33.

18. A detailed analysis of the spatial organization of *The Dead Secret* would immediately reveal how scrupulously and attentively Collins structured the spatiality of each narrative sequence, bearing in mind the fact that the Myrtle Room
had to be the centripetal topological pivot of the whole narration. Regarding
the hiding place discovered by Sarah for the letter, it may be useful to focus
on the way the house is depicted: "Shadowed by its position, this ruinous side
of the house had a dark, cold, wintry aspect, even on the sunny August morning, when Sarah Leeson strayed into the deserted northern garden" (Ibid.,
30). As to the interior's description: "At length she succeeded in opening the
door. Thicker clouds of dust than she had yet met with flew out the moment the
interior of the room was visible; a dry, airless, suffocating atmosphere almost
choked her as she stooped to pick up her letter from the floor" (ibid., 33).

19. With respect to the female typology embodied by Sarah Leeson, she can
be defined as a woman without a strong personality and devoid of a perceptive
intelligence; she passively plays her role, and, as a victim of her mistress's mach-
inations, she is barely aware of the violence concealed behind her unnatural
separation from her daughter, Rosamond. As suggested by Peter Thoms, *The
Windings of the Labyrinth: Quest and Structure in the Novels of Wilkie Collins* (Athens:
Ohio University Press, 1992), 44, Sarah is a character without an ontological
center: "Sarah Leeson, who is trapped by the secret and isolated in the smaller
illegitimate world it circumscribes, passes through life as a victim. Although she
possesses instincts of integrity and self-sacrifice, she exercises little personal authority over her life; consequently, her path is narrow, charted simply toward
death, and lacking any creative embellishment."

20. Ibid., 21.

21. Ibid., 34.

22. Here it is interesting to notice that, as early as her first physical description, Sarah Leeson is chromatically marked by grayness, which seems to be

a correlative objective of her weak and unstable personality. Significantly enough, the color gray is the most visible trait of her hair: "The one extraordinary personal deterioration which she had undergone, consisted in the unnatural change that had passed over the colour of her hair. It was thick and soft . . . but it was grey as the hair of an old woman" (ibid., 11). Needless to say, her hair is a chromatic recording of a dysphoric experience: "The ordeal of some great suffering, at some earlier period of her life" (ibid., 10). However, her countenance conveys to the reader some physiognomic signs that seem contradictory and not in coherence with the trope of grayness: "With all its haggardness and paleness, no one could have looked at it and supposed for a moment that it was the face of an elderly woman. Wan as they might be, there was not a wrinkle on her cheeks" (ibid., 11). In my view, her facial smoothness does not have the positive connotations as may appear at first glance—her wrinkleless face is indeed closer to spectrality than to beauty and health. As is known, the theme of a woman in flight was also textualized by Gaskell in her tale *The Grey Woman*, published in *All the Year Round* in January 1861. Characteristically, the young woman who is escaping from her villainous husband will eventually discover that her hair has turned gray because of the trauma of her terrorized escape. Both in *The Dead Secret* and in *The Grey Woman* the escape brings about a psychic disorder and a gradual shrinking of self.

23. Ibid., 35.

24. Ibid., 127.

25. Ibid., 48. In Dr. Chennery's words: "Well, he had a turn for mechanics (I am telling you all this to make you understand about his blindness), and after veering from one occupation of that sort to another, he took at last to watchmaking. Curious amusement for a boy, but anything that required delicacy of touch and plenty of patience and perseverance, was just the thing to amuse and occupy Leonard" (ibid., 47–48).

26. Ibid., 38.

27. Ibid., 123.

28. As suggested by Lyn Pykett, *Wilkie Collins* (Oxford: Oxford University Press, 2005), 117, behind such a complex and shifting character as Sarah Leeson lies Collins's literary intention of "explor[ing] the grounds on which class and social identities were constructed in Victorian England."

29. Collins, *Dead Secret*, 152.

30. It is well known that one of the behavioral aspects of a person affected by neurosis is an exceedingly great emphasis laid on events and things that, at least retrospectively, should be considered unimportant. This obsessive-compulsive focus on something/somebody manifests itself as chronic anxiety, which, in Sarah Leeson's case, entails repetition of thoughts, change of places, and a low sense of self-worth. From a more general angle, it is not exaggerated to maintain that neurosis is deep rooted in human experience, in the sense that it is part of our predicament. And if we are to follow what Carl G. Jung, "Approaching the Unconscious," in *Man and His Symbols*, (New York: Dell, 1968), 73, wrote just before his death in 1961, we can conclude that the neurosis and the disharmony of Victorian society share a common ground: "Our world is, so to speak, dissociated like a neurotic."

31. Collins, *Dead Secret*, 350, italics mine.

32. Ibid., 351.

33. Ibid., 77.

34. In other words, here dust must be intended not as a metaphorical impediment to clarity. Rosamond aims at a truth that rejects the melodramatic imagination, while she is determined to solve the riddle of Mrs. Jazeph's mysterious behavior: "Mind, Lenny, you must be with me in all my investigations. I lend you my eyes, and you give me your advice. You must never lose patience, and never tell me that you can be of no use. How I do wish we were starting on our voyage of discovery at this very moment" (ibid., 245). It is clear that she is anxious to start her detection not only because of thirst for truth, but also because of a sort of inner impulse to face mystery and show to herself that, in a way, she can impose order on chaos.

35. On the way Collins construed Rosamond as a character whose behavioral and racial-cultural codes did not comply with the Victorian norms and literary conventions, see Mariaconcetta Costantini, *Venturing into Unknown Waters: Wilkie Collins and the Challenge of Modernity* (Pescara: Tracce, 2008), 214–17.

36. Leonard Frankland's blindness—with a quotation from *Paradise Lost*, and notably to the lines in which blindness is explicitly evoked ("so thick a drop serene," 3, 25)—and the particular role played by Rosamond as his guide seem to be an allusion to the final section of *Jane Eyre* (1848), in which Rochester, blind and psychologically tamed and weakened, is ready to follow Jane's lead.

37. Collins, *Dead Secret*, 112 (italics mine).

38. Ibid.

39. Sarah Leeson's story has many analogies with the diegetic organization of *Ruth* (1853) by Elizabeth Gaskell. Both protagonists live the sad condition of *fallen woman* by assuming a false identity and, in Ruth's case, by playing the role of a widow. In *Ruth*, despite a strong effort to attain a moral dignity alongside a social rebirth, the eponymous heroine is doomed to die at the end—a conclusion that is in line with the literary trope derived from the need to show to society that only death is the punishment for a fallen woman. Needless to say, death often leads to a final reconciliation with society and God.

40. Collins, *Dead Secret*, 114–15.

41. Ibid., 275.

42. Ibid., 281.

43. Ibid., 286.

44. Ibid., 340.

45. Ibid., 362.

46. Ibid., 282.

47. Ibid., 284.

48. Ibid., 285.

CHAPTER 3. *COUSIN PHILLIS*

1. Martin Greenberg, *The Terror of Art: Kafka and Modern Literature* (London: André Deutsch, 1971), 86, argues that "*The Metamorphosis* does not unfold an action but a metaphor; it is the spelling out of a metaphor. It does not end in

an Aristotelian dénouement, but draws the metaphor out to its ultimate conclusion which is death."

2. Alan Shelston, "Education in the Life and Work of Elizabeth Gaskell," *Gaskell Journal* 20 (2008): 64, astutely observes that *Cousin Phillis* "at the beginning of the story [is] a place apparently untouched by time" and adds that "one dimension of *Cousin Phillis* is pastoral rather than realistic fiction. . . . The timelessness will be broken, of course, and the outside world, most obviously in the form of the railway, will impose itself on the self-contained community. The whole theme of the story is that change cannot be resisted, whether on the personal, the family, of the communal level, but the references to that world will be of their nature limited to what relates to the story itself. Social documentation therefore is not a priority, and on the face of it the story has little to tell us about the process of education as such."

3. Elizabeth Gaskell, *Cousin Phillis and Other Tales*, ed. Angus Easson (Oxford: Oxford University Press, 1981); 266.

4. John Lucas, *The Literature of Change* (Brighton, England: Harvester Press, 1980); 27, notes that "Phillis is . . . the classical name for the innocent country girl—often enough the victim of a false-hearted lover."

5. Gaskell, *Cousin Phillis*, 278.

6. Ibid., 267–68.

7. From his narrative standpoint, Paul Manning feels that the real parallel is between Isaac and him, whereas Phillis is seen as Rebekah (Genesis 24). However, the narrator is also aware that he is introducing the marriage motif, which involves not the centrality of his role but that of his friend and head engineer, Holdsworth.

8. Gaskell, *Cousin Phillis*, 278.

9. Ibid., 283.

10. Ibid., 286.

11. Ibid., 294.

12. Thomas Hardy, *Jude the Obscure*, ed. Patricia Ingham (Oxford: Oxford University Press, 1989); 85.

13. Gaskell, *Cousin Phillis*, 297 (italics mine).

14. Ibid., 299 (italics mine).

15. Ibid., 310.

16. Thomas E. Recchio, "A Victorian Version of the Fall: Mrs. Gaskell's *Cousin Phillis* and the Domestication of Myth," *Gaskell Society Journal* 5 (1991): 44.

17. Gaskell, *Cousin Phillis*, 348.

18. Ibid., 346.

19. Ibid., 289.

20. Ibid., 315.

21. Ibid.

22. Ibid., 314.

23. Ibid., 316–17.

24. Ibid., 317 (italics mine).

25. Ibid., 282.

26. All this is shown clearly at the beginning of part 2: "I read and read, unregardful of the words I was uttering, thinking of all manner of other things;

of the bright colour of Phillis's hair, as the afternoon sun fell on her bending head; of the silence of the house, which enabled me to hear the double tick of the old clock which stood half-way up the stairs. . . . The tranquil monotony of that hour made me feel as if I had lived for ever, and should live for ever droning out paragraphs in that warm sunny room, with my two quiet hearers [Phillis and her mother]" (ibid., 282).

27. Ibid., 320.

28. Ibid., 321.

29. Ibid., 321 (italics mine).

30. Ibid., 323.

31. Ibid., 324.

32. Referring to this episode and to the role of Paul Manning as mediator, Athena Vrettos, *Somatic Fictions: Imagining Illness in Victorian Culture* (Stanford, CA: Stanford University Press, 1995), 37, observes: "He is implicated in Holdsworth's betrayal of emotional truth by his own attempts at mediation; at the same time, Paul demonstrates his faith in these confidences as accurate reflections of Holdsworth's feelings and lasting expressions of his intentions. Paul subscribes, in effect, to the same interpretative values that Phillis and her family do, and is indirectly betrayed by his faith." In my view, Paul is well aware that he is offering to Phillis, if not a lie, certainly a "curative" version of Holdsworth's leave taking—his consciousness of linguistic indeterminacy is much higher than Phillis's and her parents' simply because his words of comfort are totally functional to his desire to be of help. Thus, at the beginning of part 4, we can read words that well express Paul's doubts concerning his revelation: " I had an uneasy feeling sometimes when I thought of what I had done in the excitement of seeing Phillis so ill and in so much trouble" (Gaskell, *Cousin Phillis*, 325).

33. Ibid., 333.

34. On the theme of womanhood, secrecy, and body language, see Jane Ward, *Passion and Pathology in Victorian Fiction* (Oxford and New York: Oxford University Press, 2001); 36–37: "The fear that one's emotional secret might be read, or inadvertently given away, through body language, or worse, misread and misinterpreted in the public domain, unsurprisingly led women to be ever vigilant of their bodies. The fear of hysteria or madness was as much a fear of interpretation as of disease itself. Anxieties about the externalization of psychological distress only served to strengthen belief in the pathological consequences of repression."

35. Gaskell, *Cousin Phillis*, 342.

36. Ibid., 346.

37. Ibid.

38. Ibid., 347.

39. Ibid., 352.

40. On this point it may be useful to quote the following passage: "Once I saw Phillis through the open door; her pretty golden hair had been cut off long before; her head was covered with wet cloths, and she was moving it backwards and forwards on the pillow, with weary, never-ending motion, her poor eyes shut, trying in the old accustomed way to croon out a hymn tune, but perpetu-

ally breaking it up into moans of pain. Her mother sate by her, tearless, changing the cloths upon her head with patient solicitude. I did not see the minister at first, but there he was in a dark corner, down upon his knees, his hands
clasped together in a passionate prayer. Then the door shut, and I saw no more"
(Gaskell, *Cousin Phillis*, 349).

41. Ibid., 354.

42. Ibid.

CHAPTER 4. THE CURSED HEARTH

1. On this point see Tessa Brodetsky, *Elizabeth Gaskell* (Leamington Spa,
England: Berg, 1986), 104: "In her novels, Elizabeth Gaskell frequently delineates a close father-daughter relationship; obvious examples are those between
John and Mary Barton, Mr. Hale and Margaret, Daniel and Sylvia Robson, and
Mr. Gibson and Molly. In each case, it is a loving relationship, in which the
daughter loyally supports her father, even when (as in the cases of John Barton
and Daniel Robson) he is guilty of a criminal act. The relationship is portrayed
uncomplicated, almost without tension, virtually ideal."

2. Rosemary Jackson, *Fantasy: The Literature of Subversion* (London: Methuen,
1981), 126.

3. For an analysis of this story see Francesco Marroni, *La fabbrica nella valle:
Saggio sulla narrativa di Elizabeth Gaskell* (Bari: Adriatica, 1987), 119–128.

4. Elizabeth Gaskell, *Lois the Witch*, in *Cousin Phillis and Other Tales*, ed. Angus Easson (Oxford: Oxford University Press, 1981), 124.

5. Ibid., 162.

6. Ibid., 171.

7. Ibid., 190.

8. Elizabeth Gaskell, *The Old Nurse's Story*, in *Cousin Phillis and Other Tales*,
52.

9. Ibid., 52.

10. Ibid.

11. Ibid., 36.

12. "Well! I told you I had a brave heart; and I thought it was rather pleasant
to have that grand music rolling about the house, let who would be the player"
(ibid., 42).

13. Ibid., 40.

14. Ibid., 41.

15. In Lord Furnivall's case, the description of this dominant psychological-
behavioral feature of the whole family is most explicit, and from a linguistic
point of view, hyperbolic: "The old lord was eaten up with pride. Such a proud
man was never seen or heard of; and his daughters were like him" (ibid., 50).
There is a confirmation of this reiterated "scornful pride," which can be seen as
a key to interpret the story, when Grace Furnivall's ghost appears on the scene
"with a look of relentless hate and triumphant scorn . . . with a soft, white hat
drawn down over the proud brows, and a red and curling lip" (ibid., 55–56).

16. Ibid., 47.

17. Ibid., 56.

18. Enid L. Duthie, *The Themes of Elizabeth Gaskell* (London: Macmillan, 1980); 50, acutely observes: "The past history of the houses which had sheltered the same family for generations made a powerful appeal to her historical sense."

19. Gaskell, *Old Nurse's Story*, 38.

20. Ibid., 39 (italics mine).

21. What Carla Casagrande and Silvana Vecchio, *I sette vizi capitali: Storia dei peccati nel medioevo* (Turin: Einaudi, 2000): 11, write on the theme of pride as a capital vice that is significant: "It is . . . a vice which, in itself, bears the sign of a contradiction, from the moment the movement of ascension which animates it is, in reality, a descending movement and a fall" (my translation).

22. As regards General Monck, the first duke of Albermarle (1608–70), it must be mentioned that in *Morton Hall*, Gaskell only mentions his name once, using the less familiar spelling *Monk*. To understand Monck's ambiguous role before, during, and after the civil war, what Mark Kishlansky, *L'età degli Stuart: L'Inghilterra dal 1603 al 1714* (Bologna: il Mulino, 1999): 279–80, writes is most informative: "A European war veteran, Monck served the King, Parliament and finally the Protectorate. Skillful and taciturn, his military career followed the typical motto of the professional soldier: always be on the winner's side" (my translation).

23. Elizabeth Gaskell, *Morton Hall*, in *The Moorland Cottage and Other Stories*, ed. S. Lewis (Oxford: Oxford University Press, 1995): 169.

24. Gaskell, *Morton Hall*, 176.

25. Ibid., 176–77 (italics mine).

26. Ibid., 188.

27. Ibid., 189.

28. Elizabeth Gaskell, *The Grey Woman*, in *A Dark Night's Work and Other Stories*, ed. Suzanne Lewis (Oxford: Oxford University Press, 1992), 257.

29. Gaskell, *Grey Woman*, 261.

30. Ibid., 302.

31. Ibid., 251.

32. Ibid., 262.

33. Ibid., 263.

34. Ibid., 278.

35. Ibid., 286.

36. Interestingly enough, Alan Shelston, "The Supernatural in the Stories of Elizabeth Gaskell," in *Exhibited by the Candlelight: Sources and Developments in the Gothic Tradition*, ed. Valeria Tinkler-Villani, Peter Davidson, and Jane Stevenson (Amsterdam: Rodopi, 1995); 144, has pointed out that the theme of curse can be interpreted as a response to the emergence of a new dynastic genealogy, that of the bourgeoisie: "If a dyachronic as well as a synchronic view of the family is adopted the ideal must be one of moral, economic and genetic development: the issue was an important one for the new middle-class, establishing its own dynasties against those of the traditional past."

37. Elizabeth Gaskell, *The Poor Clare*, in *My Lady Ludlow and Other Stories*, ed. Edgar Wright (Oxford: Oxford University Press, 1989), 277.

38. Ibid., 281.

39. Ibid., 304.

40. Ibid., 304–5.

41. M. T. Reddy, "Female Sexuality in 'The Poor Clare': The Demon in the House," in *Studies in Short Fiction* 21, no. 3 (Summer 1984): 261, quite rightly observes that the story "is a frightening depiction of the consequences of expressing female sexuality in a culture that insists that all good women are sexless angels and that therefore requires women to repress their sexuality, under threat of ostracism or death." Admittedly, before Reddy, Edgar Wright, *Mrs. Gaskell: The Basis for a Reassessment* (London: Oxford University Press, 1965), 185, had spoken of "latent sexuality." With reference to "The Poor Clare," the idea is taken from Patsy Stoneman, *Elizabeth Gaskell* (Brighton, England: Harvester Press, 1987), 66, who observes: "In psychological terms . . . Lucy's double, which is seen by everyone, makes visible the repressed sexuality of a whole society."

42. Significantly, the spatial displacement to Flanders leads to a change in the character, who, in Antwerp while there is a popular uprising against Austrian rule (around 1750), gains a reputation as a saint—which proves that the accusation of witchcraft is always an effect of the environment in which one lives: "Sister Magdalen is either a great sinner, or a great saint. She does more, as I have heard, than all the other nuns put together; yet, when last month they would fain have made her mother-superior, she begged rather that they would place her below all the rest, and make her the meanest servant of all" (Gaskell, *Poor Clare*, 326).

43. Ibid., 317.

44. Elizabeth Gaskell, *The Doom of the Griffiths*, in *My Lady Ludlow and Other Stories*, 230.

45. Ibid., 230.

46. Ibid., 240.

Chapter 5. *The Whirlpool*

1. For a well-documented review of the novel's coeval reception, see Pierre Coustillas and Colin Partridge, eds., *Gissing: The Critical Heritage* (London: Routledge and Kegan Paul, 1972), 276–305. In particular, in a review that appeared in *Harper's Weekly* (July 31, 1897), Henry James observed: "He seems to me above all a case of saturation, and it is mainly his saturation that makes him interesting—I mean especially in the sense of making him singular. The interest would be greater were his art more complete; but we must take what we can get, and Mr. Gissing has a way of his own" (*Gissing: The Critical Heritage*, 291).

2. See Jacob Korg, *George Gissing: A Critical Biography* (Brighton, England: Harvester Press, 1980), 209: "It was a greater success, both with the public and the critics, than any other books. The first edition of two thousand copies was sold out in a month. The puzzled critics now sought to account for the fact that a novelist of Gissing's talent had failed to win much attention in his years of work." As to the main thematics of *The Whirlpool*, Korg rightly observes: "Like

Hardy's novels, *The Whirlpool* gives the impression that life is ruled by a malevolent determinism. In social affairs, as in business, trivial causes produce grotesquely disproportionate effects" (208).

3. P. F. Mattheisen, A. C. Young, and Pierre Coustillas, eds., *The Collected Letters of George Gissing,* 9 vols. (Athens: Ohio University Press, 1992); 6:230. Letter to A. H. Bullen dated February 8, 1897. On the artistic significance of *The Whirlpool,* Loyd Fernando, "Gissing's Studies in 'Vulgarism': Aspects of His Anti-Feminism," in *George Gissing: Critical Essays,* ed. J. Michaux (London: Vision and Totowa, NJ: Barnes & Noble, 1981), 114, notes: "When in *The Whirlpool* (1897) Gissing at least dealt centrally and at three-volume length with a foundering marriage-relationship, he had therefore devoted much thought to the problem and had the benefit of repeated preparation, as it were, for its literary presentation. *The Whirlpool* is Gissing's most skilful novel in every respect, but it has rarely been discussed. It embodies his mature vision with a technical assurance that must rank it very high among novels of the final decade of the nineteenth century."

4. Coustillas and Partridge, eds., *Gissing: The Critical Heritage,* 299. H. G. Wells's article appeared in *Contemporary Review* 72 (August 1897): 192–201.

5. Mattheisen, Young, and Coustillas, eds., *Collected Letters of George Gissing,* 6:123. Letter to Eduard Bertz dated May 9, 1896.

6. With respect to the way contemporary reviewers responded to Gissing's pessimism, see an unsigned review published in *Pall Mall Gazette* (April 27, 1897), now in Coustillas and Partridge, eds., *Gissing: The Critical Heritage,* 277: "Mr. Gissing's persistent pessimism is but the more annoying by reason of its obvious sincerity, and doubly dangerous because it is so convincing. In *The Whirlpool* his art almost convinces us that it does not much matter what we do, since everything is certain to turn out badly. If you marry your life will be wrecked, and if you do not marry that abstention will probably wreck your life as completely as the most reckless love-match of them all. That your life is going to be wrecked is a foregone conclusion, and not bothering about; it is the question of how the wreck is to be accomplished that lends to life its interest"

7. Peter Keating, *The Haunted Study: A Social History of the English Novel 1875–1914* (London: Fontana Press, 1991), 128.

8. Of course, some reviewers of the novel did not omit to note its Zolaesque title, a literary connection that was by no means a good starting point for potential readers. Interestingly enough, an unsigned review in the *New York Tribune—Illustrated Supplement* (June 27, 1897) was very explicit in its rejection of the Zolaesque tradition: "The novel of sordid motives and prosaic characters has been made so revolting by Zola and his followers that the reader who gives a brief preliminary glance to Mr. Gissing's *The Whirlpool* feels tempted to put the book down. But if he has remembered any of this author's other books he perseveres through the many pages of the present volume and relinquishes it unwillingly at the end. For Mr. Gissing is one of those rare writers who, without professing to find romance or beauty in every-day life, nevertheless wrest from such unpromising material a certain human and spiritual significance which is in its way beautiful and romantic. *The Whirlpool* is persistently and superabundantly sordid." Coustillas and Partridge, eds., *Gissing: The Critical Heritage,* 285.

9. Colin Partridge, "The Humane Center: George Gissing's *The Whirlpool*," *Gissing Newsletter*, 9, no. 3 (July 1973): 3. For an acute discussion of the novel's title, see John Goode, *George Gissing: Ideology and Fiction* (London: Vision, 1978); 184: "The whirlpool of high capitalism then, but equally the whirlpool of metropolitan culture—the round of concerts, hit shows, agents and soirées, touching the demi-monde. Beyond this it is the whirlpool of modernity, of a new ethic, emancipated, tolerant, subjective, which throws all assumptions into the melting-pot. And above all, the image conjures up the place itself, the metropolis, the bustling outside, crowded and confused, within which or against which one has to contrive a privacy."

10. George Gissing, *The Whirlpool*, ed. William Greenslade (London: J. M. Dent, and Rutland, VT: Charles E. Tuttle, 1997), 147 (italics mine). All references will be to this edition. I have also consulted the following edition: *The Whirlpool*, Introduction by Gillian Tindall (London: Hogarth Press, 1984).

11. Gissing, *Whirlpool*, 145–46 (italics mine).

12. Ibid., 5.

13. Ibid., 47. Here it may not be an exaggeration to note in Rolfe's words a scriptural allusion: "And the fifth angel sounded, and I saw a star fall from heaven unto the earth: and to him was given the key of the bottomless pit" (Revelation 9:1).

14. Jenni Calder, *Women and Marriage in Victorian Fiction* (London: Thames and Hudson, 1976), 163. With respect to the marriage of Harvey Rolfe and Alma Frothingham, we may fruitfully apply what Mona Caird writes in her article "The Morality of Marriage" published in the *Fortnightly Review* (March 1, 1890): "In a marriage true to the modern spirit, which has scarcely yet begun to breathe upon this institution, husband and wife regard one another as absolutely free beings; they no more think of demanding subordination on one side or the other than a couple of friends who had elected to live together" (quoted in Calder, *Women and Marriage*, 167).

15. Gissing, *Whirlpool*, 34.

16. Regarding this weakness of Alma's personality, see Wood, *Passion and Pathology in Victorian Fiction*, (Oxford: Oxford University Press, 2001), 187: "Her inability to withstand the lure of fashionable society or to see if for what it is worth is put down to constitutional weakness and gradually, but inexorably, she is drawn toward the contaminating source of social and individual devitalization."

17. Gissing, *Whirlpool*, 31. The father/daughter relationship is one of the elements that will determine the pathological development of Alma's personality. In her neurosis, she feels that the words of society on her father's dishonorable death are always echoing in her mind: "In a crowded drawing-room she had heard someone draw attention to her—'the daughter of Bennet Frothingham.' That was how people thought of her, and would it not have been wiser if she had so thought of herself? Daughter of a man who had set all on a great hazard; who had played for the world's reward, and, losing, flung away his life. What had she to do with domestic virtues, and the pleasures of a dull, decorous circle? Could it but come over again, she would accept the challenge of circumstance, which she had failed to understand; accept the scandal and the hereditary shame; welcome the lot cast for her, and, like her father, play boldly

for the great stakes. His widow might continue to hold her pious faith in him, and refuse to believe that his name merited obloquy; his child knew better. She had mistaken her path, lost the promise of her beauty and her talent, led astray by the feeble prejudice of those who have neither one nor the other. Too late, and worse than idle now, to recognise it. She would be a good woman, rule her little house, bring up her child, and have no will but her husband's" (Gissing, *Whirlpool*, 388–89).

18. Ibid., 31.

19. Ibid., 63.

20. Ibid., 128.

21. Ibid., 290.

22. Ibid., 293.

23. Ibid., 335.

24. Ibid., 329.

25. Ibid.

26. Ibid., 223.

27. Ibid., 414.

28. Ibid., 32.

29. On Gissing's deep-rooted misogyny see David Grylls, *The Paradox of Gissing* (London: Allen and Unwin, 1986), 148–49: "The peak period of Gissing's antipathy to women occurred in the 1890s. Wretchedly unhappy in his marriage to Edith, he discharged his bile in a series of works, from *Born in Exile* to his book on Dickens, which offer a crescendo of misogyny. Given such a context, it is scarcely surprising that the *Odd Women* fails of its purpose in parts: the wonder is rather that it ever got written. Its successors—especially *The Whirlpool* and *In the Year of Jubilee*—are bristling with venomous attacks on women, for their coarseness, their credulity, their neglect of children, and above all their reckless extravagance."

30. Gissing, *Whirlpool*, 129.

31. W. Francis Browne, "Marriage as a Symbol of Alienation in *The Whirlpool*," *Gissing Newsletter* 13, no. 2 (April 1987): 3.

32. Gissing, *Whirlpool*, 228 (italics mine).

33. Ibid., 32 (italics mine).

34. Ibid., 70 (italics mine).

35. Ibid., 80.

36. Ibid., 81.

37. Ibid., 57.

38. Ibid., 60.

39. Ibid.

40. Ibid., 178.

41. Ibid., 74.

42. Ibid., 210.

43. Ibid., 94.

44. Ibid., 107.

45. Ibid., 108.

46. J. Hillis Miller, "Thomas Hardy, Jacques Derrida, and the 'Dislocation of Souls,'" in *Taking Chances: Derrida, Psychoanalysis, and Literature*, ed. Joseph H.

Smith and William Kerrigan (Baltimore: Johns Hopkins University Press, 1988), 136.

47. Thomas Hardy, *Jude the Obscure*, ed. Patricia Ingham (Oxford: Oxford University Press, 1989), 171.

48. Gissing, *Whirlpool*, 419.

CHAPTER 6. *JUDE THE OBSCURE*

1. Thomas Hardy, *Jude the Obscure*, ed. Patricia Ingham (Oxford: Oxford University Press, 1989). All references will be to this edition. I have also consulted the following editions: *Jude the Obscure*, introduction by T. Eagleton, notes by P. N. Furbank, "New Wessex Edition" (London: Macmillan, 1978); *Jude the Obscure*, ed. N. Page (New York: W. W. Norton, 1978); *Jude the Obscure*, ed. C. C. Sisson (Harmondsworth, England: Penguin, 1985); *Jude the Obscure*, introduction by T. R. Wightman, notes by P. N. Furbank, "New Wessex Edition" (London: Macmillan, 1986); *Jude the Obscure*, introduction by J. H. Miller, "Everyman's Library" (London: David Campbell, 1992); *Jude the Obscure*, afterword by A. Alvarez (New York: New American Library, s.d.). A study of the coeval reception of Hardy's novel is not among the scopes of this chapter. However, I cannot omit to emphasize that *Jude the Obscure* aroused a number of negative responses, often imbued with irritation, reproach, and moralistic indignation: "The book's reception traumatized Hardy, over Christmas 1895 and for the rest of the following year" (Ralph Pite, *Thomas Hardy: The Guarded Life* [Basingstoke: Picador, 2006], 356). After a long and depressing list of scandalized reviews and letters, Hardy made a drastic decision: he would communicate with no one and change his literary direction. An entry in Hardy's *Life* is quite worth mentioning: "The Bishop of Wakefield announced in a letter to the papers that he had thrown Hardy's novel into the fire" (Millgate, ed., *Life*, 294). Not only did the bishop burn Hardy's book, but he also aimed at "persuading W. H. Smith to withdraw if from their circulating libraries. The public took less notice of the Bishop than Hardy did, and three months after publication 20,000 copies had been sold. Scandal had brought success" (Claire Tomalin, *Thomas Hardy: The Time-Torn Man* [London: Viking, 2006], 260). For an analysis of the reception of Hardy's works, also see R. G. Cox, ed., *Thomas Hardy: The Critical Heritage* (London: Routledge & Kegan Paul, 1970).

2. Hardy, "Preface to the First Edition," *Jude the Obscure*, xxxv (italics mine).

3. Edward W. Said, *Beginnings: Intention and Method* (New York: Columbia University Press, 1985), 138, has perceptively underlined the value of Hardy's novelistic innovations: "Hardy's case in *Jude the Obscure* is . . . the recognition by a great artist that the dynastic principle of traditional narrative now seemed somehow inappropriate. Narrative was no longer, as before, first fashioned by the writer according to the sequential character of time, and thereafter given to the reader to be read, or possessed, along the printed line in which his eyes and mind repeated by miraculous multiplication the sense and direction of life." According to Janet Burstein, "The Journey beyond Myth in *Jude the Obscure*," *Texas Studies in Language and Literature* 15, no. 3 (Fall 1973): 503, *Jude* is structured

around the supremacy of the narrator's voice: "His is actually the only voice left to speak the richness of a vanished life and time." Always observed from an ironic aloofness, in *Jude the Obscure* the main characters are far from the harmony of "the mythic world" and, paradigmatically, embody a feeling of broken order: "Characters within the novel who hear no voices like the narrator's seem curiously adrift in time and lost in a world where phenomena may have many contradictory meanings—or none at all."

4. R. L. Purdy and Michael Millgate, eds., *The Collected Letters of Thomas Hardy*, 7 vols. (Oxford: Clarendon Press, 1980), 2:99. In the same letter, Hardy rejects any analogy with Émile Zola and naturalism, while underlining that his readings of Zola's works are very few. Conversely, he is ready to admit that he has learned a lot from Fielding, whose influence reviewers and critics have not detected. Ironically, he concludes, "Your everyday critic knows nothing of Fielding."

5. On the coeval reception of *Tess*, it is worthwhile citing what James Gibson, "Introduction," in *Tess of the d'Urbervilles*, notes by P. N. Furbank, "New Wessex Edition" (London: Macmillan, 1985), 13, notes: "Its appearance in a complete and unbowdlerized form created a literary sensation and the review were mixed. On one side Hardy was viciously attacked by those who saw him as an immoral influence. *The Quarterly Review* described it as a 'clumsy sordid tale of boorish brutality and lust' and 'a coarse and disagreeable story'. *The Saturday Review* criticized Hardy's grammar and thought that the book was an 'unpleasant story' written in 'a very unpleasant way'. Another reviewer described the sentence in the last chapter about the 'President of the Immortals' as 'the most dreadful sentence in modern English literature.' *The Independent* disliked this 'study of adultery.' But there were many to defend and praise Hardy."

6. Hardy, "Preface to the First Edition," in *Jude the Obscure*, xxxv–xxxvi.

7. Dale Kramer, *Thomas Hardy: The Forms of Tragedy* (London: Macmillan, 1975), 137.

8. We may note here that Roger Ebbatson, *Heidegger's Bicycle: Interfering with Victorian Texts* (Brighton, OR: Sussex Academic Press, 2006), 7, in his most perceptive investigation of *A Laodicean* (1881), has detected some modernist intimations in Hardy's novel: "The coalescence in this novel of erotic desire, money and property serves to hollow out the past whilst eliciting an empty or homogeneous present. The labyrinthine structure of the castle, taken together with the plot reliance on telegraphy and gambling, points enigmatically toward the existential 'moment' of modernism."

9. Shalom Rachman, "Character and Theme in Hardy's *Jude the Obscure*," *English* 22, no. 113 (Summer 1973): 45, has rightly observed: "Both in date of publication, 1895, and in the vision of the world it embodies, *Jude* marks the point of division between nineteenth-century moderate optimism and twentieth-century pervasive gloom. The book looks back to nineteenth-century Romanticism, and foreshadows the restlessness, the isolation of the individual, the collapse of old values, and the groping toward new ones, all of which have become the hallmarks of serious twentieth-century fiction. Jude himself is the last full-blooded romantic." With respect to Hardy's innovative contributions in the development of the novel, one of the few critics who have noted the modernist valence in

his fiction is Gilles Deleuze, whose philosophical approach, albeit concise, is very stimulating. He has emphasized the way rupture assumes a particular significance in Hardyan imagination since it postulates a new departure and a new world: "Hardy invokes a sort of Greek destiny for this empiricist experimental world. Individuals, packets of sensations, run over the heath like a line of flight or a line of deterritorialization of the earth" (Gilles Deleuze and Claire Parnet, *Dialogues II*, trans. Hugh Tomlinson and Barbara Habberjam [London: Continuum, 2002], 30).

10. Jurij M. Lotman, *Cercare la strada: Modelli della cultura*, ed. Maria Corti (Venezia: Marsilio, 1994), 38 (translation mine).

11. Carl J. Weber, *Hardy of Wessex: His Life and Literary Career* (New York: Columbia University Press, 1965), 206. In my opinion, Hardy's capacity of controlling the narration is by no means a weakness in *Jude*. More simply, I believe that, in this stage of his literary career, Hardy responded in a drastic way to the crisis of representation. Indeed, from a narratological angle, *Jude* testifies to Hardy's painstaking search for new modes of artistic expression. In part, I concur with the analysis by Perry Meisel, *Thomas Hardy: The Return of the Repressed* (New Haven, CT: Yale University Press, 1972); 157: "In *Jude the Obscure*, his imagination has driven him to the boundaries of his limitations in the writing of prose while, at the same time, it has rescued this last precarious vision by calling on the creative resources he did possess. That we must search for his final judgment on man, nature, and society in his last work of fiction in a philosophical distinction suggests that he gave up novel-writing for a reason more profound than is usually offered. It seems that the sustained tension during the years in which he fashioned a constantly evolving imaginative universe brought him to an irresolvable, if not unbearable, conflict."

12. The textual history of *Jude* is scrupulously analyzed by John Paterson, "The Genesis of *Jude the Obscure*," *Studies in Philology* 57 (1960): 87–98. Important though it may be, this article draws conclusions that, from a critical and methodological angle, are rather misleading: "It is known . . . that in spite of his meticulous preparation, Hardy had not got far into the actual writing of the novel before he lost control of it altogether" (97). It is perhaps superfluous to add that the reorganization of the diegetic development of *Jude* entails by no means a loss of control of the narration, but more precisely it testifies to a thematic dynamic as a response to a constant control of the perfect equilibrium between narrative structures and overall design. The plot changes, the re-orientation of the main characters, and even the modifications of the temporal order are part of Hardy's need to realize a model of the world perfectly in line with his own imaginary.

13. Cf. Michael Millgate, *Thomas Hardy: A Biography* (Oxford: Oxford University Press, 1985), 349–50.

14. On the history of the title, see Patricia Ingham, "The Evolution of *Jude the Obscure*," *Review of English Studies*, 27, no. 105 (February 1976): 29–30, and Cedric Watts, *Thomas Hardy: "Jude the Obscure"* (Harmondsworth, England: Penguin, 1992); esp. 52–53.

15. Deleuze and Parnet, *Dialogues II*, 27.

16. Hardy, *Jude the Obscure*, 3.

17. Ibid., 4–5.

18. Regarding the negative valence of kindness, see Alexander Fischler, "An Affinity for Birds: Kindness in Hardy's *Jude the Obscure*," *Studies in the Novel* 13, no. 3 (Fall 1981): 261: "[*Jude*] developed episodically around a simplistic argument: kindness does not pay. Jude is pronounced fatally weak from the start because he cannot hurt anything, because he has kindness to excess. To be sure, kindness is not his only weakness of character, but it is chief, and the others are generally made to seem related. Jude is unable to overcome it for reasons which Hardy suggests are temperamental and hereditary."

19. Hardy, *Jude the Obscure*, 335.

20. Ibid., 5.

21. Ibid., 9. On the significance of ornithological tropes in Hardy's imagination, see Francesco Marroni, "The Poetry of Ornithology in Keats, Leopardi and Hardy: A Dialogic Analysis," *Thomas Hardy Journal* 14, no. 2 (May 1998): 35–44.

22. Hardy, *Jude the Obscure*, 10.

23. Ibid., 11.

24. Ibid., 13.

25. Ibid. (italics mine). According to Lewis B. Horne, "Pattern and Contrast in *Jude the Obscure*," *Études Anglaises* 32, no. 2 (April–June 1979): 143, "The controlling symbols of *Jude the Obscure* are the journey and the cell. From Jude's decision to emulate Phillotson toward knowledge to his final coming to rest in his coffin, Jude travels in search of a sanctuary—a place that will provide peace through the satisfaction of desire, a condition in which 'the little cell of your life' will not be shaken and warped by 'something glaring, garish, rattling.'"

26. Hardy's *Life* confirms that the episode is founded on an autobiographical experience: "One event of this date or little later stood out, he used to say, more distinctly than any. He was lying on his back in the sun, thinking how useless he was, and covered his face with his straw hat. The sun's rays streamed through the interstices of the straw, the lining having disappeared. Reflecting on his experiences of the world so far as he had got, he came to the conclusion that he did not wish to grow up. Other boys were always talking of when they would be men; he did not want at all to be a man, or to possess things, but to remain as he was, in the same spot, and to know no more people that he already knew (about half a dozen)" (Millgate, ed., *Life*, 20). Such an experience occupies a stable chamber in Hardy's memory; its intense iconicity establishes a point of intratextual intersection with the poem "Childhood among the Ferns." Here I like to quote at least the last two strophes (lines 10–15): "The sun then burst, and brought forth a sweet breath / from the limp ferns as they dried underneath: / I said: 'I could live on here thus till death'; // And queried in the green rays as I sate: / 'Why should I have to grow to man's estate, / And this afar-noised World perambulate?' " (Thomas Hardy, "Childhood among the Ferns," in *The Complete Poems*, ed. James Gibson [London: Macmillan, 1983], 864).

27. Hardy, *Jude the Obscure*, 11.

28. Ibid., 17.

29. Ibid., 8, 14.

30. Ibid., 18.

31. Ibid., 17.

32. On this point, see Jean Brooks, *Thomas Hardy: The Poetic Structure* (London: Elek, 1971); 257: "The personal movement of Jude's life, the modern Everyman caught in the violent contrasts of his own being and the changing world, gains poetic depth from its power to represent the larger mythical, historical and evolutionary rhythms of the cosmos."

33. John Bunyan, *The Pilgrim's Progress*, ed. N. H. Keeble (Oxford: Oxford University Press, 1990), 126. According to Gary Adelman, *"Jude the Obscure": A Paradise of Despair* (New York: Twayne, 1992); 34, the novel is rife with allusions to Jesus aiming at delineating a strongly spiritual dimension in Jude's self-definition: "The sacramental imagery and identification of Jude with Christ, if hyperbolic, underscore Jude's sense of mission."

34. Among Jude's and Sue's weaknesses, the excess of sensibility is certainly the most dangerous. In a society based on a cash nexus and insensitiveness, personal realization is always hampered by a sensitive temperament. Significantly, in his *Life*, Hardy emphasizes the contrast between mind and body: "A woeful fact—that the human race is too extremely developed for its corporal conditions, the nerves being evolved to an activity abnormal in such an environment. . . . This planet does not supply the material for happiness to higher existences. Other planets may, though one can hardly see how" (Millgate, ed., *Life*; 227). The same notion is presented in *Jude*, in line with the flesh/spirit dichotomy, which is a crucial factor in Jude and Sue's characterization: "Vague and quaint imaginings had haunted Sue in the days when her intellect scintillated like a star, that the world resembled a stanza or melody composed in a dream; it was wonderfully excellent to the half-aroused intelligence, but hopelessly absurd at the full waking; that the First Cause worked automatically like a somnambulist, and not reflectively like a sage; that *at the framing of the terrestrial conditions there seemed never to have been contemplated such a development of emotional perceptiveness among the creatures subject to those conditions as that reached by thinking and educated humanity*. But affliction makes opposing forces loom anthropomorphous; and those ideas were now exchanged for a sense of Jude and herself fleeing from a persecutor" (Hardy, *Jude the Obscure*, 361, italics mine).

35. On the contrast between Sue Bridehead and Arabella Donn, see Elizabeth Hardwick, "Sue and Arabella," in *The Genius of Thomas Hardy*, ed. M. Drabble (London: Weidenfeld and Nicolson, 1976), 67–73. As far as Arabella's role is concerned, Hardwick remarks: "Arabella is as much a convention in the history of the novel as Sue is an original. It is the rule of conventions to ask us to accept as given a certain gathering of traits and motives. Arabella represents the classical entrapment by sex: the entrapment of an 'innocent' sensual man by a hard, needy, shackling woman. Arabella's coarseness is a mirror of Jude's weakness" (69).

36. Hardy, *Jude the Obscure*, 46. As to the meaning of Η ΚΑΙΝΗ ΔΙΑΘΗΚΗ, it is the Greek title of the New Testament. See the beginning of the same chapter (40–41).

37. Ibid., 68.

38. Ibid., 102.

39. Ibid., 79–80.

40. Ibid., 81.

41. Ibid., 84.

42. Ibid.

43. Ibid., 121.

44. Ibid., 120.

45. With reference to Jude's mobility and its social relevance, Terry Eagleton, *The English Novel: An Introduction* (Oxford: Blackwell, 2005), 188, suggests that such a condition is characteristic of the lower middle class—"one trapped between aspiration and anxiety, and therefore typical of some of the central contradictions of the age. In this sense, Hardy could attend to the plight of this obscure social grouping without losing grip on broader issues."

46. Hardy, *Jude the Obscure*, 126–27 (italics mine).

47. As is known, in Hardy's fiction the road always assumes a functional centrality in the definition of the psychological code belonging to the protagonists—the road is the place where change and self-fashioning occur; the road is the topology that embodies a desire understood as the end of distance, as a reunion and a movement toward belongingness. In *Jude the Obscure*, the road entails all these aspects, but also a way of experiencing a peculiar relationship with the Wessex landscape, a modality of visual appropriation of the objects. In this sense, it is significant that Jude decides to cover on foot the last four miles that separate him from Christminster: "He had that afternoon driven in a cart from Alfredston to the village nearest the city in this direction, and was now walking the remaining four miles rather from choice than from necessity, having always fancied himself arriving thus" (Hardy, *Jude the Obscure*, 77). Christminster will produce in Jude only a bitter disappointment, but, in his first visit, the road toward the university city is the place where his expectations become greater and greater.

48. Ibid., 127.

49. Ibid., 128.

50. Paterson, "Genesis of *Jude the Obscure*," 89.

51. See Hardy, *Jude the Obscure*, 8: "'The boy is crazy for books, that he is. It runs in our family rather. His cousin Sue is just the same, so I've heard, but I have not seen the child for years, though she was born in this place, within these four walls, as it happened. My niece and her husband, after they were married, didn' get a house of their own for some year or more; and then they only had one till—Well, I won't go into that. Jude, my child, don't *you* ever marry. 'Tisn't for the Fawleys to take that step any more. She, their only one, was like a child o' my own, Belinda, till the split come. Ah, that a little maid should know such changes!'"

52. For a detailed analysis of the use of photographs in *Jude*, see Rebecca Warburton Boylan, "Phantom Photographs: The Camera's Pursuit and the Disruption of Consciousness in *Jude the Obscure*," *Thomas Hardy Journal* 22 (Autumn 2006): 79: "Quite simply, Jude reads the photograph as a reflection of his own dream, finding within not only a blood kinship, but the word made flesh. It is the word, ecclesiastical and classical, that Jude longs to study at the university. Sue's youthful face assures Jude of the embodiment of the ideal, for he reads

the light surrounding her face as the sacred luminescence associated with divine knowledge and inspiration which Jude believes he will find for himself at Christminster. Thus, Jude reads within Sue's photograph his dream that Christminster's sacred and secular words will illuminate his mind and soul."

53. Hardy, *Jude the Obscure*, 89–90.

54. Ibid., 90 (italics mine).

55. Ibid., 26.

56. Ibid., 90. As is evident, both Jude and Sue are shaped by a paradigm of mobility that is their dramatic way of experiencing modernity—especially what modern life implies in terms of uprootedness, desire, and restlessness. Admittedly, Sue Bridehead's sexual identity is deeply ingrained in modernity since it seems to have lost its natural coordinates. On this point, Philip M. Weinstein, *The Semantics of Desire* (Princeton, NJ: Princeton University Press, 1984); 139, astutely has remarked: "The world of *Jude the Obscure* has become unmoored from this natural certitude. In the portrait of Sue Bridehead Hardy suggests that, to the unappeased spirit in search of articulated paradigms, nothing—not even the body's native stresses—can be reliably categorized. Life is a something foreign to the classificatory demands made by the spirit. In its utterances, its values, and even its bodily grounding, life is a phenomenon of stain, illogic, and obscurity."

57. Hardy, *Jude the Obscure*, 153.

58. As to the meaning of the concept of *explosion*, Jurij M. Lotman, *La cultura e l'esplosione: Prevedibilità e imprevedibilità* (Milano: Feltrinelli, 1993), 155–171, uses this term to convey the idea of cultural change that occurs when a culture is invaded by one or more texts of the external world. In this connection, "the moment of the explosion is the moment of the unpredictability" (155, translation mine). Needless to say, Sue Bridehead is the repository of a new language (J. S. Mill, etc.), which, admittedly, clashes with Victorian cultural orthodoxy. See also Robert Langbaum, *Thomas Hardy in Our Time* (Basingstoke: Macmillan, 1995), 16: "In *Jude the Obscure*, Sue Bridehead is the best example of explosive characterization. Sue's crucial decisions are never prepared for; it requires the deepest psychology to understand them and many remain unfathomable." Here Langbaum seems to adopt the term *explosive* in line with Lotman's theoretical suggestions.

59. With respect to Sue Bridehead's peculiar ambivalence, see Maria DiBattista, *First Love: The Affections of Modern Fiction* (Chicago: University of Chicago Press, 1991), 103: "Sue Bridehead's proper name, which defines her with an inspired if characteristically overdetermined linguistic precision, suggests that she is such an enigmatic figure precisely because she would both conceal and expose this partiality for maidenheads. Her name defines the logically untenable wish to be neither wife nor maiden, but to define a place or status between these two states."

60. See Francesco Marroni, "Thomas Hardy and the Landscape of Melancholy," in *Literary Landscapes, Landscape in Literature*, ed. Michele Bottalico, Maria Teresa Chialant, Eleonora Rao (Roma: Carocci, 2007), 80–87; esp. see 83–87 on Eustacia Vye as an embodiment of the landscape of melancholy.

61. Hardy, *Jude the Obscure*, 85.

62. Ibid., 93.

63. Ibid., 285.

64. Ibid, 410.

65. Ibid., 174.

66. Ibid., 101 (italics mine).

67. Ibid., 36–37 (italics mine).

68. Ibid., 36.

69. Ibid., 290. Interestingly, Edward W. Said, *On Late Style* (London: Blooms-bury, 2007), 135, establishes a direct link between modernism and Little Father Time: "Modernism has come to seem paradoxically not so much as a movement of the new as a movement of aging and ending, a sort of 'Age masquerading as Juvenility,' to quote Hardy in *Jude the Obscure*. For indeed the figure in that novel of Jude's son, Little Father Time, does seem like an allegory of modernism with its sense of accelerated decline and its compensating gestures of recapitulation and inclusiveness."

70. Ibid., 294.

71. On the symbolic valence of Father Time, Rachman, "Character and Theme in Hardy's *Jude the Obscure*," 51, notes that "on the symbolic level his creation is not a failure at all. Little Father Time is the concrete expression of the im-personal dislocating forces of the time and of the very personal and conscious reaction to the problem of existence of his father, a man whose impulses have been thwarted and whose lurking wish the boy enacts. The boy looks old, partly because the problem of existence is old and timeless, and partly because he as well as Jude never really experienced the joy of youth. His death foreshadows the equally untimely death of his father, but more important still it signifies the end of Jude's brand of idealism as well as the end of the race of Judes. The name Little Father Time is another way of pointing to the agency that is most respon-sible for the tragedy."

72. Hardy, *Jude the Obscure*, 314.

73. William E. Buckler, *The Victorian Imagination: Essays in Aesthetic Exploration* (New York: New York University Press, 1980), 368.

74. Hardy, *Jude the Obscure*, 312.

75. Ibid., 350.

76. Ibid., 351–52.

77. Ibid., 355.

78. Ibid., 361.

79. Ibid., 355–56 (italics mine).

80. Before regarding Father Time as a crucial exemple of modernist sensibil-ity in *On Late Style*, Edward W. Said, *Beginnings: Intention and Method*, 139, had acutely noted the deviant and upsetting valence of this character: "He is an al-teration in the course of life, a disruption of the archeology that links genera-tions one to the other. His death is the affirmation, or realization, of this indis-putable role he plays."

81. Hardy, *Jude the Obscure*, 345. According to George Wotton, *Thomas Hardy: Toward a Materialistic Criticism* (Goldenbridge: Gill and Macmillan, and Towota, NJ: Barnes & Noble, 1985), 106: "What defeats Hardy's characters time and

again is their inability to find a suitable ideological structure to replace that from which they have become detached." In my view, the origin of Hardyan characters' defeats is always deeply ingrained in a complex combination of social and personal factors. In this sense, they invariably embody the ideologeme of social and cultural change without showing an adequate capacity for adaptation.

82. Hardy, *Jude the Obscure*, 20.

83. Ibid., 428.

Select Bibliography

Abbott, C. Colleer, ed. *The Letters of Gerard Manley Hopkins to Robert Bridges.* London: Oxford University Press, 1935.

Adams, James Eli. *Dandies and Desert Saints: Styles of Victorian Manhood.* Ithaca, NY: Cornell University Press, 1995.

Adelman, Gary. *"Jude the Obscure": A Paradise of Despair.* New York: Twayne, 1992.

Alter, Robert. "The Demons of History in Dickens' Tale." *Novel* 2, no. 2 (1969): 135–42.

Arnold, Matthew. *Culture and Anarchy.* Edited by J. Dover Wilson. Cambridge: Cambridge University Press, 1990.

———. *Poetical Works.* Edited by C. B. Tinker and H. F. Lowry. London: Macmillan, 1969.

———. *Selected Prose.* Edited by P. J. Keating. Harmondsworth, England: Penguin, 1970.

Ashley, Robert. *Wilkie Collins.* Brooklyn, NY: Haskell House, 1976.

Barmby, Goodwyn. "Universal Language and Phonography." *Howitt's Journal of Literature and Popular Progress* 1 (February 1847): 94–96.

Blake, William. *The Complete Poems.* Edited by W. H. Stevenson. London: Longman, 1989.

Briggs, Asa. *Victorian People.* Harmondsworth, England: Penguin, 1971.

Brodetsky, Tessa. *Elizabeth Gaskell.* Leamington Spa, England: Berg, 1986.

Brontë, Charlotte. *Shirley.* Edited by Andrew Hook and Judith Hook. Harmondsworth, England: Penguin, 1978.

Brooks, Jean. *Thomas Hardy: The Poetic Structure.* London: Elek, 1971.

Browne, Francis. "Marriage as a Symbol of Alienation in *The Whirlpool.*" *Gissing Newsletter* 13, no. 2 (April 1987): 1–13.

Buckler, William E. *The Victorian Imagination: Essays in Aesthetic Exploration.* New York: New York University Press, 1980.

Buckley, Jerome H. *The Victorian Temper: A Study in Literary Culture.* London: Frank Cass, 1966.

Bunyan, John. *The Pilgrim's Progress.* Edited by N. H. Keeble. Oxford: Oxford University Press, 1990.

Burstein, Janet. "The Journey beyond Myth in *Jude the Obscure.*" *Texas Studies in Language and Literature* 15, no. 3 (Fall 1973): 499–515.

Caird, Mona. "The Morality of Marriage." *Fortnightly Review* 53 (March 1, 1890): 310–30.

Calder, Jenni. *Women and Marriage in Victorian Fiction.* London: Thames and Hudson, 1976.

Canetti, Elias. *Crowds and Power.* Translated by Carol Stewart. Harmondsworth, England: Penguin, 1981.

Carey, John. *The Intellectuals and the Masses.* London: Faber and Faber, 1982.

Carlyle, Thomas. *The French Revolution: A History.* Edited by K. J. Fielding and David Sorensen. 2 vols. Oxford: Oxford University Press, 1991.

———. *Sartor Resartus.* Edited by Kerry McSweeney and Peter Sabor. Oxford: Oxford University Press, 1999.

———. *Selected Writings.* Edited by Alan Shelston. Harmondsworth, England: Penguin, 1987.

Casagrande, Carla, and Silvana Vecchio. *I sette vizi capitali: Storia dei peccati nel medioevo.* Torino: Einaudi, 2000.

Chambers, Robert. *Vestiges of the Natural History of Creation* Edited by Gavin de Beer. Leicester, England: Leicester University Press, 1969.

Chapman, Raymond. *The Sense of the Past in Victorian Literature.* London: Croom Helm, 1986.

Chapple, John A. V. *Science and Literature in the Nineteenth Century.* Basingstoke: Macmillan, 1986.

———, and Arthur Pollard, eds. *The Letters of Mrs. Gaskell.* Manchester: Manchester University Press, 1966.

Chesney, Kellow. *The Victorian Underworld.* Harmondsworth, England: Penguin, 1970.

Childers, Joseph W. "Industrial Culture and the Victorian Novel." In *The Cambridge Companion to the Victorian Novel,* edited by Deirdre David, 77–96. Cambridge: Cambridge University Press, 2004.

Christensen, Allan Conrad. *Nineteenth-Century Narratives of Contagion: 'Our Feverish Contact.'* Abington: Routledge, 2005.

———. "Sick Mothers and Daughters: Symptoms of Cultural Disorder in Novels by Manzoni, Dickens, Kingsley, Bulwer-Lytton, James." *Rivista di Studi Vittoriani* 4, no. 7 (January 1999): 5–32.

———. "Writing and Unwriting in *The Caxtons,* '*My Novel*', and *A Strange Story.*" In *The Subverting Vision of Bulwer Lytton.* Newark: University of Delaware Press, 2004.

Collins, Wilkie. *Basil.* Edited by Dorothy Goldman. Oxford: Oxford University Press, 1990.

———. *The Woman in White.* Edited by John Sutherland. Oxford: Oxford University Press, 1996.

———. *The Dead Secret.* Edited by Ira B. Nadel. Oxford: Oxford University Press, 1997.

Costantini, Mariaconcetta. "'Strokes of havoc': Tree-Felling and the Poetic Tradition of Ecocriticism in Manley Hopkins and Gerard Manley Hopkins." *Victorian Poetry* 46, no. 4 (Winter 2008): 487–509.

————. *Venturing into Unknown Waters: Wilkie Collins and the Challenge of Modernity.* Pescara: Tracce, 2008.

Coustillas, Pierre, and Colin Partridge, eds. *Gissing: The Critical Heritage.* London: Routledge & Kegan Paul, 1972.

Cox, R. G., ed. *Thomas Hardy: The Critical Heritage.* London: Routledge & Kegan Paul, 1970.

Dale, Peter Allan. *The Victorian Critic and the Idea of History: Carlyle, Arnold, Pater.* Cambridge, MA: Harvard University Press, 1977.

Darwin, Charles. *The Origin of Species.* Edited by Gillian Beer. Oxford: Oxford University Press, 1996.

Deleuze, Gilles, and Claire Parnet. *Dialogues II.* Translated by Hugh Tomlinson and Barbara Habberjam. London: Continuum, 2002.

Dennis, Barbara, and David Skilton, eds. *Reform and Intellectual Debate in Victorian England.* London: Croom Helm, 1987.

Dentith, Simon. *Society and Cultural Forms in Nineteenth-Century England.* Basingstoke: Macmillan, 1998.

DiBattista, Maria. *First Love: The Affections of Modern Fiction.* Chicago: University of Chicago Press, 1991.

Dickens, Charles. *Dombey and Son.* Edited by Peter Fairclough. Introduction by Raymond Williams. Harmondsworth, England: Penguin, 1970.

————. *Hard Times.* Edited by David Craig. Harmondsworth, England: Penguin, 1984.

————. *Our Mutual Friend.* Edited by Michael Cotsell. Oxford: Oxford University Press, 1991.

————. *A Tale of Two Cities.* Edited by G. K. Chesterton. London: Dent, 1970.

————. *A Tale of Two Cities.* Edited by Andrew Sanders. Oxford: Oxford University Press, 1988.

————. *A Tale of Two Cities.* Edited by Richard Maxwell. Harmondsworth, England: Penguin, 2000.

Duthie, Enid Lowry. *The Themes of Elizabeth Gaskell.* London: Macmillan, 1980.

Eagleton, Terry. *The English Novel: An Introduction.* Oxford: Blackwell, 2005.

Ebbatson, Roger. *Heidegger's Bicycle: Interfering with Victorian Texts.* Brighton, England: Sussex Academic Press, 2006.

Eliot, George. *Adam Bede.* Edited by Valentine Cunningham. Oxford: Oxford University Press, 1996.

————. *Felix Holt, The Radical.* Edited by Peter Coveney. Harmondsworth, England: Penguin, 1975.

Fernando, Loyd. "Gissing's Studies in 'Vulgarism': Aspects of His Anti-Feminism." In *George Gissing: Critical Essays,* edited by J. Michaux, 108–20. London: Vision and Totowa, NJ: Barnes & Noble, 1981.

Fischler, Alexander. "An Affinity for Birds: Kindness in Hardy's *Jude the Obscure.*" *Studies in the Novel* 13, no. 3 (Fall 1981): 250–65.

Forster, E. M. *Howards End.* Edited by Oliver Stallybrass. Harmondsworth, England: Penguin, 1976.

Foucault, Michel. *The Order of Things: An Archaeology of Human Sciences.* London: Routledge, 2006.

Frank, Lawrence. "Dickens' *A Tale of Two Cities*: The Poetics of Impasse." *American Imago* 36, no. 3 (1979): 215–44.

Gaskell, Elizabeth. *Cousin Phillis and Other Tales.* Edited by Angus Easson. Oxford: Oxford University Press, 1981.

———. *A Dark Night's Work and Other Stories.* Edited by Suzanne Lewis. Oxford: Oxford University Press, 1992.

———. *My Lady Ludlow and Other Stories.* Edited by Edgar Wright. Oxford: Oxford University Press, 1989.

———. *The Moorland Cottage and Other Stories.* Edited by Suzanne Lewis. Oxford: Oxford University Press, 1995.

———. *North and South.* Edited by Angus Easson. Oxford: Oxford University Press, 1987.

———. *Sylvia's Lovers.* Edited by Andrew Sanders. Oxford: Oxford University Press, 1986.

Gibson, James. "Introduction." In *Tess of the d'Urbervilles.* Notes by P. N. Furbank. London: Macmillan, 1985.

———. *Thomas Hardy: A Literary Life.* Basingstoke: Macmillan, 1996.

Gilbert, E. L. "'To Awake from History': Carlyle, Thackeray, and *A Tale of Two Cities.*" *Dickens Studies Annual* 12 (1983): 247–65.

Gilmartin, Sophie, and Rod Mengham. *Thomas Hardy's Shorter Fiction.* Edinburgh: Edinburgh University Press, 2007.

Gilmour, Robin. *The Idea of the Gentleman in the Victorian Novel.* London: Allen and Unwin, 1981.

Gissing, George. *Demos: A Story of English Socialism.* Edited by Pierre Coustillas. Brighton, England: Harvester Press, 1972.

———. *The House of Cobwebs.* Introduction by Thomas Seccombe. London: Constable, 1931.

———. *The Nether World.* Introduction by Walter Allen. London: J. M. Dent and New York: Dutton, 1973.

———. *The Whirlpool.* Introduction by Gillian Tindall. London: Hogarth Press, 1984.

———. *The Whirlpool.* Edited by William Greenslade. London: J. M. Dent and Rutland, VT: Charles E. Tuttle, 1997.

Glancy, R. *A Tale of Two Cities: An Annotated Bibliography.* New York: Garland, 1993.

Goldberg, Michael. *Dickens and Carlyle.* Athens: University of Georgia Press, 1972.

Goode, John. *George Gissing: Ideology and Fiction.* London: Vision, 1978.

———. "Gissing, Morris, and English Socialism." *Victorian Studies* 12 (1968): 206–26.

Greenberg, Martin. *The Terror of Art: Kafka and Modern Literature.* London: André Deutsch, 1971.

Grylls, David. *The Paradox of Gissing.* London: Allen and Unwin, 1986.

Halloran, William. "'The French Revolution': Revelation's New Form." In *Blake's Visionary Forms Dramatic*, edited by David V. Erdman and John E. Grant, 30–56. Princeton, NJ: Princeton University Press, 1970.

Hardwick, Elizabeth. "Sue and Arabella." In *The Genius of Thomas Hardy*, edited by M. Drabble, 67–73. London: Weidenfeld and Nicolson, 1976.

Hardy, Barbara. *The Moral Art of Dickens.* London and Dover: Athlone Press, 1985.

Hardy, Thomas. *The Complete Poems.* Edited by James Gibson. London: Macmillan, 1983.

———. *Jude the Obscure.* Afterword by A. Alvarez. New York: New American Library, 1961.

———. *Jude the Obscure.* Edited by N. Page. New York and London: W. W. Norton, 1978.

———. *Jude the Obscure.* Introduction by T. Eagleton. Notes by P. N. Furbank. London: Macmillan, 1978.

———. *Jude the Obscure.* Edited by C. C. Sisson. Harmondsworth, England: Penguin, 1985.

———. *Jude the Obscure.* Introduction by T. R. Wightman. Notes by P. N. Furbank. London: Macmillan, 1986.

———. *Jude the Obscure.* Edited by Patricia Ingham. Oxford: Oxford University Press, 1989.

———. *Jude the Obscure.* Introduction by J. H. Miller. London: David Campbell, 1992.

Hartley, Lucy. *Physiognomy and the Meaning of Expression in Nineteenth-Century Culture.* Cambridge: Cambridge University Press, 2001.

Heller, Tamar. *Dead Secrets: Wilkie Collins and the Female Gothic.* New Haven, CT: Yale University Press, 1992.

Hill, Robert W. Jr., ed. *Tennyson's Poetry.* New York: W. W. Norton, 1999.

Horne, Lewis B. "Pattern and Contrast in *Jude the Obscure.*" *Études Anglaises* 32, no. 2 (April–June 1979): 143–53.

House, Humphrey, ed. *The Journals and Papers of Gerard Manley Hopkins.* London: Oxford University Press, 1959.

Hughes, Winifred. *The Maniac in the Cellar: Sensation Novels of the 1860s.* Princeton, NJ: Princeton University Press, 1980.

Ingham, Patricia. "The Evolution of *Jude the Obscure.*" *Review of English Studies* 27, no. 105 (February 1976): 27–37.

Ives, Maura. "Housework, Mill Work, Women's Work: The Function of Cloth in Charlotte Brontë's *Shirley.*" In *Keeping the Victorian House: A Collection of Essays,* edited by Vanessa D. Dickerson. 259–89. New York: Garland, 1995.

Jameson, Fredric. *The Political Unconscious: Narrative as a Socially Symbolic Act.* London: Methuen, 1986.

Jefferies, Richard. *After London.* Edited by John Fowles. Oxford: Oxford University Press, 1988.

Jung, Carl G. "Approaching the Unconscious." In *Man and His Symbols.* New York: Laurel Books/Dell, 1968.

Keating, Peter. *The Haunted Study: A Social History of the English Novel 1875–1914.* London: Fontana Press, 1991.

Kebbel, T. E., ed. *Selected Speeches of the Late Right Honourable the Earl of Beaconsfield.* London: Longmans, Green, and Co., 1882.

Kishlansky, Mark. *L'età degli Stuart: L'Inghilterra dal 1603 al 1714.* Bologna: Il Mulino, 1999.

Korg, Jacob. *George Gissing: A Critical Biography.* Brighton, England: Harvester Press, 1980.

Kramer, Dale. *Thomas Hardy: The Forms of Tragedy.* London: Macmillan, 1975.

Kundera, Milan. *The Art of the Novel.* Translated by Linda Asher. London: Faber, 1990.

Langbaum, Robert. *Thomas Hardy in Our Time.* Basingstoke: Macmillan, 1995.

Letwin, Shirley Robin. *The Gentleman in Trollope: Individuality and Moral Conduct.* Basingstoke: Macmillan, 1988.

Lippincott, Benjamin Evans. *Victorian Critics of Democracy.* New York: Octagon Books, 1964.

Lotman, Jurij M. *Cercare la strada: Modelli della cultura.* Edited by Maria Corti. Venezia: Marsilio, 1994.

———. *La cultura e l'esplosione: Prevedibilità e imprevedibilità.* Translated by Caterina Valentino. Milano: Feltrinelli, 1993.

———. *Universe of the Mind. A Semiotic Theory of Culture.* Translated by Ann Shukman. Bloomington: Indiana University Press, 1990.

Lucas, John. *The Literature of Change.* Brighton, England: Harvester Press, 1980.

———. *The Melancholy Man: A Study of Dickens's Novels.* Brighton, England: Harvester Press, 1980.

Lukács, Georg. *The Historical Novel.* Translated by Hannah and Stanley Mitchell. London: Merlin Press, 1989.

Lyell, Charles. *Principles of Geology.* Edited by James A. Secord. London: Penguin, 1997.

Mallett, Phillip. "Carlyle and Ruskin: Work and Art." In *Victorian Keats and Romantic Carlyle: The Fusion and Confusions of Literary Periods*, edited by C. C. Barfoot, 223–34. Amsterdam: Rodopi, 1999.

Manheim, Leonard. "A Tale of Two Characters. A Study in Multiple Projection." *Dickens Studies Annual* 1 (1970): 225–37.

Marcus, David D. "The Carlylean Vision of *A Tale of Two Cities.*" *Studies in the Novel* 8, no. 1 (1986): 56–68.

Marroni, Francesco. *La fabbrica nella valle: Saggio sulla narrativa di Elizabeth Gaskell.* Bari: Adriatica, 1987.

———. *La poesia di Thomas Hardy.* Bari: Adriatica, 1987.

———. "The Poetry of Ornithology in Keats, Leopardi and Hardy: A Dialogic Analysis." *Thomas Hardy Journal* 14, no. 2 (May 1998): 35–44.

———. "The Shadow of Dante: Elizabeth Gaskell and *The Divine Comedy.*" *Gaskell Society Journal* 10 (1996): 9–13.

———. *Spettri senza nome: Modelli epistemici e narrativa vittoriana.* Roma: Carocci, 2007.

———. "Thomas Hardy and the Landscape of Melancholy." In *Literary Landscapes, Landscape in Literature,* edited by Michele Bottalico, Maria Teresa Chialant, and Eleonora Rao, 80–87. Roma: Carocci, 2007.

———. "Thomas Hardy e l'"esplorazione della realtà': Una lettura di *The Darkling Thrush." Strumenti critici* 8, no. 1 (1993): 87–111.

Marx, Karl, and Friedrich Engels. *The Communist Manifesto.* Edited by David McLellan. Oxford: Oxford University Press, 1998.

Mattheisen, Paul F., Arthur C. Young, and Pierre Coustillas, eds. *The Collected Letters of George Gissing.* 9 vols. Athens: Ohio University Press, 1992.

Matus, Jill L., ed. *The Cambridge Companion to Elizabeth Gaskell.* Cambridge: Cambridge University Press, 2007.

Meisel, Perry. *Thomas Hardy: The Return of the Repressed.* New Haven, CT: Yale University Press, 1972.

Messinger, Gary S. *Manchester in the Victorian Age: The Half-Unknown City.* Manchester: Manchester University Press, 1985.

Miller, J. Hillis. "Thomas Hardy, Jacques Derrida, and the 'Dislocation of Souls.'" In *Taking Chances: Derrida, Psychoanalysis, and Literature,* edited by Joseph H. Smith and William Kerrigan, 135–45. Baltimore: Johns Hopkins University Press, 1988.

Millgate, Michael, ed. *The Life and the Work of Thomas Hardy.* Basingstoke: Macmillan, 1989.

———. *Thomas Hardy: A Biography.* Oxford: Oxford University Press, 1985.

Morgan, Rosemarie. *Women and Sexuality in the Novels of Thomas Hardy.* London: Routledge, 1988.

Morton, A. L., and George Tate. *The British Labor Movement, 1770–1920: A Political History.* New York: International, 1957.

Nussbaum, Martha C. *Poetic Justice: The Literary Imagination and Public Life.* Boston: Beacon Press, 2004.

Oddie, William. *Dickens and Carlyle: The Question of Influence.* London: Centenary Press, 1972.

Orwell, Sonia, and Ian Angus, eds. *The Collected Essays, Journalism and Letters of George Orwell.* 4 vols. Harmondsworth, England: Penguin, 1971.

Partridge, Colin. "The Humane Centre: George Gissing's *The Whirlpool." Gissing Newsletter* 9, no. 3 (July 1973): 1–10.

Paterson, John. "The Genesis of *Jude the Obscure." Studies in Philology* 57 (1960): 87–98.

Pite, Ralph. *Thomas Hardy: The Guarded Life.* Basingstoke: Picador, 2006.

Plotz, John. *The Crowd: British Literature and Public Politics.* Berkeley: University of California Press, 2000.

Purdy, R. L., and Michael Millgate, eds. *The Collected Letters of Thomas Hardy.* 7 vols. Oxford: Clarendon Press, 1980.

Pykett, Lyn. "Ruinous Bodies: Women and Sexuality in Hardy's Late Fiction." *Critical Survey* 5, no. 2 (1993): 157–66.

————. *Wilkie Collins*. Oxford: Oxford University Press, 2005.

Rachman, Shalom. "Character and Theme in Hardy's *Jude the Obscure*." *English* 22, no. 113 (Summer 1973): 45–53.

Radford, Andrew, and Mark Sandy, eds. *Romantic Echoes in the Victorian Era*. Aldershot, England, Ashgate, 2008.

Recchio, Thomas E. "A Victorian Version of the Fall: Mrs Gaskell's *Cousin Phillis* and the Domestication of Myth." *Gaskell Society Journal* 5 (1991): 37–50.

Reddy, Maureen T. "Female Sexuality in 'The Poor Clare': The Demon in the House." *Studies in Short Fiction* 21, no. 3 (1984): 259–65.

Rignall, J. M. "Dickens and the Catastrophic Continuum of History in *A Tale of Two Cities*." *English Literary History* 51, no. 1 (1984): 575–87.

Rosenberg, John D. *The Darkening Glass: A Portrait of Ruskin's Genius*. New York: Columbia University Press, 1962.

————. *Elegy for an Age: The Presence of the Past in Victorian Literature*. London: Anthem Press, 2005.

Rossetti, Christina. *The Complete Poems*. Text by R. W. Crump, Notes and Introduction by Betty S. Flowers. Harmondsworth, England: Penguin, 2001.

Ruer, Jean. "Charles Dickens, Wilkie Collins et *The Frozen Deep*." *Études Anglaises* 23, no. 2 (1970): 183–89.

Ruskin, John. *The Works of John Ruskin*. Edited by Edward Tyas Cook and Alexander Wedderburn. 39 vols. London: George Allen, 1903–12.

Said, Edward W. *Beginnings. Intention and Method*. New York: Columbia University Press, 1985.

————. *Culture and Imperialism*. London: Vintage, 1993.

————. *On Late Style*. London: Bloomsbury, 2007.

Sanders, Andrew. *The Victorian Historical Novel 1840–1880*. London: Macmillan, 1978.

Secord, James A. *Victorian Sensation: The Extraordinary Publication, Reception, and Secret Authorship of "Vestiges of the Natural History of Creation."* Chicago: University of Chicago Press, 2000.

Shelston, Alan. "Education in the Life and Work of Elizabeth Gaskell." *Gaskell Journal* 20 (2008): 56–71.

————. "The Supernatural in the Stories of Elizabeth Gaskell." In *Exhibited by the Candlelight: Sources and Developments in the Gothic Tradition*, edited by Valeria Tinkler-Villani, Peter Davidson, and Jane Stevenson, 137–46. Amsterdam: Rodopi, 1995.

Stephen, Leslie. *An Agnostic's Apology and Other Essays*. London: John Murray, 1908.

Stoehr, Taylor. *Dickens: The Dreamer's Stance*. Ithaca, NY: Cornell University Press, 1965.

Stoneman, Patsy. *Elizabeth Gaskell*. Brighton, England: Harvester Press, 1987.

Tambling, Jeremy. *Dickens, Violence and the Modern State: Dreams of the Scaffold*. Basingstoke and London: Macmillan and New York: St. Martin's Press, 1995.

————. *Going Astray. Dickens and London*. Harlow and London: Pearson/Longman, 2009.

Thomas, Donald. *The Victorian Underworld*. New York: New York University Press, 1998.

Thoms, Peter. *The Windings of the Labyrinth: Quest and Structure in the Novels of Wilkie Collins*. Athens: Ohio University Press, 1992.

Tomalin, Claire. *Thomas Hardy: The Time-Torn Man*. London: Viking, 2006.

Trodd, Anthea. *Domestic Crime in the Victorian Novel*. Basingstoke: Macmillan, 1989.

Trollope, Anthony. *An Autobiography*. Edited by Michael Sadleir and Frederick Page. Oxford: Oxford University Press, 1989.

———. *Can You Forgive Her?* Edited by Stephen Wall. Harmondsworth, England: Penguin, 1972.

Uglow, Jenny. *Elizabeth Gaskell: A Habit of Stories*. London: Faber and Faber, 1993.

Vrettos, Athena. *Somatic Fictions: Imagining Illness in Victorian Culture*. Stanford, CA: Stanford University Press, 1995.

Warburton Boylan, Rebecca. "Phantom Photographs: The Camera's Pursuit and the Disruption of Consciousness in *Jude the Obscure*." *Thomas Hardy Journal* 22 (Autumn 2006): 72–84.

Ward, Jane. *Passion and Pathology in Victorian Fiction*. Oxford: Oxford University Press, 2001.

Watts, Cedric. "Hardy's Sue Bridehead and the 'New Woman.'" *Critical Survey* 5, no. 2 (1993): 152–56.

———. *Thomas Hardy: "Jude the Obscure."* Harmondsworth, England: Penguin, 1992.

Weber, Carl J. *Hardy of Wessex: His Life and Literary Career*. New York: Columbia University Press, 1965.

Weinstein, Philip M. *The Semantics of Desire*. Princeton, NJ: Princeton University Press, 1984.

Welsh, Alexander. *The City of Dickens*. Cambridge, MA: Harvard University Press, 1986.

Wood, Jane. *Passion and Pathology in Victorian Fiction*. Oxford: Oxford University Press, 2001.

Wordsworth, William. *The Poems*. Edited by John O. Hayden. 2 vols. Harmondsworth, England: Penguin, 1977.

———. *The Prelude 1799, 1805, 1850*. Edited by Jonathan Wordsworth, M. H. Adams, and Stephen Gill. New York: W. W. Norton, 1979.

Wotton, George. *Thomas Hardy: Towards a Materialistic Criticism*. Goldenbridge: Gill and Macmillan and Towota, NJ: Barnes & Noble, 1985.

Wright, Edgar. *Mrs Gaskell: The Basis for a Reassessment*. London: Oxford University Press, 1965.

Young, Arlene. *Culture, Class, and Gender in the Victorian Novel. Gentlemen, Gents and Working Women*. Basingstoke: Macmillan, 1999.

Index